ARIZONA NATIONAL PARKS AND MONUMENTS

Arizona National Parks and Monuments

Scenic Wonders and Cultural Treasures

of the Grand Canyon State

ROGER NAYLOR

University of New Mexico Press • Albuquerque

© 2024 by Roger Naylor
All rights reserved. Published 2024
Printed in the United States of America

ISBN 978-0-8263-6702-0 (paper)
ISBN 978-0-8263-6703-7 (ePub)

Library of Congress Control Number: 2024942001

Founded in 1889, the University of New Mexico sits on the traditional homelands of the Pueblo of Sandia. The original peoples of New Mexico—Pueblo, Navajo, and Apache—since time immemorial have deep connections to the land and have made significant contributions to the broader community statewide. We honor the land itself and those who remain stewards of this land throughout the generations and also acknowledge our committed relationship to Indigenous peoples. We gratefully recognize our history.

Cover photograph courtesy of Roger Naylor
Designed by Felicia Cedillos
Composed in Minion Pro

To my friend Mike Koopsen, because one of the joys of writing
all these crazy books is sharing an adventure or two along the way.

Contents

Introduction . . . xi

SOUTHERN ARIZONA

Butterfield Overland National Historic Trail . . . 3

Chiricahua National Monument . . . 11

Coronado National Memorial . . . 19

Fort Bowie National Historic Site . . . 27

Ironwood Forest National Monument . . . 33

Juan Bautista de Anza National Historic Trail . . . 39

Organ Pipe Cactus National Monument . . . 47

Saguaro National Park . . . 55

Santa Cruz Valley National Heritage Area . . . 63

Tumacácori National Historical Park . . . 71

Yuma Crossing National Heritage Area . . . 77

CENTRAL ARIZONA

Agua Fria National Monument . . . 85

Casa Grande Ruins National Monument . . . 91

Hohokam Pima National Monument . . . 96

Montezuma Castle National Monument . . . 99

Sonoran Desert National Monument . . . 105

Tonto National Monument . . . 111

Tuzigoot National Monument . . . 117

NORTHERN ARIZONA

Baaj Nwaavjo I'tah Kukveni—Ancestral Footprints of the Grand Canyon National Monument . . . 125

Canyon de Chelly National Monument . . . 133

Glen Canyon National Recreation Area . . . 139

Grand Canyon National Park . . . 147

Grand Canyon–Parashant National Monument . . . 163

Hubbell Trading Post National Historic Site . . . 171

Lake Mead National Recreation Area . . . 177

Navajo National Monument . . . 187

Old Spanish National Historic Trail . . . 193

Petrified Forest National Park . . . 199

Pipe Spring National Monument . . . 207

Sunset Crater Volcano National Monument . . . 213

Vermilion Cliffs National Monument . . . 219

Walnut Canyon National Monument . . . 227

Wupatki National Monument . . . 233

STATEWIDE ARIZONA

Arizona National Scenic Trail . . . 241

Acknowledgments . . . 247

About the Author . . . 249

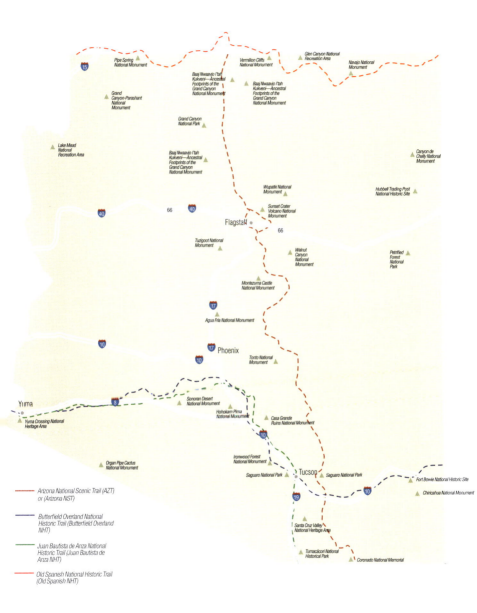

The long winding slot canyon of Buckskin Gulch cuts through Vermilion Cliffs National Monument. Courtesy of Mike Koopsen, Sedona.

Introduction

Arizona is the Grand Canyon State. We are literally defined by wonder.

Keep that sense of astonishment handy when you begin to explore Arizona's 34 national park units. You will rely heavily on it time and time again. Our two signature features—Grand Canyon and the saguaro cactus—are both protected as national parks. But that's just the beginning of the story.

An extraordinary array of national parks and monuments blanket Arizona from border to border. They range from the volcanic sprawl of stone hoodoos crowning Chiricahua National Monument to the badlands of Petrified Forest National Park colored like blood and peaches to the miles of seductive shoreline at Lake Mead National Recreation Area. There is something here to pique everyone's interest. National monuments like Tonto, Tuzigoot, Wupatki, and Montezuma Castle hold on tight to our past. Others like Sonoran Desert and Vermilion Cliffs preserve our precious wide-open spaces. And all the parks reconnect us to nature. We hike, bike, kayak, ride mules, bounce down dirt roads, slither through slot canyons, and camp under skies dripping with stars.

Forces That Shaped Us

Look, nothing comes easy in Arizona. This is a land that snarls. It is a land of ferocious sun and earth-jarring violence. Volcanoes and uplifts and the grinding of tectonic plates and the sloshing of shallow seas and a long colorful symphony of erosion have created a world of startling diversity, worthy of preservation and protection—worthy of wonder. Geologic history and human history are entwined in Arizona national parks.

The parks are where you'll hear the soft voices of ancient cultures that left behind stone cities, mysterious artwork, and an intricately engineered network of canals. This is where you'll find remnants of New World explorations, the missions, presidios, and trails of the Spanish. And this is where you'll find forts, battlegrounds, and graveyards, reminders of the clashes that spilled too much blood on America's last frontier. These parks bear our scars and carry our memories.

They are also our adventures and our salvation. The parks provide unspoiled scenery and feature some of our wildest country. They pull us outdoors and away from the tiny screens that hold us captive. We breathe fresh air again. We have room to move. We can fall off the grid if we want, immerse ourselves in the present. Here we reawaken youthful spirits. Here we are restored. Arizona national parks contain an unmatched blend of natural beauty, vivid history, recreational opportunities, and pure, sweet solitude beneath a broad, horizon-bending sky.

People from around the globe scrape, save, and plan for that once-in-a-lifetime opportunity just to come and play in our backyard. And it's all because of Arizona's legendary and life-altering parks.

My Park Story

When I first began exploring Arizona, I started with the national parks. They were the jewels, the irresistible places. I saw my first rattlesnake at Chiricahua National Monument, my first desert tortoise in Organ Pipe Cactus National Monument, and my first bighorn sheep deep in the Grand Canyon. The first time I thought I might die on a trail was at the Grand, and I couldn't wait to go back. I hiked, I camped amid luscious moonlight, I fell in love. I hiked some more.

Yet one tiny spot changed my perspective and made me see the national park system in a whole new light. Pipe Spring National Monument is a 40-acre sliver of a park dropped amid the endless expanse of the Arizona Strip, that piece of state cut off by the Grand Canyon.

I was probably 20 years old at the time, still living in Ohio. Each year I would work for a few months and when I pocketed enough money, go rambling around Arizona all through the fall and winter. While researching an upcoming trip I came across a cryptic description of Pipe Spring. I don't remember what it said, but it made it sound like the loneliest place on the planet. In those pre-Internet days, I wrote to the monument requesting they mail me a brochure. I still have that 1970s-era pamphlet in my files.

A few weeks later I was barreling across the Arizona Strip toward Pipe Spring, an old Mormon fort built atop an unexpected water source. It was a revelation. I didn't know it was possible to travel so far without falling off the edge of the world. I was intrigued by the Pipe Spring story and mesmerized by the location. Suddenly my vision of national parks was upended. I thought they were all supposed to be immense, Grand Canyon–esque. I didn't know that a place so small could tell such a large story.

I wanted to see more, to learn more. I began to embrace all the national parks and monuments. That launched a new phase of exploration for me, visiting each of the parks, savoring the details, and appreciating them for what they are. It's a phase that's still going, all these decades later.

So park chasers beware. Once you start venturing to these parks, the majestic and the modest, the accessible and the remote, it becomes hard to stop. Trust me. I know what I'm talking about.

What's in a Name?

Arizona features 34 national park units. These include 3 national parks and 19 national monuments, which is more than any other state. The National Park Service (NPS) actually supports several other types of "park," and Arizona contains plenty of those as well.

In Saguaro National Park, hikers climb the Sendero Esperanza Trail through fields of spring wildflowers. Photo by the author.

Different designations of national park units can sometimes be confusing. Here's how the NPS defines its holdings and where they exist in Arizona.

NATIONAL PARK: Large natural places having a wide variety of attributes, at times including significant historic assets.
- Grand Canyon
- Petrified Forest
- Saguaro

NATIONAL MONUMENT: Landmarks, structures and other objects of historic or scientific interest situated on lands owned or controlled by the government.

- Agua Fria
- Baaj Nwaavjo I'tah Kukveni—Ancestral Footprints of the Grand Canyon
- Canyon de Chelly
- Casa Grande Ruins
- Chiricahua
- Grand Canyon–Parashant
- Hohokam Pima
- Ironwood Forest
- Montezuma Castle
- Navajo
- Organ Pipe Cactus
- Pipe Spring
- Sonoran Desert
- Sunset Crater
- Tonto
- Tuzigoot
- Vermilion Cliffs
- Walnut Canyon
- Wupatki

An angler and a kayaker have a piece of Lake Mohave all to themselves in the Lake Mead National Recreation Area. Photo by the author.

NATIONAL HISTORIC SITE: Generally, such sites contain a single historic feature directly associated with its subject.
    Fort Bowie
    Hubbell Trading Post

NATIONAL HISTORICAL PARK: This designation generally applies to historic parks that extend beyond single properties or buildings.
    Tumacácori

NATIONAL MEMORIAL: To commemorate a person or event, although it need not occupy a site historically connected with its subject.
    Coronado

NATIONAL RECREATION AREA: Most often centered on large reservoirs with emphasis on water recreation. These combine open spaces with the preservation of historic resources and natural areas in locations that provide recreation for large numbers of people.
    Glen Canyon
    Lake Mead

NATIONAL TRAIL: National trails are linear parklands that encompass historic, scenic, and recreational trails.

   Arizona Trail (Scenic)
   Butterfield Overland Trail (Historic)
   Juan Bautista de Anza Trail (Historic)
   Old Spanish Trail (Historic)

NATIONAL HERITAGE AREA: Places where historic, cultural, and natural resources combine to form cohesive, nationally important areas. Unlike national parks, national heritage areas are large lived-in landscapes.

   Santa Cruz Valley
   Yuma Crossing

What to Know

Carry plenty of water.

That's the number one rule of just about any Arizona activity. Carry lots of water and drink it. Electrolytes are good too. If you start feeling thirsty, you're already a little dehydrated.

In each chapter I try to provide all the information you need before visiting that specific park, including some Special Notes at the end on tips and safety issues. Occasionally, I remind you about the water thing, but not always just because it's exhausting to write the same thing over and over again. So consider this your all-encompassing blanket reminder to always travel with water. Arizona is often hot, but even when it is not, it's still dry. This is an arid climate, and for those not accustomed to it, dehydration can happen quickly even on the mildest days.

Most of Arizona's national parks and monuments are easily accessible and contain all the amenities we've come to expect when traveling. Yet there are a few that are the opposite of accessible, and they sneer at your amenities. I'm looking at you, Grand Canyon–Parashant National Monument.

A handful of parks, all clearly identified in the book, involve backcountry travel. They present a special set of challenges, and you need to be ready to face them. Travel into these areas is not to be taken lightly. You're often without cell service and far from any assistance. You're responsible for your own safety and must be prepared to self-rescue.

Otherwise, the most important thing—and this really is crucial—is don't be a jerk. Recreate responsibly. You're visiting our truly special places; be respectful. Respect the park, the park staff, and the other visitors. Whether you're just driving through or camping for a week, leave the park as clean or cleaner than you found it. Follow the Leave No Trace principles.

Here are just a few of the Leave No Trace highlights. If you fear you might secretly be a jerk, please delve deeper into the principles. Memorize and adhere to them.

Plan Ahead and Prepare

Know the regulations and special concerns for the area you'll visit. Prepare for extreme weather, hazards, and emergencies.

Travel and Camp on Durable Surfaces

Durable surfaces include maintained trails and designated campsites, rock, gravel, sand, dry grasses, or snow. Protect riparian areas by camping at least 200 feet from lakes and streams.

Dispose of Waste Properly

Pack it in, pack it out. Inspect your campsite, food preparation areas, and rest areas for trash or spilled foods. Pack out all trash, leftover food, and litter. Utilize toilet facilities whenever possible. Otherwise, deposit solid human waste in catholes dug 6 to 8 inches deep, at least 200 feet away from water, camp, and trails. Pack out toilet paper and hygiene products.

Leave What You Find

Preserve the past: examine, photograph, but do not touch cultural or historic structures and artifacts. Leave rocks, plants, and other natural objects as you find them.

Minimize Campfire Impacts

Campfires can cause lasting impacts to the environment. Use a lightweight stove for cooking and enjoy a candle lantern for light. Where fires are permitted, use established fire rings, fire pans, or mound fires. Burn all wood and coals to ash, put out campfires completely, and then scatter cool ashes.

Respect Wildlife

Observe wildlife from a distance. Do not follow or approach them. Never feed animals.

Be Considerate of Other Visitors

Respect other visitors and protect the quality of their experience. Be courteous. Yield to other users on the trail.

National Park Passes

Of the 34 national park units in Arizona, only 14 charge an entrance fee. The rest are free all year round. That's a lot of bargains to be had for Arizona travelers.

Each year, the National Park Service selects five free admission days to guarantee the national parks are available to everyone. On those days the entrance fees will be waived. Since the fee-free days vary from year to year, be sure to check the NPS website to plan your trip. www.nps.gov.

Of course, if you're like me and tend to drop by various parks at every opportunity, those entrance fees can add up. That's why there is always a National Park pass stuffed in my wallet.

The NPS has created a variety of passes, both annual and lifetime, to encourage Americans to visit their national parks, monuments, and federal recreational lands. The passes are honored at sites managed by the US Army Corps of Engineers, US Forest Service, US Fish and Wildlife Service, Bureau of Land Management, Bureau of Reclamation, and the National Park Service.

Visit the park website to see which pass is best for you. Passes are free for veterans, current military and dependents, Gold Star families, and anyone with a medically determined permanent disability. For those between the ages of 16–62, the America the Beautiful annual pass costs $80.

For seniors, there's finally some good news about getting older. If you're over the age of 62, the Senior Annual pass will set you back $20. A Senior Lifetime pass that never expires is a bargain at $80.

Each pass covers the pass owner and all occupants in a private vehicle at sites that charge per vehicle, or the pass owner and up to three additional adults (16 and over) at sites that charge per person. Children ages 15 and under are admitted free.

Most national parks and many other federal agencies issue the passes on-site.

Yuma

Yuma Crossing National Heritage Area

Organ Pipe Cactus National Monument

― Butterfield Overland National Historic Trail (Butterfield Overland NHT)

― Juan Bautista de Anza National Historic Trail (Juan Bautista de Anza NHT)

SOUTHERN ARIZONA

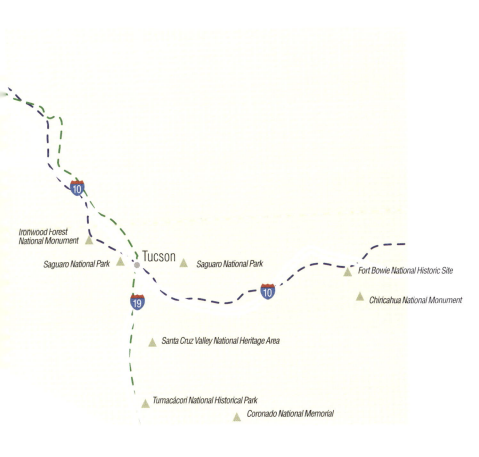

The crumbling walls of Dragoon Springs Station define a significant piece of Arizona and American history. Photo by the author.

Butterfield Overland National Historic Trail

Overview

The world's longest stage route carved a defining path through Arizona history.

Nearest Cities

San Simon, Bowie, Willcox, Benson, Tucson, Eloy, Maricopa, Gila Bend, Yuma.

Established

January 5, 2023.

Size

3,292 miles, including multiple alignments (approximately 400 miles in Arizona).

In this age of instant communication it's almost impossible to comprehend what a massive commitment of resources and manpower was brought to bear to simply send or receive a letter on the Arizona frontier.

Before the telegraph clickety-clacked its message across the miles—the pioneer version of text messaging—and before trains chugged into the territory, our links to the rest of the world were fast-riding stage wagons stuffed with mail and bleary-eyed passengers.

In 1857, businessman John Butterfield won a $600,000-a-year federal contract to transport mail between St. Louis and San Francisco. The agreement stipulated that the route was to be traversed in no more than 25 days. That thin thread of a stage line knitted the two civilized halves of the United States together despite the nearly 2,000 miles of undeveloped wilderness that separated them.

Pounding Hooves

It took a year to prepare the infrastructure, choosing routes, grading roads, securing water sources, stocking animals, and constructing stations. In September 1858, the first stages rolled out, and the Overland Mail Company was in business. Their route swooped south in a long arc to avoid snowy mountain passes in wintertime, earning the nickname the Oxbow Route. The journey of approximately 2,800 miles started in the east from two locations, St. Louis, Missouri, and Memphis, Tennessee. They converged in Fort Smith, Arkansas, then continued through Arkansas, Oklahoma, Texas, the Territory of New Mexico, and into Southern California. At this time, Arizona was still part of New Mexico.

The Overland Mail Company used two types of stages to carry mail, freight, and passengers. They would start out in Concord stagecoaches, which are tall, wide, and sturdy. The driver sat high above the team in an elevated seat. These are the classic melon-shaped coaches seen in every cowboy movie ever filmed. But the big Concords only saw use at either end of the Butterfield stage line. Concord stagecoaches were used in the east until reaching Fort Smith, Arkansas, and in California between Los Angeles and San Francisco. Those areas were more settled, and the roads were reasonably well maintained.

Between Fort Smith and Los Angeles, drivers switched to stage wagons of the celerity class. Designed for rough conditions, celerity wagons were lightweight with open-frame sides, a canvas top, and a lower center of gravity. Leather curtains draped over the sides, the only thing separating passengers from the elements. The wide wheels often churned up so much earth, they were known as "mud wagons." The celerity wagons used by the Overland Mail Company were designed by John Butterfield himself and were better equipped to handle the rocky terrain, sand, and steep grades across the still untamed west.

No matter which conveyance was used, the name of the game was speed. Coaches and wagons alike traveled at breakneck speed around the clock for 24 straight days. They needed to average more than 100 miles each and every day to make their deadline. The only stops were at regularly spaced stations along the way to change horses or mules. That's when passengers sometimes had a chance to grab a hurried meal. The seats on the stage wagons broke down so passengers could try sleeping in shifts along the rattling, bouncing roads. Make no mistake; the mail was the priority. Passengers were an afterthought. The smaller celerity wagons could fit six souls inside, so naturally there were often nine crammed together. Often passengers on the ends had to ride with a leg hanging out the side.

The Arizona Portion

Twice a week, Butterfield's stage wagons came galloping through southeastern Arizona, the land of cactus, Chiricahua Apache, and scarce waterholes. They crossed into what is now Arizona through West Doubtful Canyon in the Peloncillo Mountains, then angled southwest to San Simon and through the treacherous Apache Pass.

The route cut past Dragoon Springs, located at the edge of the granite ramparts of the Dragoon Mountains. It crossed the San Pedro River near the site of present-day Benson and pushed on through Tucson before swinging north to follow the Gila River the rest of the way to Fort Yuma, located on the western bank of the Colorado River. Generally, the Butterfield stage line followed what today are I-10 and I-8.

There were 26 stage stations scattered across Arizona. At least two of them became legendary for the violence that engulfed them.

Dragoon Springs Station

At Dragoon Springs the Butterfield crew built a strong secure station enclosing a large stone corral during the summer of 1858. Knowing this was Apache country, they wanted the station to be something of a fortress. As construction neared completion, most of the workers moved on down the line. Staying behind to finish were Americans James Hughes, James Laing, William Cunningham, and Silas St. John. Mexican laborers on-site were Guadalupe Ramirez, Pablo Ramirez, and Bonifacio Mirando.

About 1:00 a.m. on the morning of September 9, St. John awakened to the stirrings of animals followed by human screams. He was suddenly attacked by the three Mexican laborers wielding heavy axes and tools. While fighting them off he suffered grievous wounds—an axe blade chopped a deep gash in his right hip and nearly severed his left arm. St. John managed to grab a pistol and fire a shot, causing his attackers to flee.

St. John's companions were in even worse shape. Hughes had died instantly from a crushed skull. Laing and Cunningham suffered brutal axe wounds to the head and were immobilized yet clinging to life. St. John could not move around without gushing blood. It would be four days before help arrived. Four horrific days to endure agonizing pain, feverish thirst, the braying of starving mules, and the moans of dying men. He lay there with a pistol trying to keep the wolves, coyotes, and buzzards at bay. The other men finally succumbed to their wounds.

Once the carnage was discovered, a surgeon was brought from Fort Buchanan who amputated St. John's arm at the socket, nine days after he was attacked. The wounded man was eventually transported by wagon to the fort. Surprisingly, he recovered. Three weeks after the Massacre at Dragoon Springs, Silas St. John mounted a horse and rode into Tucson.

Apache Pass Station

Cutting a narrow cleft between the Chiricahua and Dos Cabezas Mountains, Apache Pass formed a high desert corridor for travelers, and offered a rare permanent source of water. Apache Spring fed a lush riparian area and was a favorite campsite of Cochise and his Chiricahua Apaches.

The Apache Pass Stage Station was built in July 1858. Stone walls wrapped around a kitchen–dining room, sleeping rooms, storage area, and mule corral with portholes in every stall. Stage passengers could secure a modest meal here of bread, meat, and beans for 50 cents while teams were being swapped out.

Despite venturing through the heart of the Chiricahua Apache homeland, the stage wagons operated for more than two years largely unimpeded. It was a well-known Butterfield policy that stages never transported gold or silver, so none were ever waylaid by outlaws. There were a few instances of Apaches running off Butterfield stock, but for the most part the Indians allowed safe passage of the stage wagons and even provided firewood for the stations in exchange for gifts.

That tenuous peace came crashing down in the winter of 1861.

Following the kidnapping of a young boy during an Apache raid, troops were dispatched to the area. On February 4, 1861, Lieutenant George Bascom led a detachment of 54 men into

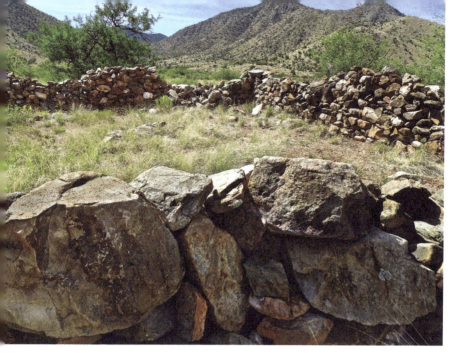

Despite only existing for a few years, a lot of blood was spilled at Dragoon Springs Station. Photo by the author.

Apache Pass with orders to recover the boy. The young lieutenant met with Cochise and accused him of kidnapping and theft. Cochise claimed to know nothing of the missing boy and even offered to help find him. But Bascom recklessly tried to place the Apache leader under arrest. Cochise escaped—but other Chiricahua people, including members of Cochise's own family, were captured. The soldiers took refuge in the rock-walled Butterfield stage station.

The resulting standoff lasted several days and ended with the deaths of hostages on both sides. What became known as the Bascom Affair infuriated Cochise, who was innocent of the kidnapping, and sparked open warfare between whites and Apaches that raged intermittently for the next 25 years. It also helped seal the fate of the southern route of the Overland Mail Company.

Because of increased Indian attacks and with rumblings of the impending Civil War, the southern route of the Overland Mail Company proved no longer viable. In March 1861, Congress directed the company change to a more northern route via South Pass and Salt Lake City.

Arizona was once again cut off from the civilized world.

Arizona's Two Wars

The frontier seemed to go up in flames in 1861. Not one but two powder kegs were lit across

Southern Arizona. Violence between whites and the Apaches erupted even as the westernmost skirmishes and battles of the Civil War were being waged along the old Butterfield stage line. And the two conflicts constantly overlapped, with Union and Confederate troops fighting each other, and Apaches attacking them both.

Hoping to seize the mineral-rich Southwest, Captain Sherod Hunter and his Arizona Rangers raised the Confederacy's Stars and Bars above Tucson in February 1862. To counteract this western incursion, the California Column was formed, consisting of several companies of infantry, cavalry, and artillery. On March 29, a vanguard of the California Column came upon a small Confederate detachment burning hay at Stanwix Station, a former Butterfield stop about 80 miles east of Yuma. A few hurried shots were exchanged, wounding one Union soldier. This encounter marked the westernmost advance of any organized Confederate force during the war.

The Confederates were burning hay at several former stage stations along the Gila River in an effort to slow the Union advance from California. On April 15, the two sides met again at Picacho Pass, near another former stage station. This time the outcome was bloodier. A Union cavalry patrol attacked a group of Confederate pickets, resulting in three Union dead, three wounded, and three Confederate soldiers taken prisoner.

There was still more blood to be spilled at Dragoon Springs on May 5, 1862. While foraging for stray cattle, a detachment of Hunter's Arizona Rangers was attacked by Chiricahua Apaches at the abandoned Dragoon Springs Station. At least two soldiers—Sergeant Samuel Ford and Richardo, a Mexican cattle drover—were killed. Some accounts set the death toll higher. Notably, these were the westernmost battle deaths of the Confederacy, and the only known Confederate soldiers killed in Arizona.

Cochise and his Apaches also ambushed Union troops in Apache Pass in mid-July 1862. This encounter led to the establishment of Fort Bowie to secure the pass and protect that source of water.

The Mail Goes Through

What John Butterfield accomplished was nothing short of astounding. He created a nationwide communication and transportation empire using 1850s technology. He started his mail service with 1,200 employees, 1,800 horses and mules, and hundreds of coaches and wagons. He built approximately 140 stage stations along the line, with dozens more added later. As he told his people: "Remember, boys, nothing on God's Earth must stop the United States mail."

And nothing ever did. According to the National Park Service, the Overland Mail was late reaching the end of the line only three times. Stages were never robbed and were only attacked once by American Indians, at Apache Pass during the Bascom Affair. The driver sustained a minor wound, but the journey continued and the mail got through.

The Overland Mail Company proved that cross-country routes were viable even across wilderness, and paved the way for the transcontinental railroad.

The site of the Apache Pass Stage Station can be visited as part of Fort Bowie National Historic Park. Signs describing the Bascom Affair are posted near a stone foundation overgrown with weeds. This is the site of the station, and the same stones used in its construction. But the ruins actually trace the remains of an 1880 trading post that was rebuilt on the site of the abandoned stage station utilizing the original materials.

With the designation of the Butterfield Overland National Historic Trail, the Dragoon Springs Station stands as the centerpiece of the Arizona experience. To reach the site, take Dragoon Road (Exit 318) off I-10, east of Benson. Follow Dragoon Road south approximately 3.5 miles. When you cross railroad tracks in Dragoon, take an immediate right onto Old Ranch Road and continue on this unpaved road for about 3 miles. If you come to a gate, be sure to close it behind you. Turn left at the Stage Station sign and continue on this rocky road for 1 mile. A high-clearance vehicle is required.

A kiosk and signs are posted to help tell the stories. You'll follow a short path to the ruins tucked away in a lonely canyon. Dragoon Springs is Arizona's only former stage structure with walls still standing. It is a quiet place, made even more haunting since it is ringed by graves. Bodies of the murdered Butterfield employees, fallen Confederates, even the amputated arm of Silas St. John were buried in the desert soil beside the crumbling rock walls, a grim reminder of the once high cost of mail on the frontier.

When You Go

www.nps.gov/buov.

Admission

Free.

Facilities

None.

Pets

It will vary from location to location.

Hiking

The site of Apache Pass Stage Station is part of Fort Bowie National Historic Park. Fort Bowie is a hike-in fort. Departing from Apache Pass Road at the park trailhead, the path follows a gentle route across grassy hills. It's 1.5 miles one-way to Fort Bowie. Along the way visitors will make numerous stops at sites of historic interest marked with informative signs. The site of the stage station is about a half-mile from the trailhead.

A segment of the Overland Mail Company cuts through the backcountry of the Sonoran Desert National Monument near Gila Bend. The monument contains hiking trails, and a network of dirt roads. Cross-country hiking is also permitted.

Camping

PICACHO PEAK STATE PARK

The campground has 85 electric sites for both tent and RV camping. All sites offer a picnic table and barbecue / fire ring. No water or sewer hookups are available. Generator use is not permitted. There are two handicap-accessible restroom and shower buildings. Site reservations can be made online or by calling (877) 697-2757. (520) 466-3183, www.azstateparks.com.

PAINTED ROCK PETROGLYPH CAMPGROUND

About 26 miles northwest of Gila Bend, a small campground at the petroglyph site offers 59 individual sites and two large group areas, featuring picnic tables and steel fire rings. There are vault toilets but no water or electric hookups. Operated by the Bureau of Land Management, the spot near the Gila River was on the Overland Mail Company route, as well as other historic expeditions, and includes interpretive signage. Fee. (623) 580-5500.

Programs/Events

None.

Special Notes

Vehicles must remain on existing roads, and hikers should stay on designated trails. Please respect all private boundaries.

Do not climb on fragile walls and mounds. Leave all artifacts where you find them. Metal detectors and digging tools are prohibited.

The author explores the carved grottoes along the Echo Canyon Trail. Courtesy of Rick Mortensen, Phoenix.

Chiricahua National Monument

Overview

The most spectacular of Arizona's Sky Island mountains bristles with an extraordinary assemblage of vertical rock spires, balanced boulders, columns, and hoodoos, creating refuge for a wide variety of plants and wildlife.

Nearest City

Willcox.

Established

April 18, 1924.

Size

12,025 acres.

Chiricahua National Monument turns every visitor into a geologist as he or she ponders an otherworldly collection of gravity-defying rock formations. These are mountains wrapped in fantasy. This is the work of primordial forces with Dr. Seuss serving as consultant. The soft chisel of the eons continues to tap away at this crust of ancient magma, creating one of the weirdest and most magnificent places in Arizona.

Waves of serrated stone spread across the landscape, wild and exotic but fiercely upright. These are mute and wounded skyscrapers. Massive columns, slender spires, and impossibly balanced boulders loom above the timber. The pinnacles seem endless and can rise hundreds of feet, yet no two are exactly the same, like fossilized snowflakes. Called the Land of Standing-Up Rocks by the Apache warriors who took refuge here and the Wonderland of Rocks by the pioneers who came later, the Chiricahuas gnaw the clouds with broken teeth.

Love at First Sight

Located in the southeastern corner of Arizona, the Chiricahua Mountains are one of the prominent Sky Island ranges. Forested mountaintop islands float above a vast sea of desert and grasslands, creating lush habitats where none should be. You'll find incredible diversity among these tightly stacked ecosystems. More than half the species of birds in North America and the highest concentration of mammals in the United States can be found amid the Sky Islands.

I have a long history with the park. These are some of my favorite hiking trails, and I've pitched my tent more nights in cozy Bonita Canyon Campground than anywhere else in the state. I saw my very first rattlesnake here, and plenty more since. The Chiricahuas are the only place where I've seen a coatimundi, which is the desert's oddest critter, like a lanky raccoon that has had some cosmetic work done. Or a pudgy lemur wearing a mask, as if planning an old-timey stickup.

This is also the first place I ever took my wife hiking in Arizona. After tying the knot in Ohio, my new bride and I honeymooned in Arizona so I could drag her around the state that would soon be our home. The first night we bunked at an elegant resort, the kind where they keep a quantum physicist on staff just to calculate the staggering thread count of the sheets. Swanky, yes, but that didn't stop me from elbowing the missus awake before dawn telling her to layer up, break out the boots, and not to worry about breakfast because we'd grab something at a gas station. Call me Mr. Romance.

I pointed the rental car toward Chiricahua National Monument. I needed her to see this stunning, startling, and profoundly strange place first—and if it didn't absolutely devastate her, well, better to know that right away. That would smack of the most irreconcilable of differences, and we could divvy up the wedding gifts and go our separate ways. I'm happy to report, she's still hanging around all these years later.

A Rain of Lava

About 27 million years ago a savage volcanic event lashed this corner of the world. The eruption, a thousand times more powerful than Mount St. Helens, spewed ash and pumice over 1,200 square miles. The mixture slowly cooled and fused into a tuff of rhyolite. More eruptions followed before sputtering quiet, then the usual suspects—ice, water, and wind—chipped away for a few eons of garden-variety erosion, carving the welded rhyolite into the multitude of curious hoodoos that intrigue us today.

These are troll bones. Stone rockets. Splintered tombstones. An army of ruddy giants on the march. The ranks of vertical rocks become almost anything. Chiricahua allows your imagination to run wild. It allows your imagination to get day drunk. This land is ripe with mystique. A thin forest squeezes between towering pinnacles as determined plants find purchase in the volcanic soil and somehow hold on.

The 8-mile Bonita Canyon Drive provides an excellent introduction to the monument. The paved road passes the visitor center and makes a twisting climb through oak, cypress, and pine woodlands with columns of stone looming overhead. A few pullouts can be found along the way. The scenic drive ends at Massai Point (elevation 6,870 feet), a high perch with 360-degree views of Rhyolite Canyon and surrounding mountain peaks.

But like all parks, Chiricahua is best enjoyed on foot. The monument features a beautiful system of trails, many of them interconnected so there's no shortage of options.

Big Balanced Rock stands 25 feet high and weighs 1,000 tons. Photo by the author.

The Punch and Judy formation adds a touch of whimsy along the Heart of Rocks Trail. Photo by the author.

A Stone Garden

My favorite spot, Heart of Rocks, lies deep in the monument. It's at the center of a web of trails, so different routes will get you there. The easiest access to Heart of Rocks comes via a trio of trails: Ed Riggs, Mushroom Rock, and Big Balanced Rock. From the Echo Canyon parking area, start on the Ed Riggs Trail, which drops gradually into a finger canyon bracketed by fractured columns and rhyolite punctuation.

Turn onto Mushroom Rock Trail where you'll soon pass the flattop fungus of stone that prompts the name. It's not an imposing formation, but don't worry, there's plenty more to come. After climbing through a forested ravine, you'll connect with Big Balanced Rock Trail. The path follows a high ridgeline with sweeping views. Look for Cochise Head, a distinctive mountain that suggests the noble profile of the Apache leader. Soon you pass through a corridor of stacked rocks and haunting hoodoos. Big Balanced Rock waits near the end of the trail. The namesake 1,000-ton boulder teeters atop what appears to be a thimble; I often tiptoe past so as not to disturb the precarious monolith.

This is the junction for the Heart of Rocks Trail, a 1.1-mile loop. Taking the short path clockwise affords more dramatic vistas and easier walking through this strange stone garden. But be alert for the signed turnoff because it's easy to miss amid all the eye candy.

Volcanic intensity still crackles within this twisty little labyrinth, undercut by a sneaky sense of whimsy. From the chaos looms the familiar as you wind through the forest. Unexpected shapes suddenly burst into sight. Behold, the formation known as Thor's Hammer! Hey, a Duck on a Rock! Visions of Punch and Judy, Camel's Head, and the Totem Pole pull you along. I love the weird verticality of this place, where the rocks seem so alert, so poised.

Reconnect with Big Balanced Rock Trail and backtrack for a total jaunt of 7.3 miles. The return is mostly downhill to the trailhead, always a nice way to end a hike.

Last of the Warriors

For centuries the Chiricahua Apaches made their home in southeastern Arizona. A nomadic people, they hunted game and gathered edible plants. They were also fearless warriors and fiercely resisted colonization. Yet with the discovery of mineral wealth across Southern Arizona more settlers streamed into the country, leading to continued clashes. American troops were dispatched to the area, and campaigns were waged. Always outnumbered, the Apaches used their fighting skill and knowledge of the rugged terrain to their advantage, returning to the mountains that provided them with shelter and food.

It finally ended in 1886 when a small band led by Geronimo surrendered to the US Army. After fighting so relentlessly to hold on to their beloved mountains, the captured Apaches were imprisoned in Florida before eventually being relocated to Fort Sill, Oklahoma.

With the Apaches removed from the equation, more settlers arrived. Swedish immigrants Neil and Emma Erickson were among the first in 1888. Their coming would make all the difference. By the 1920s, the Erickson's oldest daughter, Lillian, and her husband, Ed Riggs, were running the family homestead as a guest ranch.

While wind and water carved the rocks of the Chiricahua Mountains, another force of nature preserved the sculpted wonderland for future generations. Lillian was the strong-willed "Lady Boss" of Faraway Ranch, and she and Ed aggressively promoted the landscape as a place worthy of protection. They touted the unique beauty of the region and constructed riding and hiking trails. They gave tours to Arizona officials and wrote letters to Washington, DC. Their lobbying efforts paid off in 1924 when Chiricahua National Monument was established. Much of the infrastructure was built in the 1930s by the Civilian Conservation Corps (CCC), which gave young men work during the Great Depression.

Lillian struggled with hearing issues all her life. She went blind in 1942. Ed died in 1950 yet Lillian, sightless and almost deaf, kept the guest ranch going until 1970. She continued to live on the homestead until her death in 1977. The National Park Service purchased Faraway Ranch in 1979 and began offering tours a few years later.

Birds and Beasts

The Chiricahua Mountains exist at a rare crossroads of ecosystems, where the Sonoran and Chihuahuan Deserts overlap and the Rocky Mountains and Sierra Madre meet. Found among the varied habitats is a remarkable diversity of species. Binocular-toting birders travel from all over the world to add to their life lists. Many species such as the elegant trogon and Rivoli's hummingbird reach the northern edge of their range here.

Since nearly 90 percent of the monument has been designated as wilderness, the mountains are an excellent place to spot wildlife such as the Arizona white-tailed deer, javelina, black bear, mountain lion, all four North American species of skunks, the endemic Chiricahua fox squirrel, the black-tailed rattlesnake, and the curious coatimundi.

There's no mistaking the coatimundi, one of Arizona's most distinctive animals. Photo by the author.

Also called coati, coatimundis are social mammals that belong to the same family as raccoons. They're native to Central and South America but have found their way to the American Southwest. Females are about the size of a large house cat, and they travel in bands with other females and babies. Males can be almost twice as large and are more solitary. Active during the day, coatimundis can often be seen foraging on the forest floor sniffing with long snouts, their striped tails sticking straight up in the air like a furry periscope. Coatis are omnivores, and their diet consists of insects, reptiles, fruits, nuts, and almost anything else they can fit into their mouth. Adorable as they are, always maintain a safe distance from wildlife and never attempt to feed.

When You Go

(520) 824-3560, www.nps.gov/chir.

Admission

Free.

Facilities

The visitor center has museum exhibits and a gift shop.

Pets

Leashed pets are allowed only on the following trails: Silver Spur Trail, Faraway Ranch, Bonito Creek, and the path connecting the visitor center and campground.

Pets are not permitted on other hiking trails, inside the visitor center or public buildings, on interpretive walks/programs, or in the wilderness area.

Hiking

Chiricahua National Monument features 17 miles of trails, many of them interconnected. There's no shortage of hiking possibilities. Most of the park is designated wilderness, so bicycles are only allowed on paved roads.

Bonita Creek Trail winds along a streambed that's generally dry for 0.6 miles to the Faraway Ranch Picnic Area. Silver Spur Meadow Trail (1.2 miles one-way) dips into the park's pioneer past as it makes a gentle ramble through the Faraway Ranch Historic District to the Stafford cabin, and a few other historic structures. With another path connecting the visitor center and campground, all the lower meadows are easily accessed on foot.

NATURAL BRIDGE TRAIL

Start from a parking lot on the scenic drive and wind through oak and juniper woodlands. The trail climbs a moderate ridge and ends at an overlook of a small water-carved bridge across the canyon; 4.8 miles round trip.

SUGARLOAF TRAIL

Hike this trail (1.8 miles round trip) along a moderate ridgeline to snag the summit of Sugarloaf Mountain, one of the highest points in the monument (7,310 feet), still topped by a CCC-constructed fire lookout.

MASSAI POINT NATURE TRAIL

At the end of the scenic drive, get out and walk around to soak up the big panoramas of distant mountains and deep-cut valleys on this easy 0.5-mile loop. The paved portion from the parking area to the exhibit building is wheelchair accessible.

ECHO CANYON LOOP

This route utilizes Echo Canyon, Hailstone, and Ed Riggs Trails for a moderate 3.3-mile journey through some spectacular rock formations, into a lush cove punctuated by the splash of a stuttering little stream that flows seasonally. Hike it counterclockwise for a gentler ascent. For those who can't manage the entire loop, you can venture to the Echo Canyon Grottoes (1 mile round trip), an alluring corridor of intimate formations.

Most of the rest of the trails form multiple loops through canyons, forests, and formations to explore on their own or to access the remote little Heart of Rocks Loop. Consult the park map for trail lengths, elevation changes, and degree of difficulty to select the right outing for you.

A hiker shuttle runs periodically. Ask at the visitor center.

Camping

Tucked away in a shady pine and oak grove, Bonito Canyon Campground has 25 sites and includes restrooms with flush toilets, running water, and picnic tables. A group site can accommodate 9 to 24 people. Vehicle length limit is 29 feet. There are no hookups or showers. Make reservations at www.recreation.gov or call (877) 444-6777.

Programs/Events

Tours of Faraway Ranch are conducted when staffing permits. Faraway Ranch is the homestead built by Neil and Emma Erickson, who settled near the mouth of Bonita Canyon in the late 1880s. It's a fascinating story of surviving in the Arizona outback that continued when their two daughters turned the place into a guest ranch that would later become very successful under the management of Lillian and her husband.

Rangers conduct evening talks at the campground amphitheater and other programs such as star parties. Chiricahua National Monument is an International Dark Sky Park.

Special Notes

Please respect the formations. Rock climbing and bouldering is prohibited.

Coronado National Memorial lies at the southern end of the Huachuca Mountains on the United States–Mexico border. Photo by the author.

Coronado National Memorial

Overview

A scenic mountain perch offers incredible hiking, panoramas, and even a cave while commemorating the first European expedition of the Southwest.

Nearest Cities

Sierra Vista, Bisbee.

Established

The site was designated Coronado International Memorial on August 18, 1941. It became Coronado National Memorial on November 5, 1952.

Size

4,750 acres.

The expedition proved to be a failure. Francisco Vásquez de Coronado and his men spent two years searching for cities of gold that didn't exist.

Yet if they had set out carrying picks and shovels instead of spears and crossbows, perhaps they wouldn't have returned with empty pockets. No golden cities had yet been constructed, but the building material was right beneath the Spaniards' feet. They traveled through a mineral-rich swath of what would become Arizona, where vast deposits of silver, copper, and gold would later be discovered.

Nestled in the foothills of the Huachuca Mountains abutting the Mexican border, Coronado National Memorial commemorates and interprets the Coronado Expedition of 1540–1542 and its lasting impacts on the culture of the Southwest.

International Views

Set aside the history lesson for a minute and concentrate on the scenery, which snatches your breath. Located about 20 miles south of Sierra Vista, the memorial is part of Arizona's Sky Islands where four major ecosystems overlap—the Sonoran and Chihuahuan Deserts, the Rocky Mountains, and the Sierra Madre.

A single road enters the park and climbs from verdant grasslands into oak woodlands

A twisting narrow unpaved road climbs through a brushy canyon to reach the high perch of Montezuma Pass. Photo by the author.

and continues through heavier forest up Montezuma Canyon. Past the visitor center the road is paved for a mile and graded dirt for the upper two miles. It twists around tight switchbacks (vehicles over 24 feet are prohibited) and steep grades as the world falls away below. Montezuma Pass Overlook sits at 6,575 feet, flanked by a parking area and picnic tables.

Enjoy expansive views of Sonora, Mexico, to the south, the long sweep of the San Rafael Valley to the west, and the San Pedro River Valley to the east, which is believed to be the route taken by the Coronado Expedition. The dirt road continues northwest (as Forest Road 61), departing the memorial and angling into the Canelo Hills and on to Parker Canyon Lake for those seeking that sort of adventure, but I am content to stop at the pass. This is a place to revel in staggering panoramas. Long green meadows cloaked in high desert scrub wrap around clusters of hills. Even at less than 7,000 feet, Montezuma Pass is one of the preeminent viewpoints in Southern Arizona.

It is also a picnic spot of rare beauty, but I am too fidgety to sit still for long. From here, a network of trails fan out, including the southernmost segment of the Arizona National Scenic Trail, which stretches nearly 800 miles along the length of the state from Mexico to Utah.

To reach the southern terminus of this epic route, I start out on Joe's Canyon Trail as it

Joe's Canyon Trail leads to the southern terminus of the Arizona National Scenic Trail. Photo by the author.

skirts the rocky flank of Coronado Peak. After 0.75 miles, I reach Yaqui Ridge Trail and bear south. The trail drops steeply from the ridge through clumps of yuccas, agaves, and ocotillos with broad vistas at every step. It ends at International Boundary Marker 102. This defines the border with Mexico and also the southwestern corner of Coronado National Memorial.

The climb back to Montezuma Pass is steeper than I realized. But I don't mind pausing occasionally to catch my breath because the views are unfailingly gorgeous. This is one of the quirks of the Arizona Trail. You have to hike south before you hike north, if you want to complete the entire journey. It's just under 4 miles round trip by the time I reach Montezuma Pass. If I planned to keep walking to Utah, I would head out on the Crest Trail crossing the spine of the Huachuca Mountains.

Instead, I opt for a short scramble to the top of Coronado Peak. A 300-foot climb reaches the summit topped with a shade ramada and additional signage describing the Coronado Expedition.

Seven Cities of Gold

One fabled city of gold might not have been enough to spur a massive expedition—but seven did the trick. If you're going to dream, may as well dream big.

It started with four shipwreck survivors who wandered in what today is Texas and northern Mexico for eight long years before being rescued in 1536. They told stories of fabulous cities teeming with wealth, also known as Cibola. No one seemed to question why the men chose to loiter in the wilderness instead of relocating to one of these swanky towns. Eager to know if the tales were true, the viceroy of New Spain, Antonio de Mendoza, dispatched a Franciscan friar, Fray Marcos de Niza, to explore the new lands to the north in 1539. Acting as guide would be Esteban de Dorantes (also known as Estevancio), an enslaved African man who had been one of the shipwreck survivors.

Fray Marcos is credited with being the first European to enter what is now Arizona. The friar sent his companion ahead. Esteban reached a Zuni pueblo believed by modern scholars to be Háwikuh, south of present-day Gallup, New Mexico. He was killed when he tried to enter the village. Marcos pressed on cautiously until he could see Háwikuh from a distance. Perhaps he was fooled by a trick of the sun or an overactive imagination, but when he returned he gave a glowing report to Viceroy Mendoza. He claimed to have seen a wonderful place called Cibola that was equal in size to Mexico City.

Coronado on the March

Viceroy Mendoza chose his friend Francisco Vásquez de Coronado to lead the vast expedition that would claim this new land overflowing with wealth. Coronado set out in February 1540, leading 350 Spaniards, more than 1,000 Native allies, many servants and enslaved people, and several priests, including Fray Marcos, who would show them the way.

In July, with great anticipation Coronado arrived at Háwikuh. But instead of the gleaming golden city they expected, the Spaniards found only a stone-masonry pueblo. Of course that didn't stop them from attacking the village, killing and driving off the Zunis. Stocked with food, Coronado made the Pueblo Formerly Known as Cibola his headquarters. He branded Fray Marcos a liar and sent him back to Mexico City to escape the wrath of his men.

While recovering from wounds sustained in battle, Coronado dispatched his captains to scout the region. Don Pedro de Tovar traveled to Hopi villages in today's northeastern Arizona. Garcia López de Cárdenas reached the Grand Canyon, the first European to gaze at that rather startling sight. On the Pecos River, the Spaniards encountered a Plains Indian they nicknamed the Turk. He described a rich land to the east called Quivira. And despite their recent disappointment, the Spaniards were absolutely certain that this mysterious city of unimaginable wealth was genuine.

Coronado and his men spent a long winter battling with the Indigenous people, who were not keen on the visitors overstaying their welcome and eating all their food. Finally, in the spring the Spaniards set out for Quivira. But after a long meandering journey that took them all the way to present-day Salina, Kansas, they found only a settlement of grass houses. When confronted, the Turk admitted the tale of Quivira was a plot by the Pueblo

Indians to lure them onto the plains where they would become lost and die of starvation. Coronado ordered the Turk's execution and they began the long march back home, empty-handed. They reached Mexico City in the spring of 1542, without chests of gold and jewels. They did however bring back knowledge of the new land and its peoples. Coronado also paved the way for later Spanish explorers and missionaries to travel through the Southwest, developing the distinctive Hispanic-American culture we know today.

What to expect

Since this is a memorial site, there are no artifacts or relics of the Coronado Expedition within the park. Visitors will find plenty of signage at the visitor center and on some trails reflecting on the complete story of the expedition, from the bloody confrontations to the long-time ramifications.

The park was originally established as Coronado International Memorial in 1941, with the hope that Mexico would establish a similar park on its side of the border. When that failed to materialize, President Harry Truman renamed it Coronado National Memorial in 1952.

A highlight of the park is a visit to Coronado Cave, one of the few open, undeveloped caves in Southern Arizona. You don't have to worry about squeezing through. The large cavern is 600 feet deep and in most places about 70 feet wide. Legend has it that Chiricahua Apache leader Geronimo often hid out in the cave. It's a half-mile hike to reach the cave with an elevation gain of 500 feet. Some light scrambling over slick rocks is required to reach the cave floor.

Be prepared. Carry at least two sources of light. Do not explore the cave alone. Wear gloves. Touching the cave walls without gloves causes damage and prevents the growth of new formations. Check in at the visitor center to see if permits are required and for more information on safety and preservation of this special environment.

If you don't want to make the drive to Montezuma Pass, there is another picnic area nestled in the trees near the visitor center. But come on, the pass dishes up views worth at least one city of gold.

When You Go

(520) 366-5515, www.nps.gov/coro.

Admission

Free.

Facilities

The visitor center has informational panels and a small gift shop. There are hands-on displays of 16th-century clothing and armor for visitors to try on. Large picture windows overlook a lush desert courtyard.

Pets

Leashed pets are allowed on the Crest Trail only.

Hiking

Bicycles and motorized vehicles are restricted to developed roads only.

WINDMILL TRAIL

Follow an old ranch road through grasslands and rolling foothills to an historic windmill and corral: 2 miles round trip. Trailhead is approximately a mile east of the visitor center. Park on north side of the road near the fire danger indicator sign.

CORONADO CAVE TRAIL

The parking lot and trailhead are located 0.25 miles west of the visitor center. It's a moderate half-mile climb followed by a scramble down a steep rocky slope to enter the cave.

CORONADO PEAK TRAIL

An interpretive trail climbs from the parking area at Montezuma Pass to a distinctive summit where you'll enjoy outstanding views from shady benches; 0.8 miles round trip.

JOE'S CANYON TRAIL

This lanky route traverses Montezuma Canyon, climbing from the visitor center through the saddle atop Smuggler's Ridge before ending at Montezuma Pass; 6.2 miles round trip. The park occasionally runs a hiker shuttle so that only a one-way hike is necessary.

YAQUI RIDGE

This spur trail branches off Joe's Canyon and descends steeply to the US/Mexico border. The trail marks the southern terminus of the Arizona National Scenic Trail. It is illegal to cross into Mexico. To complete the hike from Montezuma Pass, you must first hike along Joe's Canyon Trail, making the total just under 4 miles round trip.

CREST TRAIL

Another piece of the Arizona National Scenic Trail, Crest Trail begins at the northeast corner of the Montezuma Pass parking area and climbs deeper into the Huachuca Mountains before reaching the turnoff for Miller Peak, the highest point in the range. It's 4 miles round trip to the Coronado National Memorial northern boundary along this strenuous trail, or 5.3 miles one-way to Miller Peak.

Camping

Park is day use only.

Camping is available in Coronado National Forest, or at Parker Canyon Lake, 18 miles west in the Canelo Hills. The 65-site campground sits among a stand of oaks and junipers overlooking the water. Amenities include picnic tables, fire pits, restrooms, and drinking water. No hookups. First-come, first-served. Supplies and boat rentals are available at the marina. (520) 455-7847, www.parkercanyonlake.com.

Programs/Events

Rangers offer interpretive talks, hikes, tours of Coronado Cave, and other programs as staffing permits.

Special Notes

The upper two miles of unpaved road to Montezuma Pass is narrow with tight curves but usually passable year-round for vehicles under 24 feet in length. Temporary road closures may occur after heavy rain or snowfall.

Smuggling and/or illegal entry may occur so close to the border. Be aware of your surroundings at all times. Report suspicious behavior to a park ranger or border patrol agent.

The shady porch at the visitor center makes a quiet spot for visitors to relax before beginning the return hike to their vehicles. Photo by the author.

Fort Bowie National Historic Site

Overview

A confluence of bloody conflict and beautiful scenery make the hike to this lonely park a true journey back to Arizona's frontier past.

Nearest Cities

Bowie, Willcox.

Established

August 30, 1964.

Size

999 acres.

I'm walking amid the sun-gnawed bones of Fort Bowie, one of the most significant forts on the Arizona frontier. The visitor center and its wraparound veranda lined with rocking chairs sits up the slope, flanked by picnic tables, and guarded by a howitzer. Spread across the flats, remnants of the fort still stand. Pathways weave among the stone walls. Slabs of adobe rise like broken gravestones above the tall grass.

For being the site of so much violence, it is peaceful here almost beyond words. Birdsong, the whirr of grasshoppers that launch at my every step, and the rustle of grass stalks bending in the breeze are all that I hear. It's a warm October day, still shy of the peak winter season. Not that anything changes much from month to month. Crowds are never an issue. The remote setting and a required 3-mile round-trip hike make Fort Bowie National Historic Site the least-visited park in Arizona.

During the late 1800s, Fort Bowie was the main staging point for the US Army's conflict with the Chiricahua Apaches, led by figures such as Cochise and Geronimo. At this lonely outpost much of Arizona's history was shaped. It's another instance where a clash of cultures played out, a struggle between a young emerging nation seeking its manifest destiny and a proud independent people trying to preserve their land and way of life.

Why it came to a head in this isolated spot isn't hard to figure out. In Arizona, the answer to almost any question is water.

The post cemetery can be found along the trail to enter Fort Bowie National Historic Site. Photo by the author.

An interpretive trail weaves among the ruins of the legendary frontier fort. Photo by the author.

The Echo of Water

Beneath a leafy canopy, a thin trickle spills down a rock face and flows through the sand. The small gurgle is almost inaudible amid the tangle of willow, walnut, and velvet ash trees, but don't be fooled. In this arid land, the splash of water echoes across the landscape like a thunderclap.

Or like cannon fire.

Apache Spring has quenched history's thirst in southeastern Arizona while creating a crossroads of violent conflict. The spring water tumbles down a slender ravine in Apache Pass, a high desert corridor separating the Chiricahua Mountains from the Dos Cabezas Mountains. This narrow cleft rises to an elevation above 5,000 feet and is ringed by prominent peaks like Bowie Mountain and Helen's Dome. Desert grasses mingled with brushy chaparral dominate the lower slopes of Apache Pass with oak, juniper, and pinion-pine woodlands spread across higher ground.

For hundreds of years the area was home to the Chiricahua Apaches. Since it offered the only water source for miles around, as well as firewood and grass, Apache Pass also became a noted landmark for travelers. Spanish explorers and later Mexican settlers used Apache Pass, and it was an important stop along an emigrant trail for those heading to the California goldfields.

In 1858, Butterfield's Overland Mail Company began a stage line between St. Louis and San Francisco, a route that utilized Apache Pass. A station was built in the pass to take advantage of the precious spring water.

During this time there were isolated instances of violence between the Apache people and settlers. The pass and surrounding area didn't become part of the United States until the Gadsden Purchase in 1854. For a time, Cochise and his band of Chiricahua Apaches managed a tenuous peace with the newly arrived Americans. They allowed the stage line to operate largely unhindered for more than two years. Then everything changed in the winter of 1861.

Bascom Affair

He may have just been following orders, but because of his heavy-handed and inflexible approach, Lieutenant George Bascom earned the distinction of forever having his name attached to the event that triggered America's longest war. It is known simply as the Bascom Affair.

In January 1861, Felix Martinez Ward was kidnapped during an Apache raid on his family's ranch. In February, a young inexperienced Lieutenant Bascom led a detachment of 54 men into Apache Pass with orders to recover Ward and all stolen livestock. The lieutenant invited Cochise to a meeting, which quickly turned ugly when Bascom accused him of kidnapping and theft. Despite Cochise's claims of innocence and offers to help find the boy, Bascom attempted to arrest him. Using a knife, Cochise cut through the back of the tent and escaped. The other Chiricahua people, including members of Cochise's own family, were captured. The soldiers took refuge in the rock-walled Butterfield stage station.

In the following days and weeks, Cochise took captives and attempted to exchange them for his family and warriors. When his effort failed, he killed the hostages. The army retaliated by executing the warriors in their custody. The incident sparked open warfare between whites and the Chiricahua Apache that raged for the next quarter-century.

Felix Ward had been kidnapped by Apaches, but not by Cochise's Chiricahua Apaches. He was traded to the White Mountain Apaches and raised with their children to become a warrior. As an adult he became a scout and interpreter for the US Army and changed his name to Mickey Free.

Battle of Apache Pass

Of course, 1861 was a year of conflict all around. Just a few months after the Bascom Affair, the Civil War broke out—and not all the fighting was confined to the east. A Confederate force invaded New Mexico Territory with the intention of seizing the mineral-rich Southwest and eventually seaports on the West Coast. Volunteers from California marched toward Arizona to counter the invasion. Instead, their most heated battle would come against the Chiricahua Apache.

On July 15, 1862, an advance guard of the California Column entered Apache Pass led by Captain Thomas Roberts. His force consisted of approximately 100 men, supply wagons, livestock, and two howitzers. The soldiers looked forward to fresh water and rest after a long march in the summer heat. Suddenly gunfire erupted as Apache warriors ambushed the rear of the column, hoping to capture the livestock and supplies.

While Roberts was able to reorganize his men and drive off the attackers, he now knew the spring would be heavily guarded. Cochise and his ally, Mangas Coloradas, with a combined band of about 150 warriors, controlled both hills overlooking the water. A fierce battle ensued that seesawed back and forth through the day. The howitzers made the difference, driving the Apaches away from the spring and offering cover for a bayonet charge that finally secured the commanding high ground. The Apaches attacked again the following day but quickly broke off the fighting when the howitzers were unleashed.

The battle led directly to the establishment of Fort Bowie to control the critical pass and spring. It went up quickly that summer, built by soldiers of the California Column. It began with tents and then hastily constructed adobe huts to fend off winter weather.

Built atop a hill overlooking the spring, the primitive structures had the air of a temporary camp.

In 1868, a more expansive and permanent version of Fort Bowie was built on a plateau 300 yards to the southeast. It included adobe barracks, a row of houses for officers, corrals, storehouses, a hospital, and a post trader's store. More buildings were added over the years. When it was abandoned in 1894, Fort Bowie was a modern post of about 38 structures. Those are the remnants left behind today.

Hiking through History

Fort Bowie National Historic Site is a hike-in park, the only one in Arizona, possibly the only one in the entire national park system. Visitors must take a 1.5-mile hike to enter. This helps protect natural and historical resources. It also sets the mood, allowing the sense of solitude and isolation of the frontier to seep into your consciousness. Along the way, each chapter of the story unfolds.

As you ramble across the rolling hills, the trail winds past the site of the Butterfield Stage Station, a re-created Apache wickiup, the post cemetery filled with grave markers, the original fort, and Apache Spring, which still produces a reliable supply of water. Along the way detailed signs provide information and locations. Nothing is abstract anymore. It's all right in front of me. This is the ground where they stood, where they fought and died.

As soon as you climb out of the woods surrounding the spring you get your first glimpse of what remains of Fort Bowie spread across the tablelands and ringed by rising hills. I fall in love with the location every time I'm here.

Pathways weave among the fort buildings, each identified by plaques indicating its original use. Additional signs and historic photos help bring the setting to life. There's even a photo of Geronimo and his band following their surrender in 1886. They were brought to the fort before being exiled to Florida, thus ending the Apache Wars.

The visitor center is loaded with exhibits and artifacts adding more layers to the story. There's also a small store stocked with books and souvenir items.

Yet I have to admit, my favorite part of the visitor center is the long covered porch that encircles the building. I'm a sucker for a good porch, and this one is a genuine classic. Old-fashioned enough to feel like it could have been part of the original fort. It features broad views, cooling shade, and enough rocking chairs to be mistaken for a Cracker Barrel. After a hike and a history lesson, it's the perfect place to catch my breath and savor the big quiet before starting back.

When it is time to go, you can hike back the way you came in. Another option is to take the trail behind the visitor center, which scrambles up a limestone hill known as Overlook Ridge with lovely views of the fort and valleys below. This route doesn't add any distance but offers a little more of a workout than the initial hike. Yet it more than pays for any huffing and puffing with some big panoramas of this still lonely corner of Arizona. It crosses the ridge, passing some informational signage and a couple of sitting benches before descending and rejoining the entrance trail near the Butterfield Station, a half-mile from the trailhead on Apache Pass Road.

When You Go

(520) 847-2500, www.nps.gov/fobo.

Admission

Free.

Facilities

The visitor center has museum exhibits, a gift shop, and drinking water. Visitor center hours vary seasonally. The park grounds, trails, and ruins are open daily, sunrise to sunset.

Pets

Pets must be kept on a leash no longer than 6 feet at all times.

Hiking

The hike to the fort is a relatively gentle 1.5 miles across grassy hills and a slight elevation gain at the end. Along the way visitors will make numerous stops at sites of historic interest marked with informative signs. Wear comfortable shoes, a hat, and sunscreen—and always carry water.

For the return hike, visitors can follow the same path back to their vehicle. Better still, take the trail across Overlook Ridge, behind the visitor center. This route is also 1.5 miles but involves a bit more climbing. However, the vistas of the fort and valleys below make it a beautiful, rewarding hike. There are interpretive sites along the way before the path finally descends the slopes and rejoins the entry trail.

Camping

The park is day use only. Park grounds and trails are open sunrise to sunset.

Programs/Events

Talks and guided hikes are offered during the cooler months as staffing permits.

Special Notes

The park is located 12 miles south of Bowie. The final segment of Apache Pass Road to reach the trailhead to Fort Bowie is unpaved, but generally manageable in a sedan. A hike is required just to reach Fort Bowie. Special access for mobility-impaired visitors can be obtained by calling the park ahead of time.

Do not climb on fragile walls and mounds. Metal detectors and digging tools are prohibited.

Only a short drive from Tucson, Ironwood Forest protects a scenic and vital swath of Sonoran Desert. Photo by the author.

Ironwood Forest National Monument

Overview

Solitude, scenery, and saguaros are waiting in Tucson's backcountry, along with a scraggly forest of the amazing ironwood tree.

Nearest Cities

Tucson, Marana.

Established

June 9, 2000.

Size

129,055 acres.

Saguaros may be the rock stars of the Sonoran Desert, but ironwood trees are the workhorses. They are the glue that holds the community together. Truth be told, probably half the saguaros out there owe their very existence to ironwood trees.

Desert ironwoods raise generations of plants within the protective microenvironment they create. They increase plant diversity, feed local wildlife, and replenish the soil. And they do it for centuries. Estimates show some trees to be 800 years old, and it's likely they live even longer.

Despite their impressive resume, many casual desert visitors would be hard pressed to identify the tree. That's no reflection on their observational skills. Ironwoods lack a distinctive profile like so many desert species. They can take the shape of a multi-trunked shrub or a canopy-forming tree standing nearly 50 feet tall.

Created in 2000, Ironwood Forest National Monument is an oddly configured chunk of land that was snatched away from developers northwest of Tucson. The Bureau of Land Management (BLM) manages the monument and the unusual shape is so it can encompass multiple mountain ranges including the Silver Bell, Waterman, and Sawtooth Mountains. The monument contains the densest known stand of the vital trees. Finally people began to realize, when you save the ironwoods, you save the desert.

Mines and Missiles

Don't set out for the monument expecting a welcome mat. Ironwood Forest doesn't care

Clouds wreathe the Silver Bell Mountains in Ironwood Forest National Monument. Photo by the author.

about convenience or your creature comforts. There is no visitor center, no water, and no restrooms. Cell service may not work in the remote areas. And you'll be mostly bouncing down dirt roads. If you're putting together a Pro and Con list, these should obviously go on the Pro side. Just be prepared before setting out.

This is a backcountry experience. Many of the roads are rugged. High-clearance or four-wheel-drive vehicles are recommended. Even getting in can be tricky. There are three main entry points to the monument, all are dirt, and one of them requires driving through a river. It's always a good idea to check road conditions before you go.

If you want a comprehensive overview of the monument and are equipped for a rough ride, come in on Silverbell Road from the south. This tends to be the most rugged route but bites off a nice chunk of monument as it wraps around the Silver Bell Mountains in a horseshoe shape, while passing a mine, an old cemetery, and a somewhat frightening historic site. Start from Avra Valley Road, Exit 242 off I-10, just north of Tucson in the town of Marana. Head west on Avra Valley, and you'll soon cross a bridge over the Santa Cruz River and pass the Marana Regional Airport, where the airfields were originally built during World War II to train pilots.

You'll notice a turnoff for Saguaro National Park but just ignore it. That's an adventure for a different day. Keep rolling past cotton fields and then mesquite-dotted rangeland. Near Pump Station Road, at the edge of the Silver Bells, you'll officially enter the monument.

You'll snake into the hills toward the Silver Bell Mine, still in operation. Mining began in this area in the latter half of the 1800s and continued in fits and starts. Despite the name of the mountains and two towns that sprang up, Silverbell and Silver Bell, copper proved to be the most abundant and enduring ore.

For an interesting piece of more modern history, turn left on (unmarked) Johnston Mine Road for a short jog to the Titan II Missile Interpretive Site. This was a location of one of 18 Titan II Missile silos surrounding Tucson that were manned around the clock from 1963 to 1987. Designed as a deterrent during the Cold War, each site was capable of launching a Titan II, the largest nuclear missile ever deployed in the United States, in 58 seconds if the country came under attack. At the site, several informational panels tell the tale of those tense times, and other markers illustrate the layout of the huge bunker that was once locked and loaded beneath your feet.

Journeys on Dirt

Just shy of the mine entrance, you'll bid adios to pavement and turn left onto Silverbell Road. The rutted dirt road carves a route through the desert scrub. Rocky hills crowd the landscape, their slopes thick with ocotillos waving in spindly triumph.

This takes some careful driving in my high-clearance vehicle as the road dips in and out of several arroyos. When monsoon storms chew up this section of Silverbell, it requires four-wheel drive. The road finally bends north and begins to smooth out as it passes an Ironwood Forest National Monument sign. The weathered Silver Bell cemetery lies not far beyond where 131 burials took place.

After 13 miles, Silverbell Road reaches a T-junction that highlights all the monument's main entry points. Sasco Road bears north to the community of Red Rock. Along the way it passes the ghost town of Sasco where a few foundations remain, abused by the elements and vandals. Overall the dirt road is manageable in high clearance with a word of warning. It fords the Santa Cruz River. When water is running high, the road can become impassable.

Also at the junction, Silverbell Road turns east, and this proves to be the easiest and most accessible route in the monument. Most of the time this north branch of Silverbell can be driven in a sedan. So if you prefer your driving without drama, this is the way to enter and exit the monument. (From I-10, take Exit 236 and travel west on Marana Road for 5.8 miles to Silverbell Road. Turn right on Silverbell and continue to the monument.)

The north segment of Silverbell Road is also bracketed by a remarkable sampling of Sonoran Desert—diverse, dangerous, and enticing. The valley floor bristles with a forest of gaunt trees like ironwood, palo verde, and mesquite, in addition to the sharp vertical notes of saguaros that wash up against the hard rock cliffs. It's such a dense stand of the tall cactus that this could have easily been designated as Saguaro National Monument. But that name was already taken.

The Crown Jewel

Looming over the valley is the high point of the Silver Bell Mountains, Ragged Top. Unlike neighboring peaks with clean, cactus-lined crests, Ragged Top bares its stony teeth. It rises above 3,900 feet, roofed by a jumble of sheer cliffs. The mountain is a wealth of biodiversity, harboring nearly 70 percent of the plant species that grow in the monument. The high ramparts are also home to the last herd of indigenous desert bighorn sheep in southeastern Arizona.

Ragged Top is the showpiece of the monument, one of those distinctive summits that cause peak baggers to twitch with anticipation. It looks as if a jangly collection of carabineers and coils of rope would be needed to reach the top, but there is actually a Class 2 gully on the north side that cuts a path through the summit cliffs. Class 2 means you'll be scrambling up a steep incline and may need to use your hands. Wear long pants and long sleeves because you'll be bushwhacking through some thick desert scrub. Most importantly, do not summit peaks in the Silver Bells, including Ragged Top, or the Waterman Mountains from January 1 through April 30 during bighorn lambing season.

The porous granite soil around Ragged Top (which is mostly rhyolite) and throughout the monument creates ideal conditions for ironwood trees to thrive.

Ancient Trees and People

The tree is named for its dense wood, among the heaviest in the world. Drop a piece of ironwood in water and it sinks. Visually, there's nothing remarkable about ironwood trees. They have that haggard look of many arid plants and can easily be mistaken from a distance for the more common mesquite tree. Their worth is measured in the benefits they provide to their neighbors. Ironwoods are a habitat-modifying keystone species.

As nurse plants, they provide shade and shelter beneath a dense canopy that protects young plants from harsh sun in the summer and frost in the winter. More than 230 plant species have been found starting their growth beneath ironwood branches. A member of the legume family, ironwood trees, like soybeans and peas, fix nitrogen in the soil, making it easier for nearby plants to absorb nutrients.

The ironwood's presence can dramatically increase the number of bird species in a habitat. Dozens of species of mammals and reptiles use the ironwood for forage and shelter, and its seeds are a peanut-like delicacy enjoyed by birds, rodents, and coyotes. They may not be as majestic as saguaros, but they are desert royalty nonetheless. A monument offering protection was long overdue.

Besides the rich landscape, the monument also protects numerous cultural and historical sites. Humans have occupied this desert for more than 5,000 years, leaving behind rock art and faint traces of their time here—ceramics, roasting pits, trash mounds, campsites, and villages. More than 200 sites from the prehistoric Hohokam period have been recorded, some dating back to AD 600.

Three areas—Los Robles Archaeological District, Cocoraque Butte Archaeological District, and the Mission of Santa Ana Chiquiburitac—are listed on the National Register of Historic Places. The mission was built in 1811 by Tohono O'Odham laborers for Spanish Franciscan friars, but all that remains are a few stones outlining the foundation.

Desert Rats Unite

I can't resist this patch of pristine desert, even in summer. No one becomes a desert rat because they have an abundance of common sense. I was hiking in Ironwood Forest on a late June day, a scorching day with the sun just pummeling me. As I hoofed it up some dirt road track off the flank of Ragged Top, I took out my phone just to see if I had a signal here in the outback. All that showed up on the screen was an image of a throbbing red thermometer and a warning message that the phone needs to cool down before it can be used. Even appliances have more sense than to be out in this heat. The quitters.

I'll just take a little break. I need to find some shade beneath the welcome canopy of an ironwood tree. Hey, I think I'm in the right place!

When You Go

(520) 258-7200, www.blm.gov/visit/ironwood.

Admission

Free.

Facilities

None.

Pets

Yes.

Hiking

Although there are no designated hiking trails, visitors may hike or ride horseback almost anywhere in the monument. Vehicles, including mountain bikes, must stay on existing routes. Always carry plenty of water.

Do not summit peaks in the Silver Bells (including Ragged Top) or the Watermans from January 1 through April 30 during bighorn sheep lambing season.

Camping

Primitive camping is available in the monument. Limit is 14 days. Please use existing campsites and leave no trace. There is a small group campsite along W. Silverbell Road, just east of Saco Road, and provides a pull-through for larger vehicles.

Programs/Events

Friends of Ironwood Forest National Monument offer occasional outings and events. (520) 314-1383, www.ironwoodforest.org.

Special Notes

The monument contains state trust lands and private lands. Thus, you'll encounter signs indicating different boundaries. Please be respectful of private property. Many roads are rugged. High-clearance or four-wheel-drive vehicles are recommended in those areas. Vehicles must stay on existing routes.

Target shooting is not allowed. Do not disturb flora or fauna, and do not pick up or deface any cultural artifacts.

Smuggling and illegal immigration may be encountered. Stay safe by avoiding contact with persons exhibiting suspicious behavior. If someone requires assistance, don't stop. Drive farther down the road and call 911.

Hikers can enjoy a peaceful riparian stretch of the Juan Anza Trail connecting the mission at Tumacácori and Tubac Presidio State Historic Park. Photo by the author.

Juan Bautista de Anza National Historic Trail

Overview

Connecting history, culture, and outdoor recreation, this epic trail crosses Arizona and California as it marks the route followed by Spanish men, women, and children to establish a settlement at the San Francisco Bay.

Nearest Cities

Nogales, Tubac, Tucson, Gila Bend, Yuma.

Established

August 15, 1990.

Size

1,210 miles (approximately 302 miles in Arizona).

More than two centuries after Francisco Coronado failed in his quest, Juan Bautista de Anza succeeded in his. Instead of searching for cities that didn't exist, Anza founded his own.

In 1775–1776, captain of the Tubac Presidio Juan Anza led 300 people and 1,000 head of livestock on an expedition to establish San Francisco, on the northwestern frontier of New Spain. He became the first European to create an overland route from Mexico through the unforgiving terrain of the Sonoran Desert to the Pacific Coast of California.

Unlike many national historic trails where little remains besides a vague corridor—Old Spanish National Historic Trail, for example—the Juan Bautista de Anza National Historic Trail is well documented. We know the very specific route they took, where they camped and when, all thanks to detailed diaries kept by Anza and by Father Pedro Font, chaplain of the expedition.

In Arizona, modern travelers can retrace the route Anza and his people took from Nogales to Yuma. There are auto tours as well as miles of trails suitable for hiking, biking, and horseback riding.

A Family Business

Anza was born in the summer of 1736 at Fronteras, Sonora. He was part of a military

The Juan Anza Trail passes through Canoa Ranch, which served as a campsite during the 1775 expedition. Photo by the author.

family. His father and grandfather both served Spain. In fact, Anza's father proposed the idea of finding an overland route to Alta (Upper) California. Existing sea routes were difficult and dangerous. But Anza's father was killed in 1740 before he could undertake the mission, leaving his young son with few memories but a powerful legacy.

In 1752, Anza enlisted in the army and quickly rose through the ranks to become captain and later was named as the second commander of Tubac Presidio where he served with distinction. Located south of Tucson, Tubac Presidio was founded in 1752 to protect the nearby mission at Tumacácori along the banks of the Santa Cruz River. It was the first European settlement in what is today Arizona.

Like his father before him, Anza requested permission from the viceroy of New Spain to prove a land route to Alta California was possible. Permission was granted, prompting not one but two expeditions.

Anza set out from the Tubac Presidio leading an exploratory expedition on January 8, 1774. He led a small group of 34 men—soldiers, servants, padres, and a guide. It was an arduous journey but successful thanks to aid offered by the Native people. The Pima (Akimel O'odham) people provided food. The Quechan (Yuma) Indians helped the Spaniards ford the volatile Colorado River at Yuma Crossing.

Anza formed a friendship with Quechan's Chief Palma that proved beneficial. After the

Mission San Xavier del Bac offered respite to the Anza expedition. It was where they buried a woman who had died in childbirth, baptized the baby, and celebrated three weddings. Photo by the author.

expedition became bogged down in deep sand beyond the river, Anza sent several of his men and most of the livestock back to stay at the Quechan village until his return. With lightened loads, the rest of the company pressed on and arrived at the Mission San Gabriel on March 22, near the future site of Los Angeles.

Upon his return, Anza was promoted to lieutenant colonel. He was also granted permission to lead a group of settlers to Alta California. In the spring of 1775 he began recruiting and enlisting soldiers with families, starting in the province of Sinola and moving northward. He must have been an inspiring salesman, because all he could offer would be a long perilous journey with only the hint of golden lands, lush and plentiful. The families knew they would not be returning. They were embarking on a new life.

In late September the party started from Horcasitas, the provincial capital of Sonora, bound for the Tubac Presidio, which would be their final gathering point. As the American Revolution raged on the Atlantic Coast, Juan Anza set out to find a route to the Pacific.

A Traveling Town

The journey through Arizona would be the tale of two rivers. The caravan traveled north along the Santa Cruz River to Tubac, where more people joined the group. Finally, after Mass on the morning of October 23, 1775, the expedition moved out. The company was comprised of more than 240 colonists, including 30 soldiers, their wives, and more than 100 children. It also included Indian guides, vaqueros, muleteers, and servants.

The expedition had to travel with all their supplies and belongings, almost all of it carried by dozens of mules. Each animal had to be packed and unpacked each morning and evening. The mule train followed the people and then came the horse herd, with the vaqueros and cattle bringing up the rear in this mile-long traveling village.

They continued up the Santa Cruz until they reached the Gila River and turned westward. At the junction of the Gila and Colorado Rivers, Anza and his people received a hearty welcome by Chief Palma at the Quechan village. Aided by the Native people, the party crossed the Colorado without incident. After the crossing, the caravan divided into three groups traveling a day apart to take advantage of the slow-filling desert waterholes.

Despite a desert snowstorm that killed a number of their livestock, the expedition arrived at San Gabriel in January and continued up the coast. Nearly five months after leaving Tubac they arrived at the Presidio of Monterey. They had survived numerous hardships, having faced shortages of food and water, life-threatening weather, and harsh conditions. Remarkably, only one person died on the journey, a woman after childbirth complications. Three other babies were born along the way. The livestock the expedition brought would form the foundation of the great cattle and horse ranchos of California.

While the travelers rested, Anza pushed on north with Father Font and a small party to the San Francisco Bay. Anza chose the locations for the Presidio of San Francisco and Mission San Francisco de Asis on March 28. Those sites would be settled in June, just weeks before the American colonies declared their independence from England on July 4, 1776.

Juan Anza had completed his mission. Upon his return, Anza was named governor of the province of New Mexico. He served for a decade and was appointed as commander of the Presidio of Tucson in 1788 but died before he could take office. He was 52.

Points of Interest

The journey that ingrained a rich Spanish culture into Arizona and California is memorialized today as the Juan Bautista de Anza National Historic Trail. Paved highways follow the entire route and are marked by signs. Here are a few Arizona highlights of the historic expedition.

LAS LAGUNAS DE ANZA

Located in Nogales, Las Lagunas is a secretive wetland saved and restored. Traveling from Sonora, the Anza company camped at Las Lagunas on October 14, 1775. It was their first campsite in what is now Arizona. Shaggy and shady, a small green park surrounds the wetlands. The pond is muddy at the edges, fringed with algae, full of reeds and cattails, and teeming with life. The chorus of birdsong is joyful. Butterflies wobble past and squadrons of dragonflies seem to be in constant motion. Water in the desert invites a happy chaos. There's a picnic area, a pollinator garden, some small shrines, and informational signage. This is one of the last remaining freshwater marshes in the upper Santa Cruz River Basin. Free. 966 West Country Club Drive.

TUBAC PRESIDIO STATE HISTORIC PARK

Anza served as the presidio's second commander from 1760 to 1776. Designated as Arizona's first state park, it preserves the original ruins of the fort built in 1752. The 11-acre park features gardens, several historic buildings, the state's first printing press, and an impressive museum housing original artifacts and exhibits on the long multilayered history of the Santa Cruz River Valley. The park offers some of the most detailed exhibits of the Anza Expedition to be found. Admission fee. (520) 398-2252, www.azstateparks.com, www.tubacpresidio.org.

HISTORIC CANOA RANCH

The first campsite after the expedition left its final assembly point at Tubac was at La Canoa, the "watering trough." On the evening of October 23, a woman gave birth to a son who entered the world feetfirst. The baby survived but the mother did not. La Canoa functioned as a working cattle ranch from 1820 to the 1970s. Today, the restored ranch buildings serve as mini-museums filled with photos and artifacts. A lake shimmers at the base of the Santa Rita Mountains. In the movie *Oklahoma!*, the surrey scene along the lake was filmed here. A lovely walking path circles the water, with shady picnic tables dotting the banks. Free. The ranch is located just off I-19 at Exit 56. (520) 724-6680.

MISSION SAN XAVIER DEL BAC

October 25 was a day of mixed emotions when the expedition arrived at the mission founded in 1692 by Father Eusebio Francisco Kino. The Anza Expedition buried the woman who had died. Then after a period of mourning, they celebrated three new marriages. Today's mission was built between 1783 and 1797, the oldest European structure in Arizona, and shimmers in the sun on the Tohono O'odham Nation. Known for its elegant Spanish colonial architecture and colorful art adorning the interior, the "White Dove of the Desert" remains an active parish. For visitors, docent-led tours are offered and there's a gift shop on the premises. Free. www.sanxaviermission.org.

CASA GRANDE RUINS NATIONAL MONUMENT

The company camped a few miles from the Casa Grande Ruins, and on October 31, Anza and Father Font visited the structure and recorded their impressions and measurements. Free. (520) 723-3172, www.nps.gov/cagr.

PAINTED ROCK PETROGLYPH SITE

Located about 90 miles southwest of Phoenix, Painted Rock contains an impressive collection of ancient petroglyphs scratched into boulders atop a low granite outcrop. There's also a smattering of pioneer graffiti because this would become a well-traveled route. The Gila River formed a natural travel corridor through the desert. The Anza Expedition was one of the first to camp here. In 1846, the Mormon Battalion passed through while building a wagon road, which opened the way for westward expansion. A dozen years later the Butterfield's Overland Mail Company began a stage line past the site. The site contains interpretive signs describing the Anza party's passage through the area. Free. BLM Phoenix Field Office, (623) 580-5500.

When You Go

(510) 232-5050, ext. 6702, www.nps.gov/juba. For additional information, visit the Anza Trail Coalition of Arizona at www.anzatrail.org.

Admission

Free, although other historic sites including national and state parks along the route may charge an admission fee.

Facilities

None. Passport stamp locations for Juan Anza Trail are Las Lagunas de Anza Wetlands, Tumacácori National Historical Park, Tubac Presidio State Historic Park, Historic Canoa Ranch, Tucson Presidio Museum, Saguaro National Park (East and West, same stamp), Picacho Peak State Park, Casa Grande Ruins National Monument, Gila Bend Museum and Visitor Center, and Colorado River State Historic Park.

Pets

It will vary from location to location.

Hiking

Access to the Anza Trail for hikers, bikers, and equestrians continues to expand as more Arizona communities continue building and linking pathways.

A 4-mile stretch of trail winds along the Santa Cruz River and connects Tumacácori National Historical Park with Tubac Presidio State Historic Park. The level path burrows through a riparian habitat of cottonwoods and mesquite and is popular with hikers and birders. Several panels of interpretive signage are found along the trail.

Other trailheads can be found at Santa Gertrudis Lane just south of Tumacácori, Historic Canoa Ranch, and off Elephant Head Road in Green Valley.

In Tucson, a continuous segment of trail runs from Valencia Road north to the community of Marana along the banks of the Santa Cruz River. The paved urban path is popular with everyone from joggers to bikers to moms pushing strollers.

A 12-mile section of Anza Trail passes through the Sonoran Desert National Monument. The trail follows or parallels the historic Butterfield Overland National Historic Trail through Maricopa Pass. Hikers, mountain bikers, and equestrians can all use the trail.

Camping

PICACHO PEAK STATE PARK

The campground has 85 electric sites for both tent and RV camping. All sites offer a picnic table and barbecue / fire ring. No water or sewer hookups are available. Generator use is not permitted. There are two handicap-accessible restroom and shower buildings. Site reservations can be made online or by calling (877) 697-2757. The Anza Expedition camped in the shadow of Picacho Peak on October 29. An interpretive Anza exhibit is found on the west side of the park overlooking a campsite area and the Anza route through the valley. (520) 466-3183, www.azstateparks.com.

PAINTED ROCK PETROGLYPH CAMPGROUND

A small campground at the petroglyph site offers 59 individual sites and two large group areas, featuring picnic tables and steel fire rings. There are vault toilets but no water or electric hookups. Fee. (623) 580-5500.

Programs/Events

Programs and discussions about Juan Anza, as well as other topics and guided hikes, are offered at Tumacácori National Historical Park, Tubac Presidio Historic State Park, Historic Canoa Ranch, Tucson Presidio, and Casa Grande Ruins National Monument.

Special Notes

Vehicles must remain on existing roads, and hikers should stay on designated trails. In many cases, the Juan Anza Trail crosses, or is bordered by, private lands. Please respect all private boundaries.

Almost the entire population of organ pipe cactus growing north of Mexico can be found within the national monument. Photo by the author.

Organ Pipe Cactus National Monument

Overview

This sprawling intact ecosystem shelters a surprisingly diverse community of animals and plants, and includes miles of scenic roads and hiking trails for those yearning to explore the heart of the Sonoran Desert.

Nearest City

Ajo.

Established

April 13, 1937.

Size

360,688 acres.

A pretty piece of desert perches on the border with Mexico—all spines and sunshine and solitude. Languid valleys stretch between ranges of craggy mountains. Sloping *bajadas* spill onto cactus-studded plains. This is wild country, fierce and full of secrets. This is desert to its very core. And always that imposing sky dominates. Come prepared because the summer heat here can wilt your bones. The sunsets will tattoo your heart.

Located roughly midway between Tucson and Yuma, Organ Pipe Cactus National Monument encompasses an incredible diversity of Sonoran Desert plants and animals. All told, 31 species of cactus can be found throughout the park, including the namesake organ pipe, which is rarely found in the United States.

Unlike the stately saguaro that rises in a single trunk, the organ pipe is a furious clutter of segments shooting up from the base, a cactus forever in celebratory mode—throwing its arms in the air like it just doesn't care. It can grow as high as 23 feet, second in size only to the saguaro in this country, and can live for more than 150 years. A striking resemblance to the pipes of a church organ prompted its moniker. Although the plants are common in Mexico, almost all organ pipes in this country are found in the monument. Some specimens are also scattered across the nearby Tohono O'odham Nation.

Organ pipes bloom in May and June, opening creamy white flowers only at night. That's a system designed for the seduction of their primary pollinator, the lesser long-nosed bat. It's nature's version of friends with benefits.

Good Times and Bad

President Franklin Roosevelt declared Organ Pipe a national monument way back in 1937. Those decades of added protection are evident in the towering groves of saguaro that have been allowed to flourish, the hordes of organ pipe crowding the slopes, and the numerous other species that have made a home here.

In 1976, the United Nations recognized the diversity of the monument by naming it an International Biosphere Reserve. The designation has attracted scientists from around the world conducting studies on this intact ecosystem. Two years later, 95 percent of the national monument was declared a wilderness area. Organ Pipe is now regarded as the most pristine corner of the Sonoran Desert.

Recent history has been less kind to Organ Pipe. In the 1990s, border security crackdowns in urban areas sent human and drug traffickers into the rural outback seeking new routes from Mexico to the United States. The monument became a thoroughfare for illegal activity, culminating in 2002 when park ranger Kris Eggle was shot and killed by drug smugglers. After that, most of what was deemed America's "most dangerous national park" was closed to the public.

In the ensuing years, numerous security measures have been implemented. Miles of vehicle barriers were installed along with surveillance towers and pedestrian fences. Additional law enforcement rangers were added to the monument's staff, and Border Patrol dramatically beefed up their presence. Now park rangers strive to educate visitors so they can make informed decisions about where to explore. In September 2014, all of Organ Pipe's 517 square miles were once again opened to hikers, campers, birders, and desert lovers.

I, for one, was thrilled to return, having spent many happy days hiking here, and many dark starry nights camping here.

A Lonely Landscape

Only one paved road crosses the national monument. Arizona 85 enters from the north and cleaves a long straight line through the broad desert. Traffic is usually sparse and most travelers don't bother stopping as they hurry into Mexico and the seaside community of Rocky Point. Hard to imagine the Gulf of California lies less than 2 hours away. This desert feels far removed from water.

The drive on 85 is soothing, almost hypnotic. The Bates Mountains rise to the west, the Ajo Range fills the eastern horizon, and the Puerto Blanco Mountains guide you south. You won't mistake these rough-hewn hills with the towering Sky Island mountains found farther east that support a variety of habitats. The ranges at Organ Pipe are gaunt and bony, seemingly worn down by sun and heat in one of North America's hottest, driest climates. They maintain their desert credentials from bottom to top. Still they make an impressive sight rising from the low valley floor.

The Ajo Mountain Drive offers visitors a chance to explore the desert backcountry of Organ Pipe Cactus National Monument. Photo by the author.

After entering the monument on 85, it's about 17 miles to the Kris Eggle Visitor Center, named to honor the fallen park ranger. This is where your exploration of the park begins. Inside are interpretive exhibits, a short video presentation, and a gift shop. Rangers offer talks, guided walks, and van tours during the winter months. A couple of scenic drives, hiking trails, and a campground are all located near the visitor center, creating a small hub of activity– the only spot in the park that's even remotely busy. The rest of the expanse remains open and untrammeled.

Into the Backcountry

An easy way to experience Organ Pipe's natural beauty is to take a scenic drive. There are two dirt road loops that venture deeper into the desert.

Ajo Mountain Drive is the centerpiece attraction, a 21-mile mostly gravel road that's generally manageable in a passenger car. RVs over 25 feet are prohibited, and that tells you plenty about this twisting, dipping road. After a mile it becomes one-way as it loops through dense cactus groves and across the low-shouldered Diablo Mountains. Pullouts and picnic tables offer chances to stop and savor the views. How can a land so full of cactus and rattlesnakes feel so downright peaceful? The silence helps. That's the plain simple music of Organ Pipe. Noise has no penetrative power across this broad piece of desert.

As the road reaches the foothills of the Ajo Mountains, watch for a natural arch winking at you. A short hiking trail scrambles up the slope into Arch Canyon. More picnic tables sit at the trailhead for Estes Canyon and Bull Pasture Trails, among the most popular hikes in the park. You'll skirt steep rock walls and craggy cliffs before returning through the wide Sonoyta Valley.

Puerto Blanco Drive offers a longer, more rugged outing, 41 miles total with a lot of worthwhile stops along the way. The drive provides access to the Pinkley Peak Picnic Area, Red Tanks Trail, Dripping Springs, and Quitobaquito Springs. The first few miles can usually be managed in a sedan as you meander through the foothills on the north slope of the Puerto Blanco Mountains. Make Pinkley Peak your turnaround unless you're in a high-clearance four-wheel drive. From here, the road becomes one-way and nastier. But the views are expansive as you continue to the oasis of Quitobaquito Springs and return paralleling the international border across the La Abra Plain. Expect to spend 4–5 hours completing the loop. No vehicles over 25 feet are allowed on this rough road either.

Another, gentler option is to continue south from the visitor center on paved, smooth 85. It will end in Lukeville, a small port of entry on the border. Just before reaching the burg, where gas and food are available, turn onto South Puerto Blanco Drive. This portion is two-way and graded dirt and doesn't require four-wheel drive. Another quick right turn leads you into the Senita Basin, one of the few places you can see all three of the park's columnar cacti coexisting: saguaro, organ pipe, and the senita. The most impressive groves of senita, a multi-trunked cactus topped with long hairlike spines, are along this road and near the trailhead. The monument contains the only population of senita cactus north of the border.

A Passage of Time

Humans have moved through this corner of the desert for thousands of years. Nomadic people left behind rock art, projectiles, and pottery. This was also part of a prehistoric trade route known as the Old Salt Trail. Ancient cultures journeyed to the salt beds of Sonora, Mexico, to obtain commodities like salt, obsidian, and seashells.

Some made a home here. Archaeological sites can be found within the monument, including evidence of the Hohokam culture farming this rough land. The O'odham lived here for centuries and continue to occupy the surrounding country. Early Spanish explorers passed through but found no compelling reason to linger. Starting in the 1880s miners and ranchers tried to scratch out a living. Several mines operated but none proved to be as profitable as the once booming copper mine in nearby Ajo, the first large open-pit mine in Arizona.

Many ancient artifacts have been found near Quitobaquito Springs in the southwestern corner of the monument because life always revolves around water in the desert. Just footsteps from the border, a spring flows into a pond forming a tiny but mighty oasis. This is the only place in the United States where the endangered Sonoyta mud turtle, the desert caper tree, and the Quitobaquito pupfish can be found naturally. For the tiny Quitobaquito spring snail, this reed-lined pond and its spring-fed streams are their entire world. They exist nowhere else.

This is a land full of hidden wonders. Barren mountainsides glow crimson and purple, pulsing with velvet shadows in the faltering light of sunset. Night skies glitter with a crescendo of stars. The elusive and rare Sonoran pronghorn still graze in lonely valleys. Wildflowers carpet the land with colorful blooms following wet winters. And on the sunniest slopes, the heat-loving organ pipe cactus, which migrated north from the tropics at the end of the Ice Age, reaches for the heavens with a dozen spiny arms.

When You Go

(520) 387-6849, www.nps.gov/orpi.

Admission

There is an admission fee.

Facilities

The visitor center has museum exhibits, video presentations, a gift shop, and a bookstore.

Pets

Pets are welcome at the monument, with some restrictions. They are permitted on all roads and paved campground areas. They can also join you on a handful of hiking trails: Palo Verde Trail, Campground Perimeter Trail, and Visitor Center Nature Trail. Of course, they must be leashed.

Hiking

Featuring dozens of miles of trails, Organ Pipe offers a little something for all bipeds from the casual walker to the hardcore hiker. Many trails can be combined to form loop hikes of varying length and difficulty.

Bicycles are allowed on all roads open to vehicle traffic, and travel may go in both directions even on one-way roads. Bikes are not permitted on any trails, so if you are planning to hike, be sure to carry a way to secure your bicycle if you plan on leaving it for any length of time.

Visitor Center Nature Trail is an easy brick path (0.15 mile round trip) introducing cactus varieties and includes a pond filled with Quitobaquito pupfish. The self-explanatory Campground Perimeter Loop makes an easy 1-mile circle around Twin Peaks Campground. Palo Verde Trail connects the campground and visitor center, 2.6 miles round trip. Desert View Trail is an easy 1.2-mile loop with impressive stands of organ pipe cactus and good sunrise and sunset views.

ALAMO CANYON TRAIL

Follow a dirt road to a historic ranch house and corral, while skirting a big wash that offers good birding opportunities; 1.8 miles round trip.

ARCH CANYON TRAIL

You'll make a short (1.2 miles round trip) easy climb through scrub oaks and junipers for a closer look at a sandstone arch.

BULL PASTURE

This is a difficult trail (3.2 miles round trip) with steep grade and exposed cliffs. The reward will be the spectacular views stretching into Mexico.

ESTES CANYON

Ramble across several washes before making a moderate switchback climb to a junction with Bull Pasture. It's 3.2 miles round trip as an out-and-back. Many hikers combine Estes Canyon and Bull Pasture for a more challenging but ultimately satisfying 4.2-mile loop to the high plateau and return.

VICTORIA MINE TRAIL

This moderate path (4.5 miles round trip) begins at the back of Twin Peaks Campground loop and crosses open desert, dipping in and out of washes on the way to one of the oldest historic sites on the monument. The mineshaft and ruins of the old company store remain.

DRIPPING SPRINGS

Hikers enjoy an easy jaunt back to one of the few natural water sources in the area on this 1-mile round trip outing. The trail starts from the one-way section of North Puerto Blanco Drive. Don't drink the water.

DRIPPING SPRINGS MINE

Located off the one-way section of North Puerto Blanco Drive is a moderate hike to a historic mine used by bootleggers during Prohibition; 2.8 miles round trip.

Puerto Blanco Mountains–Senita Basin Trail Complex offers a network of trails based on historic roads that connected a group of mines.

Camping

Twin Peaks Campground, open all year, contains 208 sites (174 RV and 34 tent-only sites). The campground includes water, restroom, solar showers, grills, tables, and dump station. Hookups are not available. Reservations are made through www.recreation.gov or by calling (877) 444-6777 to reserve a site the same day and up to six months in advance.

Alamo Campground provides a far more rustic experience with only four sites available with tables, charcoal grills, and a pit toilet. The primitive campground is tucked a few miles down a dirt road and is available only for tents, truck campers, and small vans. No RVs, generators, or wood fires. Reservations are made through www.recreation.gov or by calling (877) 444-6777 to reserve a site the same day and up to six months in advance.

Backcountry camping is allowed in select areas of the monument. Permit required from Kris Eggle Visitor Center.

Programs/Events

Ranger programs are offered from December through mid-April and include patio talks, a lecture series, guided hikes, van tours, night-sky parties, and full-moon hikes.

Special Notes

The monument shares 31 miles of international border with Mexico. Lock your unoccupied vehicle and keep valuables out of sight. Hike with a partner. Always be aware of your surroundings. If you see any activity that looks illegal or suspicious, do not intervene. Note your location and call 911 or report it to a ranger as quickly as possible.

The saguaro cactus is a defining feature of the Sonoran Desert and Arizona. Courtesy of Mike Koopsen, Sedona.

An easily accessed network of trails spreads out in Saguaro West, just off Picture Rocks Road. Photo by the author.

Sitting directly west of town, the Tucson Mountains offer less vertical relief than other prominent ranges surrounding the Tucson Basin. Wasson Peak is the highest summit at 4,687 feet.

It's what makes the western segment so enticing. This is pure sweet desert, bottom to top. Some of the densest stands of saguaros anywhere crowd these rugged slopes. After checking in at the Red Hills Visitor Center, experience it all on the scenic Bajada Loop drive. The 5-mile road is graded dirt suitable for sedans but not for motor homes or vehicles pulling trailers as it winds through the cactus-strewn foothills.

Along the way you'll have plenty of options to get out and stretch your legs. The Valley View Overlook Trail (0.8 miles round trip) is an easy walk across an arroyo and then topping out on a ridge with splendid vistas. Dozens of petroglyphs from the Hohokam culture can be found scratched into boulder stacks on Signal Hill, reached by a short (0.3 miles round trip) path lined with rock steps that departs from a picnic area.

My favorite trail in the park runs off Bajada Loop as well. The long lanky Hugh Norris Trail climbs through the desert scrub, snags a ridgeline, and chases it all the way to top of Wasson Peak. It's a strenuous 10-mile round trip hike but affords some of the best views in Tucson.

The Hugh Norris is one of the original trails I explored as I first succumbed to the desert's seductive spell, and I always regard it fondly. No one in his or her right mind sets out to become a desert rat. It's lunacy—a life filled with peril and impossible to rationalize. It would be like Superman starting a kryptonite collection. No good can come of it. Yet

A collection of petroglyphs are etched into the rocks at Signal Hill in Saguaro West. Photo by the author.

decades have passed, and I'm still happiest when I'm tromping around amid the cacti and rattlesnakes while my brains are being soft boiled by a blazing Arizona sun.

Of course, there are plenty of outings for those who want a smaller, gentler sample of desert. Just down the road from the visitor center, the Desert Discovery Nature Trail is a paved, wheelchair-accessible 0.5-mile loop with informational signage that provides a nice introduction to the flora and fauna around you. There's a surprising network of trails off Picture Rocks Road that twists through washes and scrambles into the foothills. These lowland hikes are drenched in wildflowers following a wet winter. There are some pullouts for trailheads, and you can also access them from the Cam-Boh Picnic Area. The trails are well marked but be sure to grab a detailed hiking map at the visitor center to help you choose the route that's right for you.

Rincon Mountain District (Saguaro East)

The much larger Rincon Mountain District lies 30 miles east on the other side of Tucson. Starting amid the desert lowlands, this section of park spreads into the higher elevations of the Rincon Mountains, leaving saguaros behind for expansive grasslands and mixed conifer forest—not the sort of thing you expect to find in the Sonoran Desert. Although to reach the lonely high country requires traveling by foot or horseback.

You can keep it simple by taking the paved Cactus Forest Loop Drive. The 8-mile scenic road starts just past the Rincon Mountain Visitor Center and weaves through stands of saguaros with excellent mountain views. Also popular with cyclists, the road offers multiple pullouts for vistas, two picnic areas, and trailheads. The main hiking area squeezes into the northeastern corner of the district, a tightly spun web of interconnected trails allowing visitors to put together all manner of routes.

The easy Freeman Homestead Trail, a 1-mile loop, takes you past a selection of giant saguaros and the site of a historic desert home. Put together a 3.8-mile loop using Loma Verde, Pink Hill, and Squeeze Pen that rambles across mostly level terrain, past the remains of an old copper mine and along the base of the Rincons, with good views of the towering wall of the Santa Catalina Mountains in the distance.

Several longer hiking trails lead into the remote backcountry. You can climb through cactus groves into woodlands of scrub oak and forests of ponderosa pine and Douglas fir. Backcountry camping is permitted only in designated sites. Camping permits are available at the visitor center. A segment of the Arizona National Scenic Trail also slices across the park here, skirting Mica Mountain.

Desert Guardians

Large groupings of saguaros are called a forest, but to me they resemble an army—an army forever slow-marching across the valleys and up the rocky slopes. Is it weird that I always think of saguaros as possessing a personality? I don't regard other plants as animate, but these slow-growing giants feel like something out of ancient times. They are positively Entish, shepherds of a harsh land. To discover they walk around Arizona desert in the deep moonlight would surprise me not at all.

Two national parks are named for iconic symbols of Arizona—Grand Canyon and Saguaro. Plenty of numbskulls think that's all Arizona has to offer, a big hole in the ground and lots of desert. But even if that were true—speaking as someone who has fallen under the spell of both—it would be more than enough.

Saguaros define the West like nothing else can. There is something compelling about the tall stately cactus with its arms forever reaching for the clouds. Saguaros possess one of the most instantly recognizable silhouettes in the plant world. For desert rats like me, it means we are home.

When You Go

(520) 733-5158 (West), (520) 733-5153 (East), www.nps.gov/sagu.

Admission

A single admission fee is good for entrance to both park districts for seven days.

Facilities

Each district has its own visitor center, which includes interpretive exhibits and a gift shop.

Pets

Pets are only allowed on roadways, in picnic areas, and on the Desert Discovery and Desert Ecology paved nature walks. Pets must always be on a leash no longer than 6 feet.

Hiking

The park has more than 175 miles of trails.

Bicycles may be used on all roadways, including the Golden Gate Multi-Use Trail in Saguaro West, and on two short trails in Saguaro East, the 2.5-mile Cactus Forest Trail, and the 2.8-mile Hope Camp Trail.

CACTUS WREN TRAIL (WEST)

After visiting the petroglyphs at Signal Hill, continue on Cactus Wren Trail across some nice open desert, then circle back on Manville Trail for a 4.3-mile loop.

KING CANYON TRAIL (WEST)

Starting from the trailhead across from the Arizona-Sonora Museum, King Canyon offers another route to the top of Wasson Peak (7.8 miles round trip), climbing through a cactus-dotted gorge. You can also combine it with the Gould Mine Trail to swing through the workings of an old copper mine with residue piles and the remains of a stone cabin in a 2.4-mile loop.

SENDERO ESPERANZA TRAIL (WEST)

Following a wide sandy path for the first mile, Sendero Esperanza climbs to a scenic ridge to join the Hugh Norris Trail (3.4 miles round trip). The lower section of trail is often ablaze with wildflowers in February and March.

DESERT ECOLOGY TRAIL (EAST)

This 0.25-mile paved trail is wheelchair accessible and offers a quick introduction to the desert with interpretive signs and exhibits.

CACTUS FOREST (EAST)

Sitting amid the desert flats at the base of the mighty Rincon Mountains, the Cactus Forest is a web of interconnected routes. Mostly level hiking makes it easy to piece together two or more trails to form customized loops like the Loma Verde option mentioned earlier.

DOUGLAS SPRING TRAIL (EAST)

Climbing into the Rincon Mountains, Douglas Spring enters the park backcountry. Make a 5.8-mile out-and-back day hike that leads to Bridal Wreath Falls, a seasonal cascade that flows after summer monsoons and winter snowmelt. It's a popular outing for birders and offers good city and mountain views.

TANQUE VERDE RIDGE TRAIL (EAST)

Along with Douglas Spring, Tanque Verde Ridge is the main route into the high elevation backcountry of the eastern district. It's steep and challenging as you pass through different life zones along the way. You climb to the top of the ridge within the first mile with excellent views of the Tucson Basin. A rare crested saguaro 2.5 miles up makes a good turn-around point for day hikers. For backpackers, the first campsite is at Juniper Basin after 7 miles.

Camping

There are no campsites in the park. Backcountry camping is available in the Rincon Mountain District only. Permits are required and available at www.recreation.gov.

Camping is available in Tucson Mountain Park (Gilbert Ray Campground), which is adjacent to Saguaro West about 4 miles south of Saguaro's Red Hills Visitor Center. The campground has RV sites with individual 30-amp electrical hookups, and a few designated tent only. It has centrally located water, picnic tables, restrooms, and an RV dumping station. (520) 403-8116 (January–March); otherwise, (520) 724-5000.

Programs/Events

Several ranger-led programs take place throughout the year with the widest variety occurring during the winter months. They include guided walks, sunset hikes, discussions on desert wildlife, petroglyphs, and celebrations of the iconic saguaro cactus.

Special Notes

Water is available only at visitor centers. Hiking in extreme heat can be hazardous. Watch out for prickly plants and venomous animals. Never put your hands and feet in places you can't see.

Cultural traditions, architectural heritage, and natural wonders are all being preserved in the Santa Cruz Valley National Heritage Area. Courtesy of Rick Mortensen, Phoenix.

Santa Cruz Valley National Heritage Area

Overview

This may be the ultimate Arizona neighborhood—a place that's scenic, historic, and multicultural, and where you can find incredible tacos.

Nearest Cities

Tucson, Marana, Tubac, Patagonia, Sonoita, Nogales.

Established

March 12, 2019.

Size

3,300 square miles.

If a single place can truly capture the essence of Arizona, it is the Santa Cruz Valley National Heritage Area.

This is the cradle of Arizona life, with traces of human occupation extending back more than 12,000 years. A confluence of cultures comes together here in a land of rare natural beauty, where sunny desert is stacked with soaring mountains and wide grasslands stretch toward the horizons. Missions and mines, ranches and vineyards, ghost towns and art communities, all have stories to tell. And everything—absolutely everything—revolves around a slender undernourished river.

If that doesn't sum up Arizona, I don't know what does.

The Santa Cruz Valley National Heritage Area was designated in 2019 to honor and help preserve that rich multifaceted character. The National Park Service describes a national heritage area as a place "where natural, cultural, historic, and recreational resources combine to form cohesive, nationally distinctive landscapes arising from patterns of past and present human activities shaped by geography."

What all that boils down to is that it's an amazing place to visit.

A River Runs through It

The Santa Cruz Valley National Heritage Area encompasses 3,300 square miles of the Santa Cruz River watershed, from Nogales and Patagonia, through Tucson to Marana and Oro Valley. So it all starts with the river.

The Santa Cruz River is an anomaly in so many ways. It exists in a desert, crosses borders then returns, and flows north instead of south. The Santa Cruz has its headwaters in the San Rafael Valley in Southern Arizona, dips into Mexico, and loops back into Arizona near Nogales. It meanders through the San Xavier District of the Tohono O'odham Nation and continues north through Tucson and Marana and eventually connects to the Gila River.

As the lifeblood of the region, human activity revolves around the river, as it always has. Archaeologists have uncovered the remains of a 4,100-year-old Indigenous farming settlement along the Santa Cruz, including charred remnants of corn. Ancient irrigation canals have been uncovered beneath the wide floodplain, including one canal believed to have been built about 3,500 years ago, making it the oldest ever found in this country.

The river sustained people for generations. When early Spanish colonizers traveled through the region, they followed the course of the river. They built missions and forts along its banks. Even through the 1800s, the Santa Cruz provided for the growing town of Tucson. But eventually decades of pumping surface and groundwater caused long stretches of the river to dry up.

For nearly a century, the only time the Santa Cruz resembled a river in Tucson was when hard rainstorms sent muddy runoff coursing down the riverbed. But in recent years, water conservation efforts and restoration projects have returned perennial flow to parts of the river.

In 2019, Tucson began discharging treated wastewater into the riverbed south of downtown. The results have been remarkable as new riparian habitat flourished almost immediately along the flowing river. Banks are shaggy with cattails and reeds. Young cottonwoods have taken root. Seep willows are growing and the area teems with life. Birds, insects, fish, turtles, and toads are all present in rising numbers. It's always a party when water nourishes the desert.

Humans are the dimwits who sucked the river dry in the first place. But at least steps are being taken to correct that blunder. Although the river's flow has diminished in modern times, there are once again about 90 miles of year-round flow in the main channel and tributary streams. Not perfect, but it's a wonderful start.

A Vibrant Neighborhood

The diverse terrain of the river's watershed creates multiple life zones in close proximity amid a setting of stunning natural beauty. This heady mix of classic Sonoran Desert interrupted by snowcapped mountains is a bewitching landscape that exists nowhere else.

Sky Island mountains rise suddenly, forming distinct habitats floating above the valley floor. Vast forests of saguaro fill the desert lands. Tree-lined streams slice across the grassy

Pronghorns graze the grasslands north of Sonoita. Photo by the author.

plains. These riparian corridors create routes for migrating birds, and with the Sky Island "archipelago," attract tropical and subtropical species, including the jaguar, ocelot, coatimundi, Mexican long-tongued bat, and elegant trogon.

Living together in this region are Native American tribes such as the Tohono O'odham (the Desert People) and the Yaqui (Yoeme) Indians, the descendants of Spanish settlers who colonized the valley in the 1600s, Mexican families who settled the area before the Gadsden Purchase of 1854 made it part of the United States, and the American pioneers who came afterward.

This tapestry of natural wonders, multiple cultures, and rich history forms the Santa Cruz Valley National Heritage Area.

Stewards of a Living Landscape

Receiving the national heritage area designation was the culmination of years of hard work by a cross section of dedicated people and organizations. The nonprofit Santa Cruz Valley Heritage Alliance spearheaded the effort and now serves as the local coordinating entity for the heritage area. It is an alliance of partners that includes local governments, nonprofit organizations, and businesses that collaborate together in the region to further the mission of the heritage area.

The work takes many forms as they seek to develop education programs; increase heritage and nature tourism; promote local foods, crafts, and other traditional products; rehabilitate historic buildings; and restore riparian areas.

Patagonia Lake State Park offers year-round fishing, birding, and camping opportunities. Courtesy of Rick Mortensen, Phoenix.

Unlike national parks, national heritage areas are large lived-in landscapes. By engaging residents and making sure their stories are told, they create a strong sense of place and regional identity. They build more inclusiveness in the community, celebrate cultural traditions, and foster better stewardship of natural resources.

Santa Cruz Valley National Heritage Area became the country's 55th national heritage area. Heritage areas do not impose federal zoning or regulations on land use, and don't involve land acquisitions. Since they are locally initiated and managed, the conservation strategy is very much community-based. It's the residents who are stepping up to protect, preserve, and promote the natural and cultural resources.

As someone who spends as much time as possible in this area, I have found it a pleasure to see the implementation of so many plans. More habitat is being restored. Trails and parks are being added. Restaurants constantly step up their game. Shops and galleries offer a strong sense of place. Festivals and events are an ongoing celebration. This is a joyful corner of the state with a delicious spirit and strong identity.

What to Do

National parks come with a certain level of expectation. When visitors show up to a place called Grand Canyon National Park, they anticipate a fair-sized hole in the ground. The Santa Cruz Valley National Heritage Area rejoices in diversity. Expect abundance. Expect surprises. There is something here for everyone. Literally.

Here are just a few of the attractions that help tell the story of this remarkable place.

MISSION GARDEN

The roots of Mission Garden run deep—4,000 years deep as it preserves the agricultural legacy of Tucson. Managed by the nonprofit Friends of Tucson's Birthplace, the garden interprets and celebrates the multicultural history of the region. Growing behind adobe walls at the foot of Sentinel Peak are heritage trees, heirloom crops, and native edible plants arrayed in unique timeline gardens such as Hohokam, Yaqui, Spanish Colonial, Mexican, Chinese, Territorial, and many more. Not only is this a delicious window into the past, but also it's an opportunity to study long-term desert farming practices. Programs, talks, and cooking demonstrations are offered through the year. Admission fee. (520) 955-5200, www.missiongarden.org.

MADERA CANYON

South of Tucson, Madera Canyon is carved from the Santa Rita Mountains. The road into the narrowing gorge climbs from desert grasslands to mixed woodlands shading a seasonal stream. More than 250 species of bird have been documented in these varied habitats. Favorite sightings include elegant trogon, elf owl, sulfur-bellied flycatcher, and painted redstart. The Madera Creek Trail follows the stream and has multiple access points. The Carrie Nation Trail branches off from Old Baldy Trail tracing the creek bed deeper into the canyon, and is a good place to see elegant trogons in April and May. Non-hikers can enjoy the various picnic areas and the free viewing area at the Santa Rita Lodge, filled with hummingbirds and other desert species. Admission fee. (520) 281-2296, www.fs.usda.gov/coronado.

TUBAC

The Spanish established a presidio, or fort, at Tubac in 1752, making it the first European settlement in what would become Arizona. It was in 1948 that landscape painter Dale Nichols opened an art school in Tubac, and the quiet little burg began an evolution into an artist colony. No wonder the town coined the slogan, "Where Art and History Meet." Today, 100-plus shops occupy the village plaza, where old adobes, Spanish courtyards, and ocotillo fences blend seamlessly with a handful of newer buildings. Yet the history still feels palpable. When you're on Calle de Iglesias in Old Town Tubac, you're traveling on one of the oldest roads in America.

PATAGONIA–SONOITA CREEK PRESERVE

The Nature Conservancy stepped in to protect a stretch of Sonoita Creek at the edge of Patagonia and the verdant floodplain adjacent to the stream as their very first project in Arizona. And it's become a beloved destination for birders. Over 250 bird species migrate, nest, and live amid this rare and beautiful Fremont cottonwood–Goodding's willow riparian forest. Several gentle paths fan out, following the creek, along the old railroad grade, and to a feeding station swarming with hummingbirds. Over 20 species of flycatchers have

Tubac is Arizona's oldest European settlement and a haven for artists. Courtesy of Rick Mortensen, Phoenix.

been recorded on the preserve as well as the thick-billed kingbird and Sinaloa wren. Guided bird-watching walks are offered on select Saturdays. Admission fee. (520) 394-2400.

CITY OF GASTRONOMY

In 2015, Tucson was the first place in the United States to be designated a UNESCO City of Gastronomy. It received the honor for its culinary distinctiveness because of its agricultural history, variety of heritage food ingredients, and traditional food preparation techniques that all combine to create the flavors of the city. Chef-driven restaurants and unique food trucks abound. In fact, approximately 63 percent of the restaurants in Tucson are locally owned compared to the national average of 37 percent. Everyone's a foodie in Tucson. Get out and sample the diverse terroir of the borderlands.

ARIZONA-SONORA DESERT MUSEUM

In a perfect world all zoos would look like Arizona–Sonora Desert Museum tucked away in the Tucson Mountains. It's a combination botanical garden, natural history museum, and zoo with natural enclosures sheltering the animals—the next best thing to seeing them in the wild. Hiking trails weave among the cactus and put you almost face-to-face with the critters. The riparian corridor offers both aboveground and underwater viewing areas. Watching the river otters frolic is worth the price of admission alone. Admission fee. (520) 883-2702, www.desertmuseum.org.

TUCSON MOUNTAIN PARK

Right next door to the Arizona-Sonora Museum is an idyllic little escape. Tucson Mountain Park is the sprawling backyard other cities can only dream about. The park protects 20,000 acres of pristine desert on the western edge of town. It shares the same mountain range, tall cactus forests, and lavish sunsets as neighboring Saguaro National Park but without an admission fee. Veined with a network of easy-to-access trails, Tucson Mountain

Park offers a standing invitation to residents and visitors alike to come outside and play. Free.

KENTUCKY CAMP

Imagine spending a night in a lonely ghost town far from civilization. Kentucky Camp sits amid the grasslands that cloak the eastern flanks of the Santa Rita Mountains northwest of Sonoita. It served as the headquarters for the Santa Rita Water and Mining Co. from 1902 to 1906. The company folded soon after the founder mysteriously plunged to his death from a Tucson hotel window. Now maintained by the Forest Service, the site includes five adobes partially restored. A small rustic cabin can be rented through the Rooms with a View program. Since the Arizona Trail is routed through Kentucky Camp, you'll enjoy daytime hiking and dark night skies laden with stars. Reservations for the cabin can be made at www.recreation.gov. (520) 281-2296, www.fs.usda.gov/coronado.

SONOITA-ELGIN WINERIES

The era of modern wine in Arizona sprang from these rolling hills beneath an immense sky. In the 1970s, a University of Arizona soil scientist opened the first commercial vineyard in the state on these high grasslands. He became fascinated with the soil here, a mixture of reddish-brownish gravelly loam, and despite virtually everyone questioning his sanity began making wine. It paved the way for a burgeoning new industry. Today a dozen or so family-owned wineries dot the hills around Elgin and Sonoita and produce a wide range of award-winning varietals.

COLOSSAL CAVE

Located 16 miles east of Tucson, Colossal Cave Mountain Park has a long and storied history. The Ancestral Sonoran Desert People once used the caverns for food storage, and outlaws hid out here between train robberies in the 1880s. During the Great Depression, the Civilian Conservation Corps built much of the infrastructure still used by visitors today. Standard tours and more adventurous outings are offered. (520) 647-7275, colossalcave.com.

When You Go

Santa Cruz Valley National Heritage Area: www.santacruzheritage.org.
Visit Tucson: 115 N. Church Ave., (800) 638-8350, www.visittucson.org.
Discover Marana: 13251 N. Lon Adams Rd., (520) 639-8040, discovermarana.org.
Sky Islands Welcome Center: 401 McKeown Ave., Patagonia, www.visitskyislands.com.
Tubac Chamber of Commerce: 1 Burruel St., (520) 398-2704, www.tubacaz.com.
Nogales–Santa Cruz County Chamber of Commerce: 123 W. Kino Park Place, Nogales,
    (520) 287-3685, thenogaleschamber.org.

While the park service has stabilized the old mission church, it endures as a haunting ruin. Courtesy of Rick Mortensen, Phoenix.

Tumacácori National Historical Park

Overview
The park protects the ruins of three Spanish colonial missions, the most prominent of these being Tumacácori with its distinctive and picturesque adobe church.

Nearest Cities
Tubac, Nogales.

Established
It became Tumacácori National Monument on September 15, 1908. It was redesignated as Tumacácori National Historical Park in 1990, and expanded to include the ruins of Guevavi and Calabazas mission units.

Size
360 acres in three units.

An old building rises above a mesquite bosque near the banks of the Santa Cruz River. Weathered and worn, the structure was never finished and has been long abandoned. Yet it remains a profoundly moving experience to stand inside amid the cool darkness, with the roof high overhead and shafts of Arizona sun creeping in through the arched doorway.

The three-story adobe church will always be the centerpiece attraction at Tumacácori National Historical Park. But the church was only one element of the mission—a planned and self-sufficient community based on European models. It was all part of Spain's goal to remake the New World in the image of the Old World.

Padre on Horseback

In the late seventeenth century, Spanish missionaries traveled from Mexico up the Santa Cruz River Valley attempting to Christianize the Natives. Father Eusebio Francisco Kino, a Jesuit missionary, arrived in 1687 and began work among Indians called Pimas by the Spaniards. In their own language, they were O'odham or "the people."

Kino founded a string of missions as he traveled through the Santa Cruz River Valley. He established Mission San Cayetano de Tumacácori in January 1691 on the east side of the Santa Cruz River. It was the first mission in what would become Arizona. Father Kino celebrated the first Mass there in a ramada, or brush shelter, that the O'odham had built for him.

The "padre on horseback," as Kino was called, made numerous excursions through the Southwest, although much of his work occurred in the Pimeria Alta—the area that now includes Southern Arizona and Sonora in northern Mexico. Respected for his kindness, Kino bridged cultural barriers to befriend the Native people and serve as their fierce advocate, where many in the Spanish hierarchy saw only a source of slave labor.

Kino was not only interested in the spiritual conversion of the Natives but also in their economic fortunes. The O'odham were an agricultural people long before the arrival of Europeans, farming the floodplain and harvesting wild plants throughout the seasons. Kino introduced them to new crops like winter wheat, and fruit trees like quince, fig, apricot, peach, and pomegranate. He also taught them to raise cattle, sheep, and goats, further expanding their food supply.

The day after founding Tumacácori, Father Kino established Mission San Gabriel de Guevavi, 15 miles upriver. In all, he established more than 20 missions including San Xavier del Bac. It's estimated that his numerous expeditions covered more than 50,000 square miles. The map he created in 1705 was the standard reference for the southwestern desert region for more than a century. His tireless efforts continued until his death in 1711.

On July 11, 2020, Pope Francis advanced the cause of Father Kino's sainthood by recognizing his life of heroic virtue and declaring him "Venerable."

Life at the Mission

The mission buildings at Tumacácori included both public and private spaces for worship, work, and daily life. It was a *visita*, a mission without a resident priest. Farm fields, orchards, gardens, and grazing lands could support a few hundred people. The O'odham who moved into the community received a measure of protection from raiding Apaches. They also learned about Spanish technology and tools, and encountered new ideas on governance, architecture, and, of course, religion.

According to the National Park Service brochure, "O'odham culture valued song and storytelling. In the chants, music, and structure of the Mass they may have found reminders of some of their own ritual ceremonies—to bring rain, or good health."

The O'odham people still carry the legacy of colonization. Many Native and Spanish traditions blended during this period of transformation. The overlapping cultures led to occasional clashes. The most notable instance was the 1751 Pima Revolt. A group of Indians, angry over increasing Spanish controls and punishments, attacked and killed two priests and more than 100 settlers, and destroyed several buildings. As a result of the rebellion, a presidio was founded at Tubac in June 1752, the first European settlement in Arizona.

The 50 cavalrymen garrisoned at the Presidio San Ignacio de Tubac were to protect the various missions in the area, quell further uprisings, and serve as a base for continued exploration of New Spain. Soldiers were encouraged to bring their families with them, giving the community of Tubac an air of permanence. Indians killed the first captain of the post in 1759. The man who would become Tubac's most famous resident, Juan Bautista de Anza, then assumed command.

Construction began on the three-story adobe church at Tumacácori in 1800. It was never completed. Photo by the author.

A Church Rises

Following the uprising of 1751, Tumacácori was moved to its current location on the west side of the river. It was renamed San Jose de Tumacácori. As part of a political upheaval, the Jesuits were expelled from New Spain in 1767. The following year, the gray-robed Franciscans were assigned to oversee the missions. They continued making improvements, expanding and adding more buildings.

The first Franciscan priest did not like living at Guevavi, so he transferred his residence to Tumacácori and made it the *cabecera*, or headquarters for other missions. There was already a small adobe church on the grounds but in 1800, they began construction on a larger, more elaborate church—the one that still stands today.

Work on the church was led by a master mason overseeing a crew of Indian and Spanish laborers. Construction proceeded in fits and starts over the next two decades. The Franciscans hoped to match the elegance of the Mission San Xavier del Bac to the north. Lack of funds led to scaled-down plans and numerous delays. Limestone for plaster and timber for roof beams needed to be hauled from the Santa Rita Mountains some 30 miles away. The church was dedicated for use although never completed, leaving the bell tower uncapped. It was only in service for a few years.

Mexico gained independence in 1821, and that would lead to changes. In 1828, the Mexican government ordered all Spanish-born residents to leave the country, which included the priest at Tumacácori. Faced with an extreme shortage of native-born Mexican priests, Tumacácori became a visita again.

The last residents abandoned Tumacácori following the end of the Mexican-American War in 1848. The mission site became part of the United States with the Gadsden Purchase in 1854.

Distinctive Bones

Weathering and vandalism took a toll on the Tumacácori church after it was abandoned. The roof was removed so the timbers could be used elsewhere. Once it was named a national monument, a replacement roof was added. Some stabilization was done to the building, but no extensive restoration was undertaken. The church remains a quiet shell, a haunting ruin rooted in Arizona's distant past. Like the mountain peaks and winding rivers of Southern Arizona, Tumacácori feels like part of the landscape.

At one time the church was brightly painted with red columns and capitals that were yellow with black markings. Statues stood against a blue background in their niches. But desert sun has peeled that away. Some of the original paint remains visible in the doorway and under the cornice below the window.

My visits to Tumacácori always start with the church because it sets the mood. I step through the arched doorway into the long narrow nave, and I can feel a sense of calm. In places the elements have gnawed at the interior walls, exposing the sun-dried adobe bricks. The remains of the choir loft are still visible, and small dark rooms branch off to the right—the baptistery, sacristy, and sanctuary that still contains remnants of original paint, picture frames, and stenciling.

Behind the church are a granary, a mortuary chapel, and the cemetery. Nearby are the *convento*, which included the priest's quarters, kitchen, classrooms, and other communal workspaces. Also on the grounds is a reproduction of a *ki*, or traditional O'odham house made of mesquite timbers, ocotillo sticks, and mud.

Walking paths lead across the grounds and through the orchard. The original orchard and garden were once surrounded by a high adobe wall to keep out animals. An irrigation ditch brought water from the river. Continue walking beneath the trees and you'll soon find yourself on the Juan Bautista de Anza National Historic Trail, the same route used by Anza when he led a group of settlers to found the city of San Francisco in 1775–1776.

When You Go

(520) 377-5060, www.nps.gov/tuma.

Admission

There is an admission fee.

Facilities

Entrance to the park is through the visitor center built in 1937. It includes museum exhibits and a gift shop. A short film tells the story of the long history and many cultures that interacted at Tumacácori. Outside is the courtyard garden, a shady oasis surrounding a central fountain. The Civilian Conservation Corps carried out the original plantings.

Pets

Tumacácori prohibits pets from the mission grounds and all buildings. Leashed pets are welcome on the Anza Trail.

Hiking

A 4-mile stretch of the Juan Bautista de Anza National Historic Trail winds along the Santa Cruz River and connects Tumacácori with Tubac Presidio State Historic Park. The level path burrows through a riparian habitat of cottonwoods and mesquite, and is popular with hikers and birders. Several panels of interpretive signage are found along the way. The trail can be accessed from the grounds or from two trailheads on the park boundary.

You can also hike south for several miles on the Juan Anza Trail as volunteers continue to expand the route. A free hiker shuttle runs on certain days during the peak season between Tumacácori and Tubac. Check with the park for details.

Camping

The park is day use only except for special evening events and activities.

Programs/Events

Tumacácori is known for their abundance of events and programs throughout the year. Cultural demonstrations highlight one of the Native cultures connected to the mission. During cooler months, rangers offer guided tours of the mission church and grounds, garden tours, river walks, and bird walks. There are moonlight hikes along the Anza Trail and stargazing parties. They even have a Firefly Fiesta in the summer (yes, we do have fireflies in Arizona). Tumacácori is an International Dark Sky Park.

The park hosts La Fiesta de Tumacácori, its most expansive event, each year on the first full weekend of December. The fiesta celebrates the many cultures associated with the Santa Cruz Valley through traditional food, crafts, music, and dance.

Tumacácori National Historical Park preserves two additional ruins at remote locations, Guevavi and Calabazas (founded in 1756). Tours of these ruins are offered from January through March on the first and third Wednesdays. Reservations are required for this guided tour.

Special Notes

Watch for uneven walkways and floors, unexpected steps, and low doorways.

The revitalization of Yuma's riverfront has made the town a welcoming destination for travelers. Photo by the author.

Yuma Crossing National Heritage Area

Overview

A natural ford on the Colorado River where so much history passed is honored in the best way possible with the preservation of landmarks, the restoration of habitat, and the uplifting of a community.

Nearest City

Yuma.

Established

October 19, 2000.

Size

21 square miles.

It would not be a stretch to claim that almost the entire history of the Southwest passed through Yuma.

Imagine the Colorado River as it was, before dams and demands and damned demands. Back then it was a beast. The river was untamed and volatile, prone to devastating floods and abrupt course changes. As it flowed through southern flatlands, the river often sprawled across 15 miles of treacherous floodplains choked with brushy marshes and patches of quicksand.

Except in one spot. Right there, two granite outcroppings squeezed the water into a narrow, predictable channel. This became known as the Yuma Crossing.

Down to the River

Europeans discovered the spot in 1540—some 80 years before the Pilgrims stepped off the *Mayflower*—when Spanish expeditions navigated up the Colorado River. Of course, they encountered established communities already on the riverbanks. These were the ancestors of the present-day Quechan and Cocopah tribes.

Father Eusebio Kino traveled through the area as he established missions in the late seventeenth century. When Juan Bautista de Anza led an expedition from the Tubac Presidio to Northern California in 1775 where he founded the city of San Francisco, he used the Yuma Crossing. During the California gold rush of 1849, tens of thousands took the rope ferry at the crossing in search of their fortunes. Almost all travel and commerce pointed for California passed through the town first named Colorado City, then Arizona City, and finally Yuma.

The 20th century marked the era of dam building up and down the Colorado River. The efforts brought hydropower and a secure source of water to the Southwest, allowing the region to grow and prosper. But there were also unintended consequences. Without the annual cycle of spring floods, native forests couldn't regenerate and soon died off. Marshes and wetlands dried up, and invasive species like salt cedar sunk roots in the degraded ecosystem and quickly took over. The thing that made Yuma special disappeared as the town lost its connection to the river.

A Watery Revival

During the 1990s, community leaders came together seeking to reestablish that connection. They also sought to restore the area's natural wetlands, establish trails and parks, and revitalize the historic downtown district. It would prove to be a massive undertaking that required numerous agencies, opposing factions, and a horde of volunteers. In 2000, Congress approved the creation of the Yuma Crossing National Heritage Area, one of the first national heritage areas west of the Mississippi River.

The community worked quickly and by 2002 had reopened the historic Ocean-to-Ocean Bridge. Built in 1915, the truss bridge was the first highway crossing of the Lower Colorado River. It had been closed since 1988 for structural deficiencies. But it was the first project undertaken by the heritage area because it reconnected Quechan tribal land to downtown Yuma. The Quechan Tribe would be an invaluable partner going forward.

Next came the riverfront, which was completely overgrown and overrun. The dense thicket was cluttered with trash dumps and hobo camps and a popular thoroughfare for smugglers. Undaunted, workers moved in. They hauled out the trash, eliminated invasive species, cleared the space, restored habitat, planted trees, and created a series of parks connected by walking and biking paths. The results have been nothing short of remarkable.

The riverfront is now divided into three segments. The centerpiece of the West Wetlands is a sprawling kid-designed creative playground, along with a lake stocked with fish, sandy beaches, hummingbird garden, woodland trails, and restored riparian habitat.

In the center of things, Gateway Park offers wonderful river views and has become the city's most popular park with beaches, picnic ramadas, and a playground. Adjacent to the park is Pivot Point Interpretive Plaza, the exact location where the first train chugged into the Arizona Territory in 1877. A 1907 Baldwin locomotive marks the spot, near the concrete pivot from the old swing-span rail bridge. Colorful panels recount all the chapters of Yuma's past. An audio system re-creates the sounds of arriving trains and passing steamboats.

Yuma Territorial Prison State Park remains a historic highlight for Yuma visitors. Courtesy of Rick Mortensen, Phoenix.

Yet most impressive of all are the East Wetlands, much of which spreads across Quechan tribal land. More than 400 acres have been returned to a natural state. Some 200,000 cottonwood and willow trees were planted and marshes were re-formed. This stretch of river now looks very much like it did a century ago. Wildlife and birds have returned, including breeding pairs of yellow-billed cuckoo and the endangered Yuma clapper rail. Multiuse paths connect all riverfront parks, a little slice of heaven for walkers, bikers, skaters, and families pushing strollers.

The Jail and the Depot

In 2010, when Arizona budget shortfalls threatened to close two state parks that bookend the riverfront development, Yuma Crossing National Heritage Area stepped up to take control. They invested money into the facilities, spruced them up, and increased visitation.

Colorado River Historic State Park tells the story of the past, present, and future of the Colorado River. The 10-acre property is the former Yuma Quartermaster Depot, established in 1864, by the US Army as a supply point for all military posts in the Southwest. Many historic buildings—some of the oldest in Arizona—have been preserved and are filled with artifacts and displays. While the quartermaster depot is still represented, the scope has widened to include all chapters of the Colorado River story, including the irrigation projects that turned Yuma into an agricultural center. (928) 329-0471, www.coloradoriverpark.com.

Yuma Territorial Prison opened in 1876, with the first few prisoners hacking their own cells out of the granite hillside. Notorious guests of the most infamous iron bar hotel of the Old West included "Buckskin" Frank Leslie, whom Wyatt Earp compared to Doc Holliday in gun skill; Pearl Hart, who committed the last Arizona stagecoach robbery; and spooky-eyed Elena Estrada, who stabbed her unfaithful lover and then cut open his chest, pulled out his heart, and threw the bloody mass into his face. Structures still standing include intact cellblocks, a guard tower, sally port, the infamous "snake den" punishment cell, and a cemetery with 104 graves. (928) 783-4771, yumaprison.org.

The Shape of Water

The heritage area also includes Yuma's charming and walkable downtown, another success story. The historic buildings house museums, restaurants, theaters, shops, and art galleries. The Sanguinetti House Museum and Gardens (240 S. Madison Ave., (928) 782-1841) is a 19th-century adobe that contains period rooms and rotating exhibits. Lavish gardens and an aviary create a colorful setting for your journey back in time. Or walk into another world entirely when entering Lutes Casino (221 Main St., (928) 782-2192, www.lutescasino.com), the state's oldest pool hall. They serve a great selection of burgers, hot dogs, and Mexican food in a funky setting where the walls and ceilings are covered with kitschy pieces of Americana.

National heritage areas create a powerful sense of place. They connect residents with the past by making sure all the stories are told, especially important in a place like Yuma with so many overlapping cultures. Yet through their efforts to preserve historical sites, conserve natural resources, create new recreational opportunities, and strengthen community pride, they improve quality of life for everyone. That's a path to the future every town should strive for.

The transformation of Yuma's riverfront has not gone unnoticed. They are considered an innovator in community-driven wetlands restoration. National, state, and local officials from all over the country make pilgrimages to this historic town that was once best known for its terrifying hoosegow. They come to study, to see what techniques and principles they can use to turn around other communities in need.

A Yuma Convert

Despite being a champion of all things Arizona, I was not a fan of Yuma in those earlier decades. There was an off-putting snarl to the riverfront and that seemed to extend through the entire town. But that all changed thanks to the vision, dedication, and hard work of hundreds of people who cared enough to get involved.

More than just a waterway, the Colorado River is the beating heart of Yuma. When it was rediscovered, an evolution began and spread throughout the town, extending far beyond the riverbanks. Yuma has done something remarkable. Any city that can complete such a massive makeover leaves me awestruck. It says something about the people who live here. This has become one of my favorite destinations. I show up not just in the winter but spring, fall, and, heaven help me, even the summer.

What I like to do most on these visits is finish dinner—so many amazing restaurants and food trucks to choose from—and then wander down to the river. I walk the pathways and listen to the birds singing in the tree branches mingled with the squeals of kids swimming and splashing nearby.

Families are spread out on the grass, an ice cream truck blares a seductive tune from the parking lot, and the low slant of sun streaks the river with shimmering fingers of gold. I bid good evening to the folks I pass, stop to watch baby quail skitter into bushes where once lay piles of rusted car parts and old mattresses. For an evening, I'm not a tourist; I'm part of a community. A welcoming embrace stretches out from the river all the way across town. That's what Yuma does just about better than any place in the state.

When Yuma made its way back to the river, it rediscovered its unique spirit. The sun's going down, and I'm glad to be back in Yuma.

When You Go

Yuma Crossing National Heritage Area: (928) 373-5198, www.yumaheritage.com.
Visit Yuma: 264 S. Main St., (928) 783-0071, www.visityuma.com.

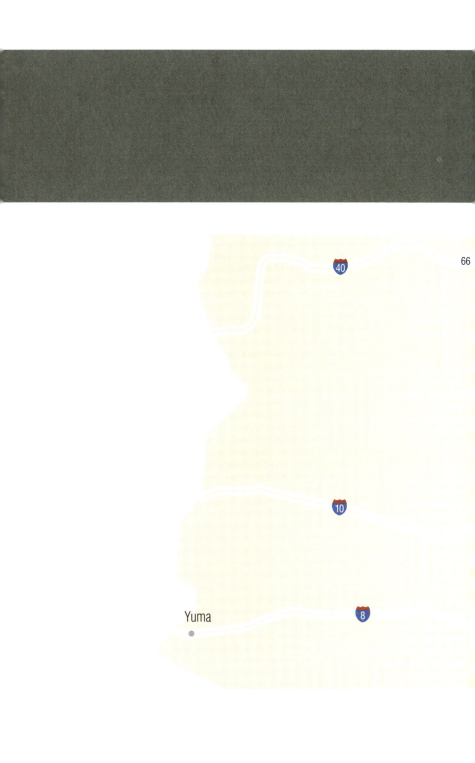

CENTRAL ARIZONA

Petroglyphs adorn the tall cliff faces at the junction of Badger Springs Wash and the Agua Fria River. Photo by the author.

Agua Fria National Monument

Overview

High desert slashed by the deep canyon of the Agua Fria River shelters numerous prehistoric sites, fragile riparian areas, and a wide variety of animal life.

Nearest Cities

Black Canyon City, Cordes Lakes.

Established

January 11, 2000.

Size

70,980 acres.

Arizona has several national parks and monuments that feature all the amenities civilized travelers have come to expect—visitor centers, gift shops, flush toilets, the whole shebang.

Then there are a handful of parks that prefer to keep things raw. They were rugged before receiving the prestigious designation, and they see no reason to change now. Why get spiffed up just because company is coming? Agua Fria National Monument, managed by the Bureau of Land Management (BLM), is like that.

Established as a national monument in 2000, the mesas and canyons of this transition zone remain as windswept and sunbaked as ever. Pronghorns still graze out on the plains. Rattlesnakes still hide under rocks adorned with ancient petroglyphs. And the Agua Fria River still tumbles from the high hills in the north through a deep canyon to create a cherished and unexpected little oasis.

Here's all you need to know. The main entry to the monument is via a rough dirt track called Bloody Basin Road, and that should provide a small clue as to what lies ahead. Perhaps the most surprising thing about Agua Fria is that it is one of our most high-profile parks. Millions of people experience it each year.

They don't actually visit, mind you, but they do see it as they hurtle past on I-17. There it is just outside their windows snugged up against the freeway, a quiet expanse that rolls away toward the eastern horizon, keeping one foot in the desert and another reaching for high chaparral.

Desert Music

Agua Fria National Monument encompasses nearly 71,000 acres of broken plateau, a deep river canyon cradled by two grassy mesas just 40 miles north of downtown Phoenix. It also contains one of the most important systems of prehistoric sites in the Southwest, revealing a significant chapter of human history. More important than any of that, it provides me with an excellent nap location.

Since the monument contains no facilities and remains just dirt-road backcountry, it's best to come prepared. This isn't a park to visit on a whim—with one minor exception.

Badger Springs Wash is a seductress, a bewitching little jaunt that's pretty much right off the freeway, and one of my favorite easy hikes in the state. It's short but with a great payoff. Just peel off the interstate at Badger Springs Road (Exit 256) and follow the gravel road for a mile to the trailhead parking.

There's a path here but it's faint, more of a hint than a trail. You just follow the wash downstream through shrubs and grasses. Sloping canyon walls rise up just enough to close out everything else, giving the spot a nice wilderness feel. You'll pass some spring-fed pools and a small channel of water flowing between boulders, adding voice to the stillness. Badger Springs Wash leads to a shady stretch of the Agua Fria River. Yet I try not to hurry, just because I love the details of this splashy little ravine.

One time I visited on a hot September day, toward the end of an active monsoon season. I had spent the morning in Phoenix hiking desert trails for an article I was writing. After 10 miles of trails and summer heat I was bushed and eager to get back to my home in the Verde Valley. Yet while zooming along on the interstate I heard the whisper of Badger Springs.

Next thing I know, I'm crunching through the wet sand listening to a symphony of birds and cascades of water. So many butterflies swarmed around me in a colorful cloud I felt a cooling breeze from their wings. They were jockeying for a medley of blooms that dotted the creek bed. I stood there feeling a moment of utter contentment, far removed from interstate travel.

The creek reaches the river in less than a mile at a lovely spot with rock walls rising overhead. Panels of petroglyphs are etched into the cliff face, and I spent time studying the drawings and symbols. Then I stretched out on a grassy slope in the lush willow shade and rested my weary feet. The Agua Fria was fat and brown and tumbled over boulders with enthusiasm. The sounds of wetness echoed from the cliff walls. A thirsty land rejoices. I fell asleep within seconds.

A Cold River Runs through It

Agua fria translates from Spanish as "cold water." Like all Arizona rivers, the Agua Fria has been battered by drought and increasing demands. An intermittent river, it is a shy, ethereal waterway. Some segments in the monument flow year-round, while other stretches need a boost of winter rains or summer monsoons for a recharge. Yet the perennial nature of the Agua Fria River, along with some of its tributaries, provided a haven for Native people and an impressive mix of wildlife.

Badger Springs Wash provides easy access to a shady stretch of the Agua Fria River. Photo by the author.

The riparian ecosystems of the river sustain a population of endangered fish like the Gila chub and Gila topminnow as well as other native fish. Nearly 200 species of birds have been recorded in the monument, and the watershed has been declared an Important Bird Area by the Audubon Society. In addition, hundreds of pronghorn call the monument home. Other residents include mule deer, white-tailed deer, javelina, and coyote. Elk and black bear occasionally venture into the area from nearby mountains.

Where I snoozed, at the confluence of Badger Springs and the Agua Fria, is one of those spots where water can almost always be found. So anyone wanting to continue a hike can explore in either direction along the riverbanks. Downstream is more scenic as the canyon deepens. There's no path—just boulder hop, bushwhack, and wade as necessary. The dark basalt rocks are courtesy of Joe's Hill, a dormant shield volcano that sits atop Black Mesa. About 2 miles from the confluence, Perry Tank Canyon flows in from the east.

People Come and People Go

Water always attracts people, thus the abundance of archaeological sites scattered across the plateau. More than 450 prehistoric sites are known to exist in the monument. While Archaic hunters and gatherers traveled seasonally through the region, small Hohokam villages were first established around AD 700 on mesa tops and along the Agua Fria River. A population influx came after 1100, as more people left the central desert to establish new villages in the uplands of Perry Mesa and Black Mesa, separated by the river's deep canyon.

Archaeologists call the late prehistoric people who lived on these mesas between 1250 and 1450, the Perry Mesa Tradition. As many as 3,000 people lived in villages and performed remarkable renovations to make agriculture viable in this rugged country. They built terraces on the slopes and check dams on the small drainages, taking advantage of rain runoff. Catch basins in the basalt rocks, springs near the cliff edges, and the deep clay soil of the mesa held moisture as well. They also cultivated agaves, gathered wild plants, and hunted game.

There were at least six large settlements. Yet by 1500, possibly due to drought, the people of the Perry Mesa Tradition had abandoned them all, leaving behind numerous questions for archaeologists today, such as who were they and where did they go? They also left behind a treasure trove of sites, including thousands of petroglyphs, symbols, and drawings etched into the rocks.

Pueblo la Plata is the most prominent site in the monument. The stone masonry pueblo once consisted of 80 to 90 rooms, an imposing village rising from the grasslands. What remains today are just low crumbling walls, although still providing significant information to researchers. Pottery sherds are scattered about. Please don't take or move them. To get there from I-17, take Bloody Basin Road (Exit 259) and travel 8.3 miles from the monument boundary. Turn north on the narrow 9023 dirt road and continue for a mile. A walk-through gate takes you from the parking area to the site on a short trail.

Bloody Basin Road

With a name like Bloody Basin, it's not surprising there's a violent backstory. Bloody Basin got its name from the Battle of Turret Peak in 1873, where the US Army tracked a band of Apaches who had attacked and killed three settlers, torturing one of them. The soldiers came upon the Apaches and launched a surprise assault. Several Indians were killed, with many more injured, and no loss of life to the troops.

Of course, there is no way of knowing whether this band of Natives was even responsible for the original killings. There has been some speculation that the reason they were so easily surprised is that they had no reason to expect an attack. Whatever the case may be, the name stuck.

Bloody Basin Road has a graded surface for the first 5 miles. It gets rougher after that and requires a high-clearance vehicle. Several small roads branch off Bloody Basin, and they may require high-clearance four-wheel drive. You can also continue driving on Bloody Basin, if you're in four-wheel drive as it exits the monument and makes a long scenic journey to a crossing of the Verde River near the historic Sheep Bridge. Be sure to check road conditions before setting out.

To experience more recent history, the northern end of the monument contains a couple of easily accessed points of interest. At the 1891 Schoolhouse Interpretive Site, visitors will find informational signage and the remnants of the old school foundation at the end of a 0.2-mile trail. The Teskey Home Site preserves the modest remains of a family ranch settled in 1925.

For both sites, leave I-17 at Exit 262, driving southeast to the small community of Cordes Lakes. Continue east on Quail Run Road, which leaves town and turns to a well-maintained dirt road. From where the pavement ends, drive 0.25 miles to a fork in the road.

For the schoolhouse, bear left at the fork and continue toward the EZ Ranch. Drive 1.25 miles to the River Bend area and look for the BLM kiosk. For the Teskey home, bear right at the fork and continue on Kelton Ranch Road. Drive 1.25 miles. Just before the bridge that goes over Big Bug Creek, turn right and park. Look for the welcome sign.

When You Go

(602) 867-5400, www.blm.gov/visit/agua-fria.

Admission

Free.

Facilities

None. Passport stamps are available at the BLM Phoenix District Office. 2020 E. Bell Road, Phoenix.

Friends of Agua Fria National Monument (www.aguafriafriends.org) maintain a presence at a small visitor center with information and maps in Black Canyon City at the Heritage Park. 33955 Old Black Canyon Highway, (623) 374-5282.

Pets

Pets must be kept on a leash no longer than 6 feet at all times.

Hiking

There are no developed trails, although Badger Springs Wash makes for a pretty gentle meander of 0.8 miles to reach the Agua Fria River.

Cross-country hiking is permitted. Terrain is rough and rocky, with steep cliffs and canyons and remote areas. Watch out for rattlesnakes and Gila monsters. Be prepared with plenty of water, supplies, and proper hiking equipment. Many of the rough four-wheel drive roads make good walking paths as well.

Camping

There are no campgrounds in the monument. Dispersed/primitive camping is allowed. Pick your own campsite—but please use existing hardened sites and protect riparian areas by camping at least 200 feet from water sources.

Programs/Events

Friends of the Agua Fria National Monument occasionally conduct events and activities such as dark sky viewing and guided hikes.

Special Notes

Travel only on designated roads. That includes mountain bikes. Driving in washes is not permitted.

Do not collect or remove pieces of pottery, stone tools, glass bottles, or other artifacts. Do not climb on walls of prehistoric sites, and don't touch or deface petroglyphs.

Check with the local BLM office for the status of fire restrictions. When campfires are permitted, use existing campfire rings. Be absolutely, 100 percent certain your fire is completely out before leaving.

Bury human waste at least 6 inches deep and 200 feet from campsites, roads, trails, and all water sources. Better yet, pack out all of your waste, including paper.

Hunting is permitted in the monument. Purchase the appropriate license and permit and follow all regulations. Target shooting is not allowed.

Pathways throughout the monument are lined with signs depicting facets of Hohokam culture. Photo by the author.

Casa Grande Ruins National Monument

Overview

One of the largest and most mysterious prehistoric structures ever built in North America became the nation's first archaeological preserve and continues to intrigue researchers and visitors alike.

Nearest City

Coolidge.

Established

President Benjamin Harrison proclaimed the 480-acre Casa Grande Reservation on June 22, 1892, making it the nation's first prehistoric and cultural site. President Woodrow Wilson made it a national monument on August 3, 1918.

Size

472 acres.

It towers above irrigated farm fields near the Gila River just like it did 700 years ago when it was first built. That's a long time to withstand desert sun and storms. Standing four stories tall, Casa Grande remains the only multistory structure from the Hohokam culture.

The first recorded mention of the imposing building came from Father Eusebio Francisco Kino, the first European to see the ruins in 1694. Traveling through the region to establish missions, Father Kino described it as *casa grande* ("great house"), and the name endured, just like the structure.

Built without the aid of metal tools, draft animals, or blueprints—built from the very desert soil itself—Casa Grande is an engineering marvel. It became the nation's first federally protected archaeological site in 1892.

People and Culture

Engineering prowess was a hallmark of Hohokam culture that was in place along the Gila and Salt Rivers by AD 450. The people who lived and farmed in this region for more than 1,000 years also built the largest and most complex irrigation system in the New World. That's how these "masters of the desert" could thrive in such an unforgiving land.

Built more than 700 years ago, Casa Grande stands as a testament to the engineering prowess of the Ancestral Sonoran Desert People. Courtesy of Mike Koopsen, Sedona.

They were long known to researchers as Hohokam, but that term is being replaced by Ancestral Sonoran Desert People. The word "Hohokam" is still accepted for the culture of the time but not when describing the people themselves.

Casa Grande was part of a collection of settlements scattered along the Gila River linked by an extensive network of canals. Corn was a primary crop for these desert farmers but over the centuries, through travel and trade, they added beans, squash, gourds, pumpkins, tobacco, and cotton. The canals diverted water to irrigate their fields. Communities living along the miles of ditches worked together to maintain the intricate irrigation system.

Barter was also an important part of Hohokam culture. Their desert villages sat along natural trade corridors that stretched to the Great Plains, into Mexico, and on to the sea. The people of Casa Grande traded cotton, pottery, and surplus crops for raw materials and other goods. Copper bells and scarlet macaws came from the south, shells from the Sea of Cortez, and turquoise and obsidian arrived from the north and east.

A Building Boom

When the Ancestral Sonoran Desert People became more reliant on agriculture, they became more settled. They built earthen homes called pit houses, dug into the desert soil and supported by interior posts. Pit houses provided protection from the weather, a sleeping space, and storage. Most daily activities took place in the courtyard.

About 800 years ago they began building larger, more complex structures including walled compounds like that found at Casa Grande. The Great House was built during 1350 in a single episode. It was, needless to say, a massive project. Layers of caliche mud, a desert subsoil with such a high lime content it dries to a concrete-like hardness, was used, 3,000 tons of it. The caliche was layered by hand-forming walls 4 feet thick at the base and tapering toward the top. Eleven large rooms were set upon a raised foundation. The central tier formed the tallest section of the structure and stood four stories.

Approximately 600 roof beams of juniper, pine, and fir were required. Even a cursory glance around will indicate a definite lack of pine forests. The timber came from at least 60 miles away, either carried or floated down the river. Saguaro ribs and reeds were laid perpendicular to the main beams and covered with wet mud. They plastered and painted the inside walls.

Careful study of the site allows archaeologists a pretty clear vision of how Casa Grande was built. The why remains more of a mystery, even after all these centuries. It is believed that Casa Grande functioned partly as an astronomical observatory. The four walls align with the four points of the compass. Carefully sized and placed openings in the upper level not only provided unobstructed views of their canals, but also matched up with key astronomical events such as solstices, equinoxes, and eclipses. For farmers, such information is vital for planting cycles.

Play Ball

The Ancestral Sonoran Desert People are identified by their heavy use of agriculture, red on buff pottery, shell work, and the presence of ball courts. The people played a game similar to those documented in central Mexico in oval basins ringed by an earthen embankment from where spectators could watch.

It's believed that ball games were a ceremonial event that tied different communities together, as they did in Mesoamerica. Some archaeologists theorize that ball games were associated with trading fairs where artisans from different villages would come together to exchange a variety of goods. Such events strengthened identity and interactions among the villages.

The Casa Grande ball court was the first to be professionally investigated. In 1918, Frank Pinkley, who was the initial caretaker at Casa Grande Ruins, identified the basin with caliche-mud plaster floors and sloped banks of packed earth. Excavations at other Hohokam sites uncovered similar structures. More than 200 ball courts have been identified across Arizona, even as far north as Wupatki National Monument near Flagstaff.

Changing Times

The popularity of ball courts waned in the 1100s, marking a gradual change in the Hohokam world. The Ancestral People left outlying settlements to gather in large villages like Casa Grande. Walled compounds were constructed. Rectangular platform mounds were built as new ritual facilities.

The Great House defining the Casa Grande village was built circa 1350. Yet it would be abandoned just a century later. Throughout the 1400s, Hohokam society returned to a previous *rancheria* lifestyle as people abandoned the large community centers and the canals to form small villages along the Gila River.

There's no clear answer on what prompted the decline of this amazing culture that numbered in the tens of thousands across the Phoenix and Tucson Basins. Theories include extreme drought, disease, devastating floods, or a general breakdown of Hohokam society. Yet they did not vanish. Today's O'odham believe they are descendants of the Hohokam.

By the time the Spanish arrived, Casa Grande and the other villages were long empty and falling into disrepair. Continued exposure to the elements and decades of souvenir hunters took a toll. The scientific community had long been intrigued by Casa Grande. High-profile anthropologists Adolph Bandelier and Frank Cushing made visits, and the push for preservation grew louder throughout the 1880s. In 1892, Casa Grande became the nation's first archaeological reserve.

Standing Tall in the Desert

The first roofed shelter to protect the ruins from weathering was built over Casa Grande in 1903. Some major excavations of the village took place in the ensuing years. It was redesignated as a national monument in 1918. More changes came during the 1930s, when the Civilian Conservation Corps constructed roads and several adobe buildings to serve as housing and administrative offices that are all still in use today.

The earlier ramada shelter was replaced in 1932 by an imposing metal roof supported by four mighty pillars. The big steel umbrella has become part of the distinctive profile of the ruins. Yet somehow the Great House survived seven centuries of scorching sun and extreme weather all on its own, a testament to the craftsmanship and engineering skill of the Ancestral People.

Each time I visit this towering skyscraper made of mud, I'm struck by how little times have changed. Small towns are still scattered through the Gila River Basin. Desert life still revolves around water. Cotton and other crops are still being grown. And ball games are still ritualized events.

Casa Grande Ruins National Monument maintains an excellent museum filled with artifacts. The Ancestral People were known not just for their architectural prowess but also as skilled artisans. Take time to watch the movie shown in the theater (good advice at all the parks), which provides an overview of the site and how it remains relevant. Six tribes in today's Southwest still have histories that link themselves to the people who once lived here. For those tribes, Casa Grande Ruins is a sacred site.

No one enters the Great House due to safety and preservation concerns. It must be admired from outside. Interpretive tours are offered during cooler months as staffing allows. A walking path leads to the Great House and continues through the remains of what was once the largest compound in the prehistoric village. Signs around the plaza help identify other features and provide information on daily life during the Hohokam era. You can continue into the picnic area across the parking lot where more sites, including the ball court, are visible from the observation deck.

When You Go

(520) 723-3172, www.nps.gov/cagr.

Admission

Free.

Facilities

The visitor center includes museum exhibits, a theater, and a gift shop.

Pets

Well-behaved pets on a leash no longer than 6 feet are welcome.

Hiking

There are no actual hiking trails in the monument but a short easy walking path that leads past the ruins and several other features.

Camping

The park is day use only.

Programs/Events

Several ranger-led programs take place throughout the year, as well as a speaker series and demonstrations by Native American artists and craftsmen. Guided tours are offered as staffing permits.

Special Notes

All ruins, artifacts, and natural features are protected by law and must be left undisturbed. Take precautions against summer heat.

Hohokam Pima National Monument

If you set out on a quest to visit all of Arizona's national park units, this one will prove problematic. It is unique among national park units in the state—probably the entire country—in that you cannot visit it.

Hohokam Pima National Monument is located within the boundaries of the Gila River Indian Community near Sacaton, about 30 miles southeast of Phoenix. Due to the sensitive nature of this site, the tribe has decided not to open the area to the public. There is no visitor center, no hiking trails, or viewpoints. There is no passport stamp, or park brochures. There is no public access to this particular national monument.

A Desert Garden

Hohokam Pima National Monument was established on October 21, 1972, to protect a large Hohokam village known as Snaketown set on the Gila River. The ancient community was inhabited from approximately AD 300 to AD 1200. As many as 2,000 people may have resided in Snaketown. It was the center of a vast trade network.

The excavations at Snaketown, first in the 1930s and again in the 1960s, provided important information and artifacts. Data gathered here helped archaeologists develop one of the earliest chronologies of Hohokam culture. The site indicated that the Ancestral Sonoran Desert People were strongly influenced by cultural groups in Mexico, including introducing patterns of "urban style" living. One theory holds that the people who settled in these desert basins were in fact migrants from Mesoamerica.

Snaketown included a central plaza, two oval-shaped fields identified as ball courts that were surrounded by pit houses, crematoriums, places to produce pottery and jewelry, and an elaborate irrigation system. Some scholars believe the ball courts may have promoted trade or competition between communities. They were skilled artisans, creating distinctive pottery and jewelry for trade. But the canals they built were their enduring legacy.

The Ancestral Sonoran Desert People designed a remarkable and sophisticated irrigation system unlike anything seen in the New World. They harnessed river water that could be funneled to nearby fields where they grew beans, corn, squash, cotton, melons, and other crops. The canals were dug by hand with stones and sticks, on average 10 feet deep and 30 feet wide, and sometimes stretching for 10 miles. They were carefully engineered to drop a few inches every mile. Woven mats were used as dams to channel and control the flow of water. Such a large-scale engineering project indicates a highly coordinated society. They would not only need to construct the canals but also maintain them, and would need to work together to regulate the flow of water that irrigated tens of thousands of acres of desert land.

It's not clear what caused the abandonment of Snaketown. Drought, flooding, disease, internal strife, and external conflicts are all possibilities. For whatever reason, the Hohokam culture that had endured in a harsh land for more than a thousand years, dispersed. The Gila River Indian Community, consisting of the Akimel O'odham (Pima) and Pee-Posh (Maricopa) people, believes the residents of Snaketown were their ancestors.

Centuries later the ancient canal system left behind would lead to the founding of another notable community.

A Surprising Rebirth

In 1867, Jack Swilling, a prospector and Civil War veteran, recognized the dusty overgrown ditches for what they were. He formed the Swilling Irrigation and Canal Company and went to work reviving old canals and digging new ones. A handful of settlers moved in and began planting crops. When it came time to name their settlement, they considered Pumpkinville and Stonewall. It was an Englishman named Phillip Darrell Duppa who suggested the fledgling community should be named Phoenix since it was a city rising from the ashes of a former great civilization.

After the excavations of the 1960s, the Snaketown ruins were backfilled to protect the site for future research, leaving nothing visible aboveground.

To learn more about Hohokam culture, visit nearby Casa Grande Ruins National Monument. Another good resource is the Huhugam Heritage Center, run by the Gila River Indian Community. Although not officially affiliated with the National Park Service or Hohokam Pima National Monument, it is an excellent resource and does contain artifacts collected from Snaketown. Huhugam Heritage Center is located at 21359 S. Maricopa Rd. in Chandler. (520) 796-3500, www.grichhc.org.

And if your quest really is to visit all of Arizona's national park units, drive east on I-10 from Phoenix. You'll pass through Hohokam Pima National Monument around mile marker 170 where Goodyear Road crosses the interstate.

You won't see anything as you drive past. Gazing across the landscape serves only as a reminder to just how ingenious these people were who envisioned a way to transform the desert into their very own garden.

Tucked in a high alcove, Montezuma Castle has survived the centuries in remarkable condition. Courtesy of Mike Koopsen, Sedona.

Montezuma Castle National Monument

Overview

Possibly the best-preserved and most dramatic cliff dwelling in the United States gazes across a shady riparian oasis.

Nearest City

Camp Verde.

Established

December 8, 1906. Montezuma Castle was one of America's first four national monuments.

Size

1,015 acres.

First, there are a couple of things you should know about Montezuma Castle. It's not and he didn't.

It's not really a castle, and Montezuma didn't build it. The imposing five-story 20-room structure is however, one of the best-preserved examples of Native American architecture in the country. The prehistoric high rise is the very definition of a cliff dwelling, tucked into a limestone alcove 100 feet above the canyon floor.

Built by the Sinagua people more than 800 years ago, Montezuma Castle sits high above the Beaver Creek floodplain, accessible only by a series of ladders. The deep-cut recess provides protection from the elements and is no doubt responsible for the excellent condition of the ancient structure. The first Euro-American explorers to discover it presumed that anything so complex must be Aztec in origin, hence the name. Actually, it was built by Indigenous people, occupied for centuries, and then abandoned decades before the Aztec emperor Montezuma was even born.

Land of the Sinagua

Sinagua comes from the Spanish words *sin agua*, or "without water." Archaeologist Harold Colton named the group in 1939 referring to the San Francisco Peaks near Flagstaff, where Colton first identified the culture. Early Spanish explorers called the mountains "Sierra Sin Agua" because they lacked flowing rivers.

Archaeologists divide the Sinagua into two groups: Northern Sinagua, who lived in the Flagstaff area, and the Southern Sinagua, who settled in the Verde Valley. The groups are similar but retain some cultural differences. Northern Sinagua villages can be found at Walnut Canyon National Monument and Wupatki National Monument. Preserving the heritage of the Southern Sinagua are Montezuma Castle and nearby Tuzigoot National Monument.

The Southern Sinagua had settled in the Verde Valley by AD 650, possibly earlier. Their first structures were partially excavated pit houses. They were farmers growing corn, beans, and squash, and also supplemented their crops with hunting and gathering. Unlike their northern counterparts, the Sinagua in the Verde Valley enjoyed an abundance of water from rivers and streams. This allowed them to utilize floodplain farming on fertile terraces and irrigation techniques learned from Hohokam villages located farther south.

The Sinagua built Montezuma Castle between AD 1100 and AD 1350. The 20 rooms are spread across five levels with staggered floors that follow a series of shallow rock ledges. Walls were made from limestone and mud mortar, 2 feet thick at the bottom, tapering a bit near the top. They were coated with a layer of adobe plaster. The roofs incorporated wood beams covered with thatch and mud. Most timbers came from Arizona sycamores that grow along Beaver Creek. Archaeologists estimate 35 people lived in the castle with another 200 living close by.

Reasons they chose to build high up on the cliff are the subject of speculation. The southern exposure meant the dwellings stayed warmer in the winter and cooler in summer. The high location kept them above a creek that was prone to flooding during summer storms. It also provided protection from potential enemies and afforded excellent views.

The Sinagua eventually began to leave Montezuma Castle and surrounding areas. By 1425 they were gone. No one knows why, but it may have been due to resource depletion, drought, social conflict, or religious reasons. The majority likely traveled north and joined Hopi villages. Others may have remained and integrated with the Yavapai and Apache that were migrating into the valley.

Castle and the Creek

President Theodore Roosevelt wasted no time. Using the newly passed American Antiquities Act, Teddy went to work. On December 8, 1906, he created America's first four national monuments. Montezuma Castle was one of those. (Another Arizona site, Petrified Forest, was also one of the original four.)

Despite damage caused by looters, the structure has held up extremely well, no doubt due to its sheltered location. Early tourists were allowed to scale ladders and explore inside the big building. When the condition of the dwelling began to noticeably deteriorate, that policy ended in 1951.

The remains of an even larger structure can be found in the monument. At the base of the same cliff wall that holds Montezuma Castle is a jumbled rock pile marking all that's left of "Castle A," a 45–50 room pueblo. Yet without the protection of the alcove, Castle A succumbed to the elements. However, a 1933 excavation uncovered numerous artifacts and greatly enhanced understanding of the Sinagua people.

Today, visitors to the monument enjoy a tranquil riparian setting. The Sinagua had an eye for location. This is one of the places I always take visitors. It's easy, accessible, and delivers a big dramatic payoff. Gazing up at that towering castle stirs the imagination.

A paved trail meanders beneath the shade of graceful sycamore trees and leads to scenic viewpoints of the towering cliff house. Along the way, informational signs fill in the ecological and cultural details as it loops past an overlook of the flowing stream.

But as satisfying as it is, your visit shouldn't end here.

Montezuma Well

Just as startling as the man-made wonder of Montezuma Castle is the natural wonder of Montezuma Well. It's an unexpected oasis carved from the earth's skin.

Located about 11 driving miles away from the castle, Montezuma Well is a detached unit of the national monument. What appears to be just a placid pond is actually a limestone sinkhole formed by the collapse of an underground cavern. Subterranean springs replenish the well, pumping out 1.5 million gallons of water each day.

Yet the well doesn't overflow because there is an opening that drains off the water. Like a bowl with a crack near the brim, water flows through a limestone cave where most of it ends up in Beaver Creek. But some is channeled off by an ancient canal system built by the Sinagua. They used this to irrigate their crops. You can still see their small cliff dwellings perched atop a sheltered ledge above the pond.

A paved, signed path climbs a short hill to an overlook of the well, which is almost 400 feet in diameter. A short spur trail comprised mostly of steps, leads down through tangled greenery and jumbled boulders to the edge of the pond, where the water spills into an underground stream. At the base of the limestone wall is a cave and the remains of a Sinagua dwelling.

Morning sun glints off the water at Montezuma Well. Ducks glide across the surface, occasionally diving with a flip of tail feathers. It's a peaceful scene, but I'm not fooled in the least. Because of the water's high concentration of carbon dioxide, fish can't live in the well. But that doesn't mean that the pond isn't teeming with life. In fact, Montezuma Well actually supports five endemic species, plants and animals that exist nowhere else in the world. It likely contains the highest concentration of endemic species of any single spring in North America—a single-celled plant called a diatom, a tiny snail, a water scorpion, an amphipod that resembles a miniature shrimp, and a predatory leech.

When the sun sets, the seemingly placid waters churn with thousands of leeches rising from the depths to feed on the amphipods. The amphipods try to survive by limiting

The limestone sinkhole of Montezuma Well is an unexpected find in the high desert of the Verde Valley. Courtesy of Mike Koopsen, Sedona.

movement and resting on plants at night. Although they can't get too comfortable because the water scorpions live in the weed beds along the shore and enter the open water in the darkness to hunt the tasty amphipods.

The thought of leech hordes snaking through dark waters searching for meat always reminds me that it's time once again to watch *Attack of the Giant Leeches*, a 1959 low-budget and unintentionally hilarious sci-fi film. I don't want to spoil it, but the leeches appear to be played by men in Hefty trash bags with suckers glued on. That's enough for me to start making popcorn.

Climb back up the steps to join the main trail, which traces the rim before gently descending a grassy slope dotted with cactus and marked by the partial walls of another Sinagua dwelling. At the bottom of the hill, the trail continues to the parking area. But if you return without taking the short spur trail to the outlet, you'll miss a magical part of your visit.

Follow the path into a dark tunnel of trees for one of those amazing Arizona moments. Step out of the scorching summer sun and immerse yourself in a cool and shady sliver of paradise. The trail hugs the cool limestone wall beneath a jungle-dense canopy of trees. Water flows past in a canal built more than 1,000 years ago. Just beyond the canal and the dense undergrowth is Beaver Creek. Temperatures plunge in this riparian refrigerator. It's often 20 degrees cooler here than on the rim.

In Arizona we're accustomed to varied climates stacked at differing elevations, but they are generally spread out over a few miles, not a few steps. In all my travels around the state, I can't think of a single place where the climate and scenery changes so abruptly. I love being here in summer, inhaling that sweet chilled air.

Around a corner of the wall, near a massive sycamore tree, is the outlet. This is where water from the well emerges from the 150-foot-long underground tunnel. The water not siphoned off by the canal ends up replenishing Beaver Creek. Today the canal still sends irrigation water to two nearby ranches.

Before you leave Montezuma Well, be sure to visit the remains of a prehistoric pit house dating back to 1050 located at a roadside pullout. Your last stop should be the picnic area down the hill near the entrance, because it's absolutely lovely. The grassy park features an abundance of shade trees sheltering the tables and a gentle meander of canal water flowing along the edge. It's a quiet spot to sit and contemplate all that you experienced at the hidden gem of Montezuma Well.

When You Go

Montezuma Castle: (928) 567-3322, www.nps.gov/moca.
Montezuma Well: Take I-17 to Exit 293. Continue through the towns of McGuireville and Rimrock, following the signs four miles to the park entrance. (928) 567-3322, www.nps.gov/moca.

Admission

Admission fee is good for seven days and grants entry to Montezuma Castle and Tuzigoot National Monument in Cottonwood. There is no admission fee to Montezuma Well.

Facilities

The visitor center at Montezuma Castle has museum exhibits and a gift shop.

Pets

Pets are allowed on trails but must be kept on a leash.

Hiking

A paved 0.3-mile loop trail winds past Montezuma Castle, through a shady grove of sycamore trees, and along spring-fed Beaver Creek.

At Montezuma Well, a 0.3-mile loop leads to an overlook of the oasis. The trail is paved but does include steps. Spur trails branch off from the main trail and lead to cool shady spots near the water at each end of a subterranean channel.

Camping

Both Montezuma Castle and Montezuma Well are day-use-only parks.

Programs/Events

A variety of interpretive programs are offered throughout the year. Some of these include cultural demonstrations and performances, guided nature walks, ranger talks, and artist-in-residence programs.

Special Notes

Stay on trails. Be alert for snakes.

Sonoran Desert National Monument protects almost a half-million acres of wide-open spaces. Photo by the author.

A network of dirt roads provides access to the backcountry of Sonoran Desert National Monument. Photo by the author.

Sonoran Desert National Monument

Overview

A vast expanse of wide-open desert protects isolated mountain ranges separated by broad plains dotted with cactus, and keeps civilization at bay.

Nearest Cities

Gila Bend, Maricopa, Casa Grande.

Established

January 17, 2001.

Size

486,400 acres.

I stood outside my idling SUV studying a chewed-up patch of dirt road in the Sonoran Desert National Monument. The arroyo must have seen a fierce little torrent of water from a late-season storm. That had been a month ago but the watery teeth marks lingered. Sand had been washed away exposing a series of drop-offs and ledges. Gauging my clearance, I was almost certain I could make it.

That's when I turned around. "I was almost certain I could make it" is the universal battle cry of Idiots.

So many stories of folks who got stranded/trapped/lost/arrested/injured/eaten began with the almost certain belief that they could make it. While I do have a longstanding relationship with Idiocy, perhaps even an honorary degree, I am older now. If I'm no wiser, at least I am lazier. No need to spend a couple of hours digging my tires out of a ditch when I could just park and walk across open desert.

Welcome to Nowhere

Containing almost a half-million acres of diverse and unspoiled tall cactus desert, the monument is a special place hiding in plain sight. An interstate highway cuts right through it, yet most travelers pass by unaware.

Located about 60 miles southwest of Phoenix, Sonoran Desert National Monument is overseen by the Bureau of Land Management (BLM). It contains three wilderness areas—North Maricopa Mountains Wilderness, South Maricopa Mountains Wilderness, and Table Top Wilderness—and several mountain ranges separated by broad valleys. Within its borders are numerous archaeological sites and the remnants of several historic trails, like Butterfield Overland National Historic Trail, the Mormon Battalion Trail, the Gila Trail, and the Juan Bautista de Anza National Historic Trail.

What it lacks is a centerpiece attraction. There are no signature sights, no defining experience. There's no official entry point, just a lot of barely marked dirt roads. You won't find a visitor center with helpful rangers to offer suggestions. Scenic overlooks? Interpretive signage? Forget about it. It's just a great patch of desert pulled safely away from the clutching claws of development.

Maybe that's why I like the monument. It challenges visitors to make their own fun. For me that means hiking. Or bird watching. Or sitting on a rock and chatting with passing lizards. Or finding a shady spot in a sandy wash to stretch out and take an impromptu middle-of-nowhere snooze.

The monument offers a whole lot of nothing. For many people that holds little interest. As a connoisseur of desert, I consider it a dusty, prickly paradise.

Embrace the Lonely

I've actually done a fair amount of hiking in Sonoran Desert National Monument and have yet to make it to an official trail. Amid this vast expanse there are only four designated hiking trails, and all are located in the interior of the monument down rough dirt roads. The 9-mile Margie's Cove Trail and the 6-mile Brittlebush Trail lie in the North Maricopa Mountains Wilderness. The Table Top Wilderness contains the 7-mile Lava Flow Trail and the 3-mile Table Top Trail.

To reach most trailheads requires high-clearance four-wheel drive, which I don't have. But a couple of the roads are supposed to be manageable during good weather in a standard high-clearance vehicle. Maybe it's just bad timing on my part that my visits seem to coincide with poor road conditions.

Or maybe it is excellent timing. Because what I've found is I can experience an incredibly peaceful day in the monument just by walking into the quiet remoteness of a lonely desert. The tangle of dirt roads that fan out in many directions make excellent hiking paths. And since vegetation is sparse, I can hike off-trail without trampling plants or stumbling over cacti. I like venturing across the acreage and making my own discoveries, savoring my own panoramas, because I'm creating a route that no one has ever taken before.

Always keep a sharp eye out for wildlife. The monument supports an impressive roster of animals including mountain lion, desert bighorn, gray fox, mule deer, javelina, bobcat, and the endangered Sonoran pronghorn. More than 200 species of birds have been observed here as well the desert tortoise and other reptiles, including rattlesnakes. One more reason to keep eyes open.

From Pavement to Dirt

The main access to Sonoran Desert National Monument is from State Route 238 or from two exits off I-8.

From the interstate, Freeman Road (Exit 140) is a rough dirt road heading south into the White Hills and Sand Tank Mountains. Visits to the Sand Tanks require a permit for crossing the Barry M. Goldwater Range. Permits are free and available online, but require the recipient to watch a safety video.

Vekol Road (Exit 144) serves as the de facto main entrance to the monument. A wide gravel track rambles south through the desert scrub. The wide plains of the Vekol Valley offer some enticing and convenient camping spots beneath a big dark sky. The sedan-quality condition of this road lasts about 2 miles. Past the Vekol Ranch turnoff it becomes more rugged.

The White Hills rise to the west, and the Table Top Mountains dominate the eastern skyline. Skinny dirt roads branch off leading across the desert. Always be alert while here. This southern segment of the monument is a corridor for drug and human smugglers.

Hwy 238 connects Maricopa to Gila Bend, as a state route on the eastern end and a county road on the western side. But no matter the designation, the twisting ribbon of pavement provides access to the northern segment of the monument—although without much fanfare. You might spot a sign or two, but mostly you just need to look for dirt roads bearing north. This is where you'll find a few of my favorite hiking and snoozing areas.

Desert Saved

This is definitely a place to show up prepared. Make sure your gas tank is full and spare tires are inflated. Carry plenty of water. But I'm not sure if a visit to Sonoran Desert National Monument requires the most planning of any of Arizona's parks, or the least.

All my plans seem to fall apart, yet I have a great time. When I turned around before reaching Margie's Cove West Trailhead, I still hiked all afternoon. I roamed among saguaro groves and scrambled into rocky hills to enjoy some choice views. Clusters of tiny yellow wildflowers bloomed, like lizard bouquets, always a welcome sight in November. I'm still trying to identify them.

Another time when I couldn't reach the Table Top Trail, I struck out for the White Hills. I discovered remnants of an old fence line and rusty horseshoes. I sat in the shade of an ancient ironwood tree studying a thoroughfare of animal tracks in a wash. On one hillside, I found a collection of saguaros striking enough fanciful poses to fill a comic strip. The quiet soothed and the solitude was healing.

We need silent places. We need sanctuaries of nature saved from urban sprawl. We need undisturbed desert where wildlife can roam and the sun can beat down all day and the heavens can splinter at night into a billion diamond points of light.

So I'll keep coming back to Sonoran Desert National Monument. And who knows. Maybe one of these days, I'll make it to an actual trail.

When You Go

(602) 867-5400, www.blm.gov/visit/sonoran-desert-national-monument.

Admission

Free.

Facilities

None. Passport stamps are available at the BLM Phoenix District Office. 2020 E. Bell Road, Phoenix.

Pets

Yes.

Hiking

Visitors may hike or ride horseback almost anywhere in the monument. Four designated trails total 26 miles.

MARGIE'S COVE TRAIL

A nearly level 9-mile trail cuts through the heart of the North Maricopa Mountains Wilderness. The trail follows a combination of former vehicle tracks and unmarked desert washes. No trail signage or directional markers are available along the route.

To access Margie's Cove West Trailhead, drive State Route 85 to Woods Road, located just south of milepost 134 (about 14 miles north of Gila Bend) and turn east. At the cattle guard/dirt road, turn left and follow the small brown trail signs that guide you along the Hwy 85 fence line, then east 3.8 miles to BLM Route 8001E. Turn right onto 8001E and drive south 1.2 miles to the trailhead. A high-clearance two-wheel-drive vehicle is generally suitable for this road but not always.

BRITTLEBUSH TRAIL

This 6-mile path also traverses the North Maricopa Mountain Wilderness, and also lacks signage. From Hwy 238 (about 12 miles east of Gila Bend) turn north on BLM Route 8004. Follow 8004 and 8004A for 6 miles to the trailhead. Motorized access to the trailhead is sometimes unavailable due to road closures. Brittlebush Trail can also be accessed via Margie's Cove West Trailhead.

TABLE TOP TRAIL

Climb from the floor of Vekol Valley to the distinctive summit of Table Top Mountain in 3.5 miles, while gaining more than 2,000 feet of elevation. Due to steep conditions, this is not a good horseback trail. From I-8, take Vekol Road (Exit 144) south for 2.1 miles to the Vekol Ranch turnoff. Stay to the right and continue south on Vekol Road (BLM Route

8007) for 8.7 miles to BLM Route 8024. Turn left and travel 4.5 miles to the trailhead. A high-clearance two-wheel-drive vehicle is generally suitable for this road but not always.

LAVA FLOW TRAIL

This moderate 7.2-mile route pieced together from old roadways skirts the basalt-covered slopes of the Black Mountains. Lava Flow can be accessed at three points. The north and west trailheads require four-wheel drive. To reach the southern trailhead, follow the same directions to Table Top. Lava Flow South is on BLM Route 8024, 0.8-miles before the Table Top Trailhead.

Camping

Dispersed camping is allowed throughout the monument unless otherwise posted. Two small campgrounds at Margie's Cove West and Table Top Trailheads offer a restroom and three small campsites with a picnic table and barbecue grill. No water or hookups are available. Campsites are on a first-come, first-served basis. Pack out all trash.

For primitive camping, choose a campsite that has been previously used and no more than 100 feet from the road. Camping is limited to 14 days within a 28-consecutive-day period. Small campfires are allowed unless otherwise posted. Put all fires out cold before you leave. Wood is scarce so bring your own or use only dead, down, and detached wood. Better yet, skip a campfire and enjoy the night skies. If you do build a fire be absolutely, positively certain it is out before you leave. And it's worth repeating, pack out all trash.

Programs/Events

None.

Special Notes

Water is not available. Carry and drink plenty of water.

Roads are primitive and not maintained. High-clearance or four-wheel-drive vehicles are recommended in most areas. Have a full tank of gas, full-sized spare tires, a tool kit, and first-aid kit. Cell phones do not work in many areas of the national monument.

Vehicles, including bicycles, must remain on existing routes. Travel only on roads and washes posted with a BLM Route number sign. Bikes are prohibited in wilderness areas and on wilderness trails.

Drug and human smuggling have occurred within the monument, south of I-8. Report any suspicious activity to BLM Federal Law Enforcement Communications Center, County Sherriff, or Border Patrol.

Rattlesnakes and scorpions may be encountered. Do not put your hands and feet in places you can't see.

A paved half-mile trail climbs the slope through cactus groves to reach the Lower Cliff Dwelling. Photo by the author.

Tonto National Monument

Overview

Tucked into alcoves of steep mountainsides, two prehistoric Salado cliff dwellings built more than 700 years ago still gaze across the broad Tonto Basin.

Nearest City

Globe.

Established

December 19, 1907.

Size

1,120 acres.

The lake is a new thing. A pretty thing. An improbable thing. Theodore Roosevelt Lake lies far below the cliff dwellings of Tonto National Monument. Commonly known just as Roosevelt Lake, because hey, we're a busy people in Arizona, the big reservoir spreads across the southern end of the Tonto Basin.

When the Theodore Roosevelt Dam was completed in 1911, it impounded the Salt River and formed the largest lake entirely within Arizona's borders. In some ways, the Salt is the state's most iconic river. The waterway that has nurtured the Phoenix valley for centuries tumbles from the forested heights of the White Mountains and courses through a steep-walled canyon before finally spilling across the saguaro-studded desert.

Roosevelt Lake is the oldest of the six reservoirs constructed and operated by the Salt River Project. But besides that big shimmering, mirage-like body of water, everything else probably looks about the same as it did when the prehistoric culture known as Salado inhabited these lands. The two cliff dwellings of Tonto National Monument provide the best-preserved architectural evidence of Salado culture, and in a memorable setting.

The Tonto Basin acts as a transition zone, a rugged landscape pinned between the high mesas and canyons of the Colorado Plateau to the north, and the low deserts stretching south. Long ago it was home to thousands, likely tens of thousands, of inhabitants from 1250 to 1450. This was the heart of the Salado Phenomenon, one of the Southwest's enduring riddles.

The Mysterious Salado

Have you ever seen two archaeologists throwing punches in the dirt parking lot of a

The centerpiece attraction of Tonto National Monument is the Lower Cliff Dwelling since it can be visited year-round. Courtesy of Mike Koopsen, Sedona.

honky-tonk? Probably not. But if you had, chances are good that they were debating the Salado Phenomenon, and things just got out of hand.

Experts are still trying to sort it. Let's start with what we know. The term "Salado" is derived from Rio Salado, the Spanish name for the Salt River. In the 13th century, years of prolonged drought were followed by years of torrential rains and flooding. Such environmental stresses prompted the migration of many peoples. One theory holds that Ancestral Puebloan peoples from the north and Mogollon peoples from the east entered the fertile Tonto Basin, encountering Hohokam communities. Here the three cultures intermixed, intermarried, and shared knowledge and technology. Salado emerged from this cultural melting pot.

Salado culture seemed to be based on a spirit of cooperation. Their pottery, architecture, textiles, and farming techniques all reflected a blending of influences. So it's no wonder Salado proves such a puzzle to eggheads today. Drought and floods are easy to understand. War is a simple concept to grasp. But a sudden spontaneous outbreak of cooperation? That's as uncommon as it is refreshing. Scholarly debate continues.

Moving on Up

Most of the inhabitants of the newly founded commune lived on the basin floor along the Salt River and its tributary, Tonto Creek. Here they built irrigation canals and grew corn, cotton, squash, beans, and amaranth, an ancient grain similar to quinoa. They supplemented their diet by hunting and gathering wild native plants like mesquite beans, saguaro fruit, pinion nuts, walnuts, acorns, jojoba beans, and prickly pear pads and fruit.

These were people living close to the land, using every resource available to them. They cultivated agave and yucca to weave sandals, mats, and baskets. They also created a distinctive black-on-white-on-red pottery. Known today as Salado polychromes, this pottery was the most widely distributed of its kind in the Southwest.

Artifacts found in the monument suggest the Salado people maintained an extensive trade network. Seashells from the California coast, obsidian from New Mexico, and macaws from Mexico found their way to this desert community.

As the population swelled on the valley floor, some took to higher ground. Around 1300, groups of people moved higher up the slopes—away from the precious water—and began construction on cliff dwellings. Archaeologists are not sure what prompted the movement. Protection from weather or hostile neighbors, or because the valley floor was overcrowded are possibilities. They may have moved simply to harvest resources found in the uplands such as deer and bighorn sheep and the variety of native plants.

Maybe these high-rise dwellers just needed a place to concentrate on their craftsmanship. Along with their beautifully decorated pottery, the Salado were highly accomplished weavers, creating textiles of intricate designs that rivaled any contemporary Southwest culture. Their closely woven cotton fabric is similar to modern cloth made by machines. Taking the extra time to add such artistic flair to functional household goods indicates a thriving and vibrant society.

It makes their departure all the more puzzling.

In the late 1300s, the Tonto Basin became drier. Although periods of drought were occasionally broken by devastating floods, the kind that that destroyed farmlands and irrigation canals. Another migration began and by 1450, the Salado had abandoned the once bountiful Tonto Basin. Modern tribes say their ancestors chose to relocate and join other communities.

Castles in the Sky

Both cliff dwellings at Tonto are built in natural caves, high up the slopes above the visitor center that houses an impressive collection of artifacts gathered from the site. The caves face east for morning sun and shade in the afternoon. The Lower Cliff Dwelling serves as the main attraction of the monument since it is open year-round.

Even without the big payoff at the end, the hike to the Lower Cliff Dwelling makes a gorgeous desert outing. The paved trail twists up the slope in a series of curves. Signs are posted along the path providing information on native plants and animals, and a good reason to pause and catch your breath. As I climb, the views across the basin widen. What starts as a slivered peek soon grows into a broad panorama with a bristling foreground of saguaros and a distant backdrop of mountains framing the big lake.

I can't help but imagine the Salado would have appreciated seeing so much water gathered and tamed. How much easier their lives would have been. The manipulation of water has been the predominant Arizona story for eons. Outlines of irrigation canals were still visible until the flooding of Roosevelt Lake.

At the top of the trail, a rough stone house fills the eye socket of a cave. It contains about 20 rooms and may have supported 40 to 60 people at its maximum habitation. Prehistoric builders used a mixture of stone and adobe to build the walls. Pine and juniper roof beams had to be carried from surrounding mountains.

Although 700 years old, the dwelling retains strong traces of the people who lived here. Pay attention to the details. Thick walls are still standing. Original wood and some of the original ceilings remain intact. Walls are blackened by smoke from cooking fires. Ancient fingerprints can still be seen in the caliche plaster. Some rooms may be entered, but please do not touch or climb on the walls. A ranger is usually present through the day to answer questions.

The Upper Cliff Dwelling is accessible by guided tour only from November through April. Reservations for tours open in October and fill up fast. So plan ahead. Rangers lead small groups on an unpaved path starting out in a wash and climbing up the slope some 1.5 miles while gaining 600 feet of elevation.

Practically the best part of the tour is the information provided by the guide about the Sonoran Desert and the Salado people. The larger Upper Cliff Dwelling built in a shallow cave with a sloping floor contains about 40 rooms, 32 on ground level, and 8–10 second-story rooms. There are some partially intact roofs, parapet walls, and two large rooms, which may have been used for ceremonies. Corncobs still litter the cave floor.

It's a remarkable tale, a hodgepodge of cultures that came together and flourished for almost as long as America has existed as a nation. The Salado prospered as a culture and proved surprisingly healthy as a people. Skeletal remains reveal little evidence of the nutritional deficiencies often found in Puebloan agricultural societies.

Yet in the end, they broke apart, leaving behind a transcendent collection of artistic craftsmanship, the splendid bones of architectural achievement, and one of the most profound mysteries of the prehistoric Southwest.

When You Go

(928) 467-2241, www.nps.gov/tont.

Admission

There is an admission fee.

Facilities

The visitor center includes museum exhibits and a gift shop. A short film tells the story of the people and cultures of the Tonto Basin.

Pets

Leashed pets are allowed only in the picnic area along the entrance road (nice views of the lake), the parking lot, and the Cactus Patch and Lower Cliff Dwelling Trails. But pets are not permitted in the Lower Cliff Dwelling. Neither are they permitted in the visitor center, museum, or on the Upper Cliff Dwelling Trail.

The Upper Cliff Dwelling is accessible only by guided tour with a reservation required. Courtesy of Mike Koopsen, Sedona.

Hiking

LOWER CLIFF DWELLING TRAIL

A paved 0.5-mile self-guided path ascends 350 feet. Views extend back down cactus-spiked slopes across the basin and Roosevelt Lake. The trail opens at 8:00 a.m. year-round. Check in at the visitor center when you arrive. From September through May, start your hike before 4:00 p.m. From June through August you must start before noon.

UPPER CLIFF DWELLING TOUR

Ranger-guided tours are offered Friday through Monday from November through April. Reservations are required for the outing, which will last 3–4 hours. The trail is 3 miles round trip on a rocky climbing path.

Camping

The park is day use only, except during special evening events, typically held between November and April. Tonto National Monument is an International Dark Sky Park.

There is camping available in the surrounding Tonto National Forest, including some at Roosevelt Lake. Windy Hill Campground is the closest to the national monument.

Programs/Events

Tonto features events and programs throughout the year, including guided bird walks.

Special Notes

Do not climb, lean, sit, or stand on the walls. Do not touch ancient walls because oils from hands can cause deterioration. Do not pick up or remove rocks that are part of a wall. Do not collect or disturb plants, animals, or archaeological objects. Do not eat in the cliff dwellings. Absolutely no fires, candles, or smoking should occur at archaeological sites.

The ancient village of Tuzigoot spreads across a hill above the Verde River. Courtesy of Mike Koopsen, Sedona.

Tuzigoot National Monument

Overview
This ancient Sinagua pueblo crowns a hilltop overlooking the Verde River and has been partially restored with rooms that can be explored.

Nearest Cities
Clarkdale, Cottonwood.

Established
July 25, 1939.

Size
812 acres.

I see Tuzigoot in ways that most visitors never do. I admire it from all angles, all approaches, and understand its connection to the Verde River. When it comes to this ancient Sinagua village, I am a virtual expert.

Heaven knows, it has nothing to do with my vast archaeological knowledge. I just get to see it all the time. Located just a few miles from my house, Tuzigoot is my friendly neighborhood national monument. It tops a hill that overlooks my unofficial backyard, Dead Horse Ranch State Park. The park is where I hike several days a week. So there I am, walking for miles and miles in the shadow of the old stone pueblo.

Low, rambling, and exposed, Tuzigoot spreads across a long ridge more than 100 feet above an oxbow of the Verde River. It may lack the drama of Montezuma Castle but instead exudes a quiet dignity, a silent connection to the rich history of the valley.

The House of Crooked Water

Montezuma Castle was incorrectly named, but Tuzigoot is both lyrical and accurate. The name was given to the site during excavation in the 1930s. Tuzigoot is a slight corruption of a Tonto Apache phrase. It generally translates to "crooked water."

The Southern Sinagua built the village between AD 1125 and AD 1400. It spread across the top of a limestone ridge, above a meander of the Verde River. The Sinagua preferred high ground for their dwellings near sources of water, on hilltops or cliffs. This may have been to preserve valuable farmland, or it may have been a defensive position, or simply because they enjoyed the views.

There was no indication the Sinagua feuded with any of their neighbors. On the contrary, they were part of a large trade network that spanned hundreds of miles. Archaeologists at Tuzigoot have uncovered painted pottery from the Hopi Mesas, seashells from the Pacific Ocean, and the remains of scarlet macaws from Mexico, hinting at the scope of goods that flowed through the Verde Valley.

The pueblo was built in stages, adapting to a growing population. The Sinagua used local materials for construction of all their dwellings. In this case, the cobble walls of Tuzigoot utilized the abundance of stone available. At its peak, Tuzigoot was 500 feet long and 100 feet wide, and contained 110 rooms spread over two levels. Most rooms contained two large posts supporting roof beams and dividing the room into halves, or thirds. The lack of doorways indicated that access to most rooms was by way of ladders through rooftop hatches. One flat section of the hilltop was left open to serve as a plaza, always an important community space in pueblo villages.

Changing Times

The Sinagua were primarily farmers. At Tuzigoot they grew corn, squash, beans, and cotton on the fertile Verde River floodplain. They supplemented their crops by hunting and also cultivated plants like agave and prickly pear cactus for food and fiber. For hundreds of years, the Sinagua thrived in the resource-rich valley.

Yet in the late 1300s, an exodus began, as it did throughout the prehistoric Southwest. People started to leave. No one knows what prompted the departure—the exhaustion of farmland, drought, or social conflict are all possibilities. Or perhaps there were no external factors. According to the Hopi, the Verde Valley was always meant to be just a temporary stop on a much longer journey. They believed the Sinagua simply continued their migration onto the Hopi Mesas to the north.

It was about this time that the seminomadic Yavapai and Tonto Apache arrived in the Verde Valley, although some researchers believe they were here much earlier. The Yavapai have always said their ancestors left stone pueblos and farms for a more mobile lifestyle of hunting and gathering.

A New Deal

Every visit to Tuzigoot begins at the visitor center and museum, housed in a rustic stone-wrapped building that emulates Sinaguan construction. Pay your entrance fee, then take a few minutes to learn more about the people who called this hilltop home centuries ago. Small but thoughtful, the museum highlights an assortment of ceramics, textiles, and tools

Tuzigoot's distinctive profile is visible from adjacent Dead Horse Ranch State Park. Courtesy of Rick Mortensen, Phoenix.

found during excavation of the pueblo. A re-created Sinagua room offers a glimpse of everyday life in Puebloan times. Descendants of the people who once lived here helped develop the exhibits.

There's yet another layer of history to Tuzigoot. Everything you see on the site and in the museum came about as a direct result of New Deal programs. Tuzigoot was excavated in 1933–1934, aided in part by labor provided by the Federal Emergency Relief Agency's Civil Works Administration, an organization created during the Great Depression to provide employment for out-of-work Americans. In 1936, local relief workers hired by the newly formed Works Progress Administration built the museum and visitor center.

Walk the paved trail that circles the remnants of the village. Informational signage is posted and most mornings a volunteer docent is on hand to answer questions. It's hard to visit this ancient place and not have some questions. While the pathway is barrier-free, there are some steep sections that may be challenging for wheelchairs and strollers.

A two-story room of the pueblo has been restored, so visitors can admire the building techniques and materials used by these resourceful people. Preservation techniques today strive to protect structures without altering original construction methods or materials. The park service uses soil-based mortars instead of cement. While much more historically accurate, it does erode easily and requires constant maintenance. So please don't sit, stand, or climb on the walls.

Take time to savor the wraparound views of the lush Verde Valley crowded with colorful hills and framed by rising mountains. Sycamore Canyon lies to the north, and the old mining town of Jerome clings to the slope of Mingus Mountain. Close by, and most significantly to the Sinagua, the Verde River courses past. You can trace the riparian corridor by following the line of cottonwood trees.

Marching to the Marsh

The Tuzigoot pueblo perches above the visitor center. Down the slope away from the village the paved path leads to an overlook of Tavasci Marsh. A cutoff meander in the Verde River created the wetland, which is one of Northern Arizona's largest remaining freshwater marshes. The Audubon Society has designated Tavasci as an Important Bird Area.

The path follows a gentle slope, with large sign panels describing everything from the creation of the wetland, to how it has been impacted by human interaction, and the bounty of wildlife such a rare gem supports in an arid landscape. Smaller signs identify plants and their uses. The trail ends at a wooden deck with seating, making for a pleasant spot to enjoy this little oasis. You'll see lots of greenery but not much water. But trust me, the water is there. Otherwise, the greenery wouldn't be. The trail is just over a half-mile round trip and is wheelchair accessible.

For those looking to explore a little more of the landscape, an unmarked gravel road crosses the Tavasci Marsh Overlook Trail just past the second large sign. Turn right down a moderate hill. The old roadbed winds through a mesquite bosque before ending at a wall of towering cattails. That's how you know you've reached the marsh. I love the aromas here, the soft spice of desert dampness. It's warm and woody, lush and earthy. You're about a half-mile from the sunbaked hilltop of Tuzigoot, but it feels like you're immersed in a different world.

A left turn soon dead-ends at private property. But turn right and it will swing around to a wide path maintained by Dead Horse Ranch State Park, which also offers access to the marsh. Follow it back to another wooden deck overlook of the wetlands, this time right on top of the cattails. Who knows, you may even pass a grizzled though still ruggedly handsome hiker on the trail. If you're carrying this book with you, I may even be persuaded to sign it.

When You Go

(928) 634-5564, www.nps.gov/tuzi.

Admission

Admission fee is good for seven days and grants entry to Tuzigoot and Montezuma Castle

National Monument. There is no admission fee to Montezuma Well, a detached unit of Montezuma Castle.

Facilities

The visitor center has museum exhibits and a gift shop.

Pets

Pets are allowed on trails but must be kept on a leash no longer than 6 feet.

Hiking

A self-guided 0.3-mile loop trail leads around and through the Tuzigoot pueblo. The trail is paved but has some steep sections. Accessing the Citadel room requires the use of stairs.

A 0.5-mile gently sloped paved trail leads to an overlook of Tavasci Marsh. Additional gravel trails lead to the marsh. The unmarked trails leading to the marsh can be a bit confusing, so be sure to consult a map or get directions beforehand.

Camping

Tuzigoot is a day-use-only park. Camping is available in adjacent Dead Horse Ranch State Park. There are more than 100 RV sites spread across several campground loops. Most pull-through sites can accommodate 40-foot motor homes and truck and trailer rigs up to 65 feet. They include potable water and electricity. Generators are prohibited. Blackhawk Loop features 17 nonelectric sites reserved exclusively for tents. All campgrounds include restrooms and showers. For reservations, (877) 697-2757, www.azstateparks.com.

Programs/Events

Ranger talks and guided walks offer a variety of interpretive programs throughout the year.

Special Notes

Do not touch the walls of the pueblo. Do not lean, sit, stand, or climb on them.

Pipe Spring
National Monument

Grand
Canyon-Parashant
National
Monument

Lake Mead
National
Recreation Area

66

——— Old Spanish National Historic Trail
(Old Spanish NHT)

NORTHERN ARIZONA

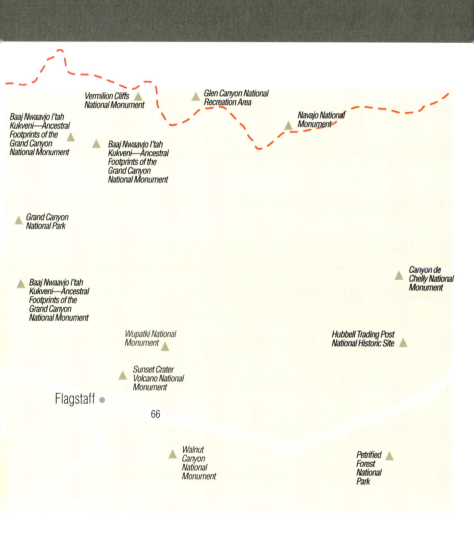

A rugged unmaintained trail in the northeastern parcel drops down through Soap Creek Canyon to the Colorado River where rafters navigate a whitewater rapid. Courtesy of Mike Koopsen, Sedona.

Baaj Nwaavjo I'tah Kukveni—Ancestral Footprints of the Grand Canyon National Monument

Overview
Big distinct tracts of land to the north and south of Grand Canyon protect diverse habitats, thousands of cultural and religious sites, and significant water sources that feed the Colorado River.

Nearest Cities
Tusayan, Fredonia, and Jacob Lake.

Established
August 8, 2023.

Size
917,618 acres.

The Baaj Nwaavjo I'tah Kukveni—Ancestral Footprints of the Grand Canyon National Monument was long overdue. For decades, Native American tribes clamored for the protection of lands they hold sacred and for waterways that are critical not just for them, but for millions of people across the Southwest.

More than just a savage tear in the earth's fabric, the Grand Canyon is the open and beating heart of Northern Arizona. This is the center of life in the region. For Indigenous peoples, the colorful canyon and its tributaries play a role in multiple creation stories. The monument honors the legacy of these Native American tribes by preserving the broader Grand Canyon ecosystem and preventing any new uranium mining operations, which risks contamination of a vast water supply.

The monument incorporates federal lands in three separate areas to the south, northwest, and northeast of Grand Canyon National Park. Baaj Nwaavjo I'tah Kukveni encompasses plateaus, canyons, forests, grasslands, flowing creeks, and springs. Wildlife like bison, elk, mule deer, pronghorn, and bighorn sheep graze among the diverse flora, including endemic and sensitive plant species such as Arizona leatherflower, Arizona phlox,

Tusayan rabbitbrush, and Morton wild buckwheat. Over 3,000 known cultural and historic sites can be found here, including 12 properties listed on the National Register of Historic Places.

The US Forest Service and Bureau of Land Management (BLM) oversee the monument, in conjunction with a commission comprised of a dozen Native American tribes. The tribes represented include the Havasupai Tribe, Hopi Tribe, Hualapai Tribe, Kaibab Band of Paiute Indians, Las Vegas Paiute Tribe, Moapa Band of Paiutes, Paiute Indian Tribe of Utah, Navajo Nation, San Juan Southern Paiute Tribe, Yavapai-Apache Nation, Pueblo of Zuni, and the Colorado River Indian Tribes.

The monument's name comes from the Havasupai words *baaj nwaavjo* for "where Indigenous peoples roam," and the Hopi words *i'tah kukveni* for "our ancestral footprints."

Geography and Geology

Baaj Nwaavjo I'tah Kukveni is made up of three distinct areas. The segment to the south of Grand Canyon National Park (GCNP) consists of the Tusayan Ranger District of the Kaibab National Forest. It also borders the Navajo Nation and Havasupai Indian Reservation. Havasupai means "people of the blue-green waters." The spectacular waterfalls and streams that comprise their lands deep within the Grand Canyon attract thousands of visitors annually. They are the only tribe living inside the Grand Canyon.

The segment that lies northwest of GCNP begins at the western edge of the Kanab watershed and stretches all the way to the Utah border at the Shinarump Cliffs. Kanab Creek creates habitat for several bird species including the threatened western yellow-billed cuckoo and endangered southwestern willow flycatcher.

The northeastern segment abuts Vermilion Cliffs National Monument and stretches from Marble Canyon past House Rock Valley to the edge of the Kaibab Plateau, rising suddenly from sagebrush flats, a great humpbacked tableland of lush forest that provides access to the Grand Canyon's North Rim. The sudden steep rise is due to the East Kaibab Monocline, a massive fold in the Colorado Plateau.

Much of the monument is a landscape broken and bent through eons of tectonic uplift. These are sweeping plateaus and deep-cut canyons. Sandstone, shale, and limestone are common here; sedimentary rocks formed millions of years ago. Extensive fractures and faults direct the flow of surface and groundwater, as well as creating seeps and springs—oases that are crucial to animal and human life in this arid terrain.

The national monument designation largely protects this complex watershed from future contamination of uranium mining. It was uranium mining during the 1950s that caused widespread health issues and death for generations of tribal members. For decades tribes and environmentalists have sought permanent bans on the practice. While no new mining claims may be filed, there are still preexisting mines that could be developed. The area of the monument is home to only about 1.3 percent of all known uranium reserves in the US.

The monument includes only previously designated federal lands and incorporates no state or private land holdings. All outdoor recreational activities such as hiking, camping, biking, fishing, and hunting are still permitted where applicable.

Exploring the Monument

These sacred lands are also natural lands. Most national monuments remain far less developed than national parks, and that's certainly the case at Baaj Nwaavjo I'tah Kukveni. Visitors are welcome but they are not coddled. While paved roads cut across the monument, access is primarily via dirt roads or rugged trails.

US Hwy 89A ventures through the two northern parcels of the monument located on the Arizona Strip, the piece of state isolated by the canyons of the Colorado River. A network of forest roads penetrates deeper corners of the monument. In the northwestern area, amid a labyrinth of canyons, there is evidence of ancient villages, including cliff houses, storage sites, granaries, and pottery. Scattered through the Kanab Creek drainage are a striking collection of pictographs and petroglyphs. One site in Kanab Creek Canyon has been used for more than 2,000 years, including for Ghost Dance ceremonies in the 19th century.

Most of the northeastern parcel lies south of 89A and is bordered along the eastern edge by the Colorado River as it flows through Marble Canyon. On the western side, near the base of the Kaibab Plateau, a finger of monument land trends north along House Rock Valley Road, which provides access to the Vermilion Cliffs National Monument. The vast sweep of the actual House Rock Valley spreads south from 89A, rolling grasslands that tumble toward the North Rim of Grand Canyon. Remnants of human history include homes, pottery, and tools. This has long been an important area to Tribal Nations for hunting and resource gathering.

House Rock Valley provides habitats for a surprising assortment of wildlife, including pronghorn, winter range for mule deer, and an important autumn raptor migration route. The sensitive Allen's lappet-browed bat, along with several other sensitive bat species, the rare House Rock Valley chisel-toothed kangaroo rat, and the endemic Kaibab monkey grasshopper can be found here. The House Rock Valley Wildlife Area also contains a herd of bison.

The southern portion of Baaj Nwaavjo I'tah Kukveni lies within the Kaibab National Forest and is the easiest to explore. State Route 64 cleaves through a mix of sagebrush prairie and conifer forest as it points toward Tusayan and the busy southern entrance of Grand Canyon National Park. Here the distinctive profile of lava-capped Red Butte rises over the landscape. This is a sacred site to the Havasupai, who refer to it as "Clenched-Fist Mountain." A hiking trail leads to the top, where a fire station is manned during summer months.

For a few decades Red Butte also served as a landmark to pilots flying into Grand Canyon's original airport. Built in the 1920s, the nearby site featured a hangar, a lodge, cabins, and two unpaved airstrips. The Red Butte Airfield attracted some notable guests, including Charles Lindbergh, Amelia Earhart, and Will Rogers. Sightseeing flights over the Grand Canyon flew out of here for decades until a new airport was constructed in Tusayan in the 1960s. Today grassy meadows have overtaken the runways, and the sagging remains of the big hangar and a few outbuildings still battle the elements.

Nearly 40 miles of the Arizona National Scenic Trail also ramble across this portion of the monument. The southern access point of the trail is at the Moqui Stage Station. Between 1892 and 1899 a stagecoach line ran between Flagstaff and the Grand Canyon. The journey took 12 hours and cost $20. There's an informational sign and remnants of an old stone well marking the site. The Arizona Trail winds north through the tall ponderosa pines—keep an eye peeled for elk—until reaching the Grandview Lookout Tower. The 80-foot tall steel tower and two-room cabin were built in 1936 by the Civilian Conservation Corps. Views from the tower stretch across the forest and the canyon.

Guardians Continue Their Work

Baaj Nwaavjo I'tah Kukveni is a rugged landscape of remarkable diversity wrapped around America's greatest natural treasure. A rich assortment of plants and wildlife flourish amid this sprawling interconnected ecosystem that has been cared for through the centuries by Indigenous peoples. These are lands that many tribes refer to as their eternal home. It's considered a place of healing and spiritual sustenance. With the designation of national monument, these original guardians can continue to use the areas for religious ceremonies, hunting and gathering of plants, medicines, and other materials, including some found nowhere else on earth.

Many of these Indigenous people were expelled from their territory when Grand Canyon National Park was established in 1919. Yet they continued to campaign to protect the lands surrounding the park, understanding that they are inextricably linked to the vast canyon. Even something so powerful and impressive as the Grand Canyon is deceptively vulnerable. Now it is less so. Through the tireless efforts of a handful of people, the Grand Canyon will stay pristine for future generations.

When You Go

Tusayan Ranger District: (928) 638-2443, www.fs.usda.gov/kaibab.
BLM: www.blm.gov/national-conservation-lands/arizona/ancestral-footprints.

Admission

Free.

Facilities

None.

Pets

Yes, in most areas. Please keep pets leashed and away from archaeological sites.

Hiking

All trails listed are in the southern section of Baaj Nwaavjo I'tah Kukveni. Hiking trails can be found in the northeastern and northwestern parcels but are more rugged and not maintained. Many require route-finding ability and should only be attempted by experienced hikers.

RED BUTTE TRAIL

Climb to the top of Red Butte (7,326 feet) on this 1.25-mile trail. It gains almost 900 feet, much of it as it traverses the upper rock layers in some steep switchbacks. The lookout tower sits atop the flat summit. From Hwy 64, turn east on Forest Road (FR) 320 and drive 1.5 miles. Turn north on FR 340, go 0.75 miles and turn right (east) onto a spur road. Trailhead is at the end of this quarter-mile road.

VISHNU TRAIL

This 1.1 mile scenic loop begins just north of the Grandview Lookout Tower. It ventures out to a point on the Coconino Rim and affords broad vistas of the Grand Canyon then returns along a section of the Arizona Trail. The Vishnu is popular with bikers, horseback riders, and hikers. From Hwy 64, take FR 302 east for about 15 miles. Turn left onto FR 310 and the lookout tower will soon appear on your right. The unpaved roads are suitable for passenger vehicles.

TUSAYAN MOUNTAIN BIKE TRAILS

These routes explore secluded forests along old logging roads. Open to hikers, bikers, and horseback riders, this is also a great opportunity to see wildlife such as elk, mule deer, pronghorn, porcupine, coyote, and wild turkey. Trail #126 is a loop of 1.1 miles, Trail #702 is a loop of 17.2 miles, and Trail #703 is a loop of 8.3 miles. Trail #702 continues to the Grandview Lookout Tower and is part of the Arizona Trail (Passage #37). Parking lot and trailhead access is at the Tusayan Ranger Station right off Hwy 64.

ARIZONA TRAIL

The Coconino Rim section (Passage #36) of the Arizona National Scenic Trail stretches for 18 miles from the Moqui Stage Station to Grandview Lookout Tower. It is open to hikers, bikers, and equestrians. To access the southern trailhead at Moqui Station, turn east on FR 320 off Hwy 64 at mile marker 224. Drive 16 miles, then turn right on FR 301 and drive 3.5

miles to the station. To reach the northern access point of Grandview Lookout Tower, follow directions from Vishnu Trail.

Camping

Ten-X Campground is found in the southern segment of the monument, 2 miles south of Tusayan just off State Route 64. Spread among a ponderosa pine / Gambel oak forest, Ten-X has 142 single sites, 18 double sites, and 2 group sites. Of these, 30 are first-come, first-served. Sites include picnic tables, fire pits, and grills, with nearby vault toilets. There's also a short nature trail. Pull-through sites can accommodate a 35-foot RV. No utility hookups or dumpsites are available. Due to a limited water supply, RVs are not allowed to fill up. The campground is generally open May through September. Reservations are available at www.recreation.gov or by calling (877) 444-6777.

Another very cool option is the US Forest Service Rooms with a View program. Historic cabins, in this case Hull Cabin, offer rustic backcountry lodging in the southern segment of the monument, just 1 mile south of the Grand Canyon. Built by sheep ranchers in 1889, Hull Cabin consists of a bedroom, living room, and fully equipped kitchen. It can sleep up to six people and includes running water in the kitchen. A separate shower house contains two solar-powered stalls, and a vault toilet. Guests must bring their own food, bedding, towels, and other necessities. Located in a secluded meadow surrounded by pines, Hull Cabin is available May through September. Reservations can be made through www.recreation.gov or by calling (877) 444-6777.

Dispersed camping is allowed within portions of the monument. For specific regulations, check with local offices. Choose a campsite that has been previously used and no more than 100 feet from the road. Always check on fire restrictions. Use a fire pan when fires are allowed. Ground fires leave scars on the landscape. Otherwise, use an existing fire ring. Put all fires out cold before you leave. Better yet, skip a campfire and enjoy the lavish night skies. If you do build a fire, be absolutely, positively certain it is out before you leave. Pack out all trash.

Programs/Events

None.

Special Notes

Treat all natural and cultural sites with respect. Leave all artifacts undisturbed. Artifacts are considered sacred to modern Indigenous people. This includes pottery pieces, stone tools, and corncobs. It is illegal to remove any artifact, including historic trash such as rusted cans, from public lands.

Archaeological sites should be viewed from a distance. Do not enter. Do not sit, stand, or climb on any walls. Don't touch rock art as natural oils from your hands damage these delicate images.

Avoid building cairns. Leave placement of trail directional signs and cairns to land managers. And if you are fortunate enough to stumble upon a cultural site, do not post GPS coordinates online. This often leads uneducated visitors to sensitive sites. Simply enjoy the moment for yourself.

Stay on existing roads. If venturing into the backcountry, be prepared. Some roads are primitive and not maintained. High-clearance or four-wheel-drive vehicles are recommended in many areas. Have a full tank of gas, full-sized spare tires, a tool kit, and first-aid kit. Cell phones do not work in some areas of the national monument. Water is rarely available. Carry and drink plenty of water.

Spider Rock rises 800 feet from the floor of Canyon de Chelly. Courtesy of Mike Koopsen, Sedona.

Canyon de Chelly National Monument

Overview

High-walled canyons cut from the plateau country of the Navajo Nation shelter green pastures, groves of cottonwood trees, and the remnants of ancient civilizations.

Nearest City

Chinle.

Established

April 1, 1931.

Size

83,840 acres.

Pastoral beauty wrapped in high sandstone walls, Canyon de Chelly serves as a wellspring of life on the Colorado Plateau.

Stand on the rim of Canyon de Chelly (pronounced de SHAY) in the heart of Navajo country where the world seems still and peaceful. Gaze down into the depths and don't be surprised if it calls to you. What you're seeing is home. It is the ultimate home, an enduring cherished home for different cultures spanning 5,000 years—longer than anyone has lived uninterrupted on the Colorado Plateau. In fact, Canyon de Chelly is one of North America's longest continuously inhabited landscapes.

The sheer walls plunge almost straight down to a sandy floor. A thin ribbon of water wends its way through stands of cottonwood trees. Horses graze in green pastures at the base of the cliffs. Gardens and orchards surround hogans, traditional Navajo dwellings, and other structures. Canyon de Chelly is still home to dozens of Navajos, or Diné, families.

The National Park Service works in partnership with the Navajo Nation to manage park resources and sustain the living Diné community.

Rim to Rim

The national monument consists primarily of two major gorges—Canyon del Muerto and Canyon de Chelly—cut from the slickrock landscape at the fringe of the Chuska Mountains. They form a rough sideways *V*, with the visitor center located at the narrow end where the

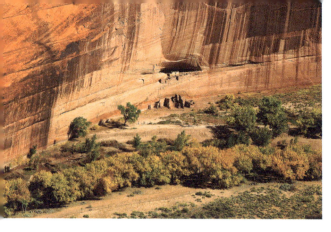

White House Ruins consists of two levels—a cliff house and a pueblo on the canyon floor. Courtesy of Mike Koopsen, Sedona.

canyons join, and the town of Chinle just beyond. Snowmelt from the Chuskas along with fierce summer rains continue to fuel the Chinle Wash flowing through the canyon complex.

Paved roads trace the rims of both canyons with Canyon del Muerto forming the northern branch and Canyon de Chelly making up the lower prong. These scenic drives are how most visitors experience the monument.

The North Rim drive (17 miles one-way) offers three panoramic overlooks and is best during the morning hours. Antelope House Overlook offers a sweeping view of the remains of a large pueblo that was built in the 1300s with a circular plaza. The name derives from animals painted on an adjacent cliff, the work attributed to Navajo artist Dibe Yazhi, who lived here in the early 1800s. The lonely red butte across the canyon is known as Navajo Fortress that once served as an important refuge for the Diné.

Also along the North Rim is the Mummy Cave Overlook, where two mummies were found in a large well-preserved pueblo. And the final stop is Massacre Cave Overlook, which reveals a sad, bloody chapter of the canyon's history. An estimated 115 Navajos, mostly women, children, and elderly, were killed here in 1805 by a Spanish military expedition when they took shelter on the ledge high above the canyon floor. The Spaniards fired shots into the cave, sending bullets ricocheting off the walls and eventually killing everyone inside in the deadly hailstorm of jagged lead.

The South Rim drive (18.5 miles one-way) also starts near the visitor center and is best during the afternoon, when the softer light floods the canyon and makes for rich photographs. The road winds along the edge of Canyon de Chelly past seven overlooks, each more spectacular than the last as the walls rise higher and higher. It culminates at the vista for Spider Rock, a slender pinnacle of rock rising 800 feet from the canyon floor. At White House Overlook, visitors can hike into the canyon on a breathtaking trail for an up close look at a multistoried pueblo. Be aware, this overlook and trail are sometimes closed due to safety concerns.

The Canyon Floor

Besides hiking the White House Ruins Trail, all other ways to explore the inner canyon require a Navajo guide. A list of tour companies is available at the Navajo Parks and

Recreation Department office at the entrance of Cottonwood Campground and on their website (www.navajonationparks.org). You can choose a tour with private operators for horseback rides, jeep tours, and hiking outings. There are also group tours offered by Thunderbird Lodge ((928) 674-5842, www.thunderbirdlodge.com).

Locals call the Thunderbird Lodge outings "shake-and-bake" tours, and for good reason. They are a jarring, jostling ride in the back of a military-style six-wheel-drive truck that is open air during the warm months, exposed to the sun. At most stops, guests stay in the vehicle while the driver stands nearby pointing out features and shares some stories. If you're looking for a more intimate personalized experience, a private tour is the way to go. But if your time and/or budget is limited, these bouncy group tours are a good option. They're scheduled at specific times of day and reasonably priced, especially for solo travelers. I went out on a summer afternoon 4-hour tour because I knew it would be less crowded than the morning or sunset outings.

No matter what option you choose, it is a memorable experience to plunge into the ancient embrace of Canyon de Chelly. We drove down the sandy wash, swallowed up by the canyon mouth as walls rise higher and higher. We wheeled past small farms, beneath a canopy of cottonwood trees with cliffs looming overhead and prehistoric pueblos tucked in alcoves and rock art adorning the walls. When we stopped to get out and stroll around, the quiet was astounding. I could listen to the breeze rustle each cottonwood leaf individually, a small and wonderful symphony. Time and space were suspended in this sacred place.

People of the canyon

The first residents of the canyon, the Archaic People (2500–200 BC), left few traces, just sheltered campsites and faint rock art. They took advantage of the canyon's abundance, living in small groups, hunting deer, antelope, and rabbit, while foraging for plants. The Basketmakers (200 BC–AD 750)—known for their extraordinary weaving skills—were the first to begin farming the canyon floor. They built communities of dispersed households, large granaries to store food, and a few public structures.

The most notable architecture of Canyon de Chelly first developed about 1,250 years ago when scattered hamlets gave way to villages. It's uncertain why this change occurred, but during the Pueblo era the many masonry structures of Canyon de Chelly sprang up. Villages offered opportunities for social interaction, trade, and ceremony.

Puebloan life ended in the canyon around 1300 as people migrated south and west, establishing new villages driven by drought, disease, or conflict. In time, these people became the Hopi. The Hopi describe these events as part of a migratory cycle. Pilgrimages and seasonal farming continued in Canyon de Chelly until the Navajo arrived in the 1700s.

The Navajo, an Athabaskan-speaking people, migrated from Canada to the Southwest. They were hunters and gatherers but quickly learned farming techniques from the Pueblo peoples. They adopted herding sheep and goats from the Spanish. The name "Navajo" comes from the Spanish. They called themselves Diné, or "The People."

Arriving in Canyon de Chelly more than 300 years ago, the Navajo flourished in the

The pueblo named Mummy Cave is one of the most beautiful and intact ruins in Canyon del Muerto. Courtesy of Mike Koopsen, Sedona.

beautiful setting. They planted corn, beans, and squash, and tended precious peach orchards left behind by the Hopi on the canyon floor. Warfare broke out among the Navajo, other tribes, and the Spanish colonists in the late 1700s. The winding canyons provided some refuge from raiding parties but were too expansive and open and largely indefensible.

That became all too clear when the US military began to move in after defeating the Mexican forces during the Mexican-American War. Forts were established in the heart of the Diné homeland, leading to additional conflict. Finally, in 1863, Colonel Christopher "Kit" Carson, under orders from General James Carleton, launched a brutal scorched-earth campaign against the Navajo, burning crops, killing livestock, and massacring men, women, and children.

Most of the surviving Navajo were rounded up in 1864 and led on a forced march more than 300 miles to the Bosque Redondo Reservation near Fort Sumner in the New Mexico Territory. Hundreds died on this Long Walk. Many more perished from the harsh conditions at the barren and overcrowded Bosque Redondo along the Pecos River. Water from the Pecos proved alkaline. Food was scarce and firewood was miles away. Finally, in 1868 after long negotiations, the Navajo were allowed to return home. Their homesteads, livestock, and crops were all gone. The Navajo now relied on a small allotment of food, supplies, and sheep. Trading posts sprang up, and the Diné began to slowly rebuild their lives.

Enduring Tranquility

The vast sweep of history of the Southwest can be viewed at Canyon de Chelly. The geological forces at work, the traces of ancient civilizations, and the living community continuing the traditions are all part of the epic story.

Despite the echoes of long-ago violence, it remains a remarkably serene and spiritual place. The pastoral setting only enhances the drama of the towering sandstone walls. It is the canyon that redefines canyons in Arizona. We are the home of Grand Canyon, a staggering, mind-bending experience. The Grand pushes you back from the rim while inspiring a sense of awe. Canyon de Chelly pulls you closer, seduces your heart with its intimacy and shy beauty. It is a place you fall in love with over and over again.

When You Go

(928) 674-5500, www.nps.gov/cach.

Admission

Free admission to the monument. Fees are charged for any private tours or permits.

Facilities

The visitor center has museum exhibits and a gift shop.

Pets

Pets must be leashed at all times. They are not allowed on the White House Trail or in the canyon.

Hiking

White House Trail (2.5 miles round trip) is the only place visitors may enter the canyon without a Navajo guide. It descends 600 feet via a series of switchbacks to the canyon floor and crosses the Chinle Wash lined by cottonwood trees. During spring and summer months the bottomland is often sprinkled with wildflowers. The trail ends at the base of the cliff, sheltering the terraced ruin known as White House. The village once contained 80 rooms. Vault toilets are available at the bottom, but there is no drinking water. Stay on the trail. Do not enter dwellings or disturb historical or natural features.

Camping

Navajo Parks and Recreation Department manages Cottonwood Campground located near the visitor center. The campground is open year-round and offers grills, picnic tables, and restrooms. Sites are first-come, first-served. No showers or hookups are available. Group sites require reservations. Maximum RV length is 40 feet. For information, call (928) 674-2106.

Programs/Events

Lectures, educational programs, cultural demonstrations, and presentations are offered as staffing permits. Ranger-led hikes are popular outings throughout the year.

Special Notes

The Navajo Nation observes daylight saving time, while the rest of Arizona and the Hopi Reservation do not. Navajo Nation law prohibits alcohol on the reservation.

The canyons are deep with very steep, vertical walls—falls can be fatal. Use extreme caution at the canyon rims. Keep control of children and pets at all times.

Lock your vehicle at overlooks. Secure valuables out of sight or take them with you.

All cultural and natural features are protected by federal and tribal law. Disturbing archaeological sites or collecting artifacts is strictly forbidden.

The towering sandstone walls of Glen Canyon cradle the shimmering waters of Lake Powell. Courtesy of Mike Koopsen, Sedona.

Glen Canyon National Recreation Area

Overview

A rare combination of deep colorful canyons cradling a large though shrinking lake remains a major outdoor recreation destination on the Arizona and Utah border.

Nearest City

Page.

Established

October 27, 1972.

Size

1,254,116 acres.

Glen Canyon National Recreation Area (GCNRA) remains in a state of flux. How it will look in the future is hard to say.

Encompassing more than 1.25 million acres, GCNRA spreads across Northern Arizona and into southern Utah. The centerpiece of the park is Lake Powell, a spectacular reservoir on the Colorado River. It's an unearthly landscape, this sparkling lake ringed by colorful sandstone buttes and rock walls rising straight out of the water. Lake Powell was formed following the completion of Glen Canyon Dam in 1963.

Standing 710 feet above bedrock, Glen Canyon Dam is the second-highest concrete arch dam in the United States. It was built to impound the reservoir and to provide hydroelectric power. At a time of rapid population growth across the Southwest, the dam seemed like a gleaming symbol of progress. Today it also feels like a relic from a bygone era. Glen Canyon Dam is trapped between centuries.

Since 2000, Lake Powell has been dwindling, the result of a devastating megadrought. Climate change brings hotter temperatures and less precipitation. A larger population means higher water demand. These factors combined are shrinking the Colorado River at a frightening pace. Water levels in Lake Powell have dropped precipitously in recent years.

Point of No Return

In its heyday, Lake Powell was more than 186 miles long and spread through a maze of slickrock canyons. Nearly 2,000 miles of meandering shoreline bordered the big reservoir, making it the second-largest artificial lake in the nation, dwarfed only by its downstream neighbor, Lake Mead.

Now many of Powell's side canyons have dried up. Some boat ramps are closed, and popular attractions are no longer accessible. Some marinas in Utah have suspended operations due to the receding water level. In addition to the water scarcity, the other concern is that Glen Canyon Dam could cease generating electricity. Once the lake drops to a level below "minimum power pool," the turbines would no longer produce hydroelectric power. About 5 million customers rely on electricity generated by the dam. Federal officials have pondered plans to overhaul the dam so it could still produce electricity and release water at critically low levels.

Of course, environmentalists have pondered demolishing the dam since before it was even built. Early detractors railed against the dam, arguing the reservoir was unnecessary and it would destroy the canyon's pristine ecosystem and Native American artifacts.

What was once a fringe idea—to drain Lake Powell and allow the flowing river water to fill Lake Mead—is now part of the mainstream conversation. While politicians will determine the fate of Glen Canyon Dam and Lake Powell, nature has the final say.

Before the Dam

The park sits amid the great uplift of the Colorado Plateau, an area characterized by high elevation and arid climate. Canyons carved by the Colorado River and its tributaries expose layers of rock deposited one on top of the other over the ages, each layer telling a story.

Human history of the region dates back almost 12,000 years when the small bands of prehistoric Indians roamed and hunted here at the end of the Ice Age. Hunters and gatherers gave way to later cultures, including those who relied on agriculture and permanent or semipermanent habitations.

For many Indigenous peoples the Glen Canyon area is a spiritually occupied landscape that is inseparable from their cultural identities and traditional beliefs. Glen Canyon–affiliated tribes are Hopi, Kaibab Paiute Tribe, San Juan Southern Paiute Tribe, Paiute Indian Tribe of Utah, Navajo Nation, Pueblo of Zuni, and Ute Mountain Ute Tribe.

The first Europeans to visit the region were members of the Spanish Dominguez-Escalante Expedition in 1776. After failing to discover an overland trail to California, the party navigated the maze of canyons along the Colorado River on their return trip, keeping detailed journals and maps.

In 1869, Major John Wesley Powell, a one-armed soldier, scientist, and explorer, led the first of his two Colorado River journeys, carefully mapping his route along the way. It was Powell who named Glen Canyon. This is what he wrote: "So we have a curious ensemble of wonderful features—carved walls, royal arches, glens, alcove gulches, mounds and monuments. From which of these features shall we select a name? We decide to call it Glen Canyon."

The lake was named to honor Powell.

Lonely Dell Ranch, home to the families who operated Lees Ferry, provides a shady oasis to modern visitors. Photo by the author.

Dry Land

Here's what's surprising. Lake Powell makes up only 13 percent of the vast recreation area that also covers rugged desert terrain, deep canyons, and rocky cliffs. So there's plenty more to be explored as well.

Start by visiting the mightiest swoop of the Colorado River, Horseshoe Bend. A famous curve, a seductive curve wraps around a sandstone escarpment some 1,000 feet below. A short trail (1.5 miles round trip) is maintained by the City of Page. The hardened path leads to a cliff-top perch, where the eye-popping drama unfolds directly beneath your feet. There are some railings at the overlook but much of the rim remains exposed, so watch your footing and keep track of children and pets.

Further west you'll find an essential piece of the Colorado River story. Navajo Bridge spans the river at Marble Canyon. When completed in 1929, it was the highest steel arch bridge in the world. In 1995 a new bridge was built similar in design just downstream to handle increased traffic. Now the twin spans stretch across the steep-sided gorge. The old bridge is open only to pedestrians and provides stunning views of the Colorado 467 feet below. It's also a great spot to watch California condors that were reintroduced to the area in 1996.

After crossing the bridge, you'll see the signed turnoff to Lees Ferry. The 5-mile road winds through sloping hills to a rare spot. This is the only place along hundreds of miles of canyon country where a wagon could reach the Colorado River and a crossing could be managed.

Mormon leaders established a ferry at the remote outpost to offer transportation between Utah and Arizona Territory. John D. Lee was the first ferryman, settling here with some of his wives. The ferry began operation in 1873. For decades, people and animals were carried across the river in small boats. It was risky business. Boats capsized and plenty of folks drowned, but it was the only game in town until it ceased operation in 1928 following a fatal accident. Since Navajo Bridge was nearing completion, the ferry was never reestablished.

Today Lees Ferry is the put-in place for Grand Canyon rafting trips, and is a popular spot for fly fishermen. A trail leads along the river past rusted equipment and stone buildings, the crumbling remains of a Mormon fort built in 1874.

My favorite part of Lees Ferry sits back from the river. The Lonely Dell Ranch was originally homesteaded by John Lee and later occupied by all the families that operated the ferry. To survive in this wilderness, they needed to be self-sufficient and grow food for themselves and their animals. Sitting beside the Paria River allowed for extensive irrigation systems that turned this harsh land productive.

Lonely Dell is such an unexpected oasis tucked away at the base of colorful cliffs. Big shade trees provide a cooling canopy for the ranch house and surrounding log cabins. An orchard spreads out from the yard, and birds flit among the tree branches. Feel free to pluck a ripe piece of fruit for a snack. Just don't be harvesting bushel baskets full to sell by the roadside.

A Cleansing Heat

This is also where I spent one of the hottest and best summer days of my life. The heat was absolutely brutal on a late June afternoon when I visited Lees Ferry and Lonely Dell Ranch. I spent the morning relaxing in the shade of the ranch but for some reason roused myself and set out into Paria Canyon, which starts wide before the walls close in. I hiked a few miles following the muddy, shallow Paria River. It was the worst possible day to hike, but I couldn't resist. Something about the thuggish heat seduced me, pulled me into its sizzling embrace.

It was absolutely foolish, but I felt safe. I'm acclimated to Arizona's special brand of heat. I carried plenty of water to drink, and had a river to wade in, to soak my hat and shirt, and cliff walls for shade. I moved slowly into the defile, watching for soaring condors, but even they were smart enough not to stir around in air that hung thick and gauzy.

The heat was a thing alive, surrounding me, clawing at me. I stepped into the river and it felt like I was knee-deep in soup. The sun perched on my shoulder and growled at me. At the same time it felt utterly purifying. I was the only man on earth, hiking in a sauna and raining sweat. When I stopped for shade, and pressed my wet back against the cool stone of the cliffs, it felt exquisite. I was dancing with madness, right on the Edge, in that quiet place where a desert rat's heart beats hardest. To walk into that raging light and emerge is a form of rebirth.

When I finally made it back to my ride, I was utterly drained. Yet my mind was as clear as a mountain stream. I drove to a rustic lodge and sat on their big shady porch swilling ice-cold beer, ate a delicious burger, and watched the final rays of sun swab the tall cliffs until they were glowing. Anytime I feel a little beaten down by a blustery winter day, that's the memory I take out to warm myself with.

When You Go

(928) 608-6200, www.nps.gov/glca.

Admission

Admission fee is good for seven days.

Facilities

Carl Hayden Visitor Center, located at the west end of Glen Canyon Dam, contains interpretive and interactive exhibits, and a gift shop. It offers impressive views of the dam and lake.

Navajo Bridge Interpretive Center, at the west end of Navajo Bridge, features outdoor exhibits, a gift shop, and a pedestrian walkway over the Colorado River.

Wahweap Marina & Lake Powell Resort, located 5 miles from the dam, is the largest marina on the lake. It offers lodging with 350 rooms, multiple restaurants, shops, swimming pools, a fitness center, and a campground. Boat rentals and boat tours are available. (888) 896-3829, www.lakepowell.com.

Antelope Point Marina is just outside of Page. The Navajo-owned business rents all manner of watercraft, from kayaks to houseboats, and offers boat tours and private charters. There's an RV park with full hookups, a floating restaurant and lounge, general store, and lakeside spa. (928) 645-5900, antelopepointlakepowell.com.

Pets

Pets are allowed in most parts of the recreation area but must be kept on a leash.

Pets are not permitted in archaeological sites; at marinas, docks, walkways, and launch ramps (except when proceeding directly to or from a boat); along the San Juan River from Clay Hills Crossing upstream to the GCNRA boundary; in the Orange Cliffs special permit area; on Rainbow Bridge NM (except for pets in vessels at the courtesy dock); the portion of Cathedral Wash between the road and the Colorado River; and Coyote Gulch within GCNRA boundary.

Hiking

HORSESHOE BEND

Treat yourself to an optical thunderbolt with this short, often crowded hike that ends atop a sheer steep cliff. Far below, the Colorado River makes a sweeping horseshoe-shaped bend. Trailhead is located off US 89, approximately 5 miles south of Carl Hayden Visitor Center. There is a fee to park in the lot, operated by the city of Page.

HANGING GARDENS

Follow a level path across a mesa to a lush alcove where a seep spring creates a miniature oasis. Rock walls are adorned in a dense mat of ferns and orchids in this cool shady hideaway; 1-mile round trip. The turnoff for the trailhead is a quarter-mile east of Glen Canyon Bridge on US 89.

CATHEDRAL WASH

Travel down a storm-carved arroyo with interesting rock formations to the river. This moderate hike, 1.25 miles one-way, involves some rock scrambling. Trail ends at picturesque Cathedral Rapid. Do not hike when there is a potential for flash flooding. Park at the second turnout on Lees Ferry Road.

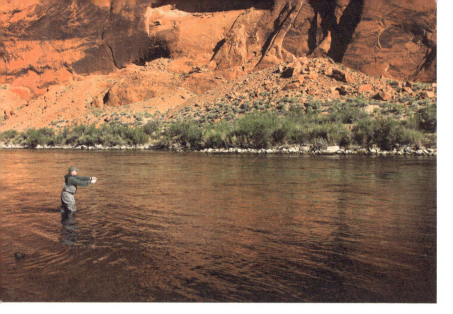

A fly fisherman tries his luck in the Colorado River near Lees Ferry. Courtesy of Mike Koopsen, Sedona.

RIVER TRAIL

Starting at the launch ramp at Lees Ferry, the mile-long path follows an old wagon road past a series of stone buildings in varying states of decline.

SPENCER TRAIL

A strenuous climb up riverside cliffs at Lees Ferry. Trail is 4.4 miles round trip and gains 1,500 feet of elevation offering commanding views of the Colorado River and Page. The Spencer Trail branches off from the River Trail.

LONELY DELL RANCH

A self-guided walking tour follows a dirt road back to the ranch and orchard, with pathways leading among the old buildings and fruit trees; 1-mile round trip.

PARIA CANYON TRAIL

Starting from the Lonely Dell Ranch parking area, follow the path upstream along the Paria River and continue for as long as you like. Paria Canyon stretches for 38 miles into Utah, and the hike through is a great backpacking expedition. Overnight hikes require a permit from the Bureau of Land Management. Day hikers can go as long as they like. Some wading may be necessary in the shallow river.

Camping

Lees Ferry Campground sits on a bench above the river. It is a NPS site but does not take reservations. There are 54 designated sites with picnic tables, grills, restrooms, and potable water. No hookups, but there is an RV dump station.

Beehives Campground is another small and primitive NPS facility located across the highway from Wahweap South Entrance. Only six designated sites with picnic tables. No hookups, dump station, or restroom. Pack it in, pack it out. Portable toilets required. No campfires or glass containers, and there's a three-night camping limit.

Wahweap Campground & RV Park includes 112 dry campsites, 90 with full hookups, and group sites. Restrooms, laundry, showers, store, launch ramp, dump station, and potable water are available. Picnic area and swim beach are nearby. (800) 528-6154, www.lakepowell.com.

Antelope Point RV Park is part of the Navajo-owned Antelope Point Marina. The RV-only site contains 100 pull-through spaces with full hookups. Maximum length is 70 feet, and there are two dump stations. (928) 645-5900, antelopepointlakepowell.com.

There is no camping fee or permit required to camp on the lake in undeveloped areas. However, entrance fees and vessel-use fees apply. You can camp anywhere on the shorelines of Lake Powell except in developed marinas.

Programs/Events

A variety of programs are offered at different locations, including ranger talks, guided hikes, and stargazing.

Special Notes

The consumption or direct possession of an alcoholic beverage by a person operating a vessel is prohibited. Always wear a life jacket when on the water. All boaters must know and follow applicable state and federal boating requirements, as well as carrying all mandated equipment on their vessels. Copies of this information are available at visitor centers.

There are no lifeguards or designated swimming areas. Swim at your own risk. Swimming is prohibited at all marinas and launch areas.

On some houseboats, carbon monoxide can collect under the swim platform. Do not allow passengers to congregate around engines or the backs of boats when engines or generators are running.

Glass bottles and Styrofoam are prohibited in the park.

The colorful layers of the Grand Canyon and a sliver of the Colorado River are visible from Moran Point on the Desert View Drive. Courtesy of Mike Koopsen, Sedona.

Grand Canyon National Park

Overview

The Grand Canyon feels like why the national park system was created.

Nearest Cities

Tusayan, Williams, Flagstaff, Cameron, Jacob Lake.

Established

President Theodore Roosevelt designated it as a national monument on January 11, 1908. It became a national park on February 26, 1919.

Size

1,201,647 acres.

And then there is the Canyon.

Nothing prepares you for the emotional and spiritual wallop of that first glimpse of the Grand Canyon. It is an epiphany lying in wait. You approach through a screen of forest until suddenly everything you thought you knew—everything that seemed safe and comfortable—is snatched away and you teeter on the edge of ruin.

Stretching before you is a sea of naked rock, an endless array of temples and terraces, castles and cathedrals, awash in reckless light. The eons are stacked in layers below, nearly 2 billion years of geology laid bare. You stand at the end of the world and gaze toward the beginning.

The size is unfathomable. You barely approach the rim, yet the canyon surrounds you, engulfs you, threatens to swallow you whole. Colors rage amid drifting cloud shadows and slanted sunlight. Cliffs of sandstone, limestone, shale, and schist are streaked red and purple, orange and yellow. These are broken mountains, propping up jagged horizons for a virtual eternity. Grand Canyon feels like a cataclysm pausing just to catch its breath.

The silence is a symphony. The silence seduces. It grabs hold of you. Wafting up from the abyss, a profound quiet eclipses the petty noise of everyday life. The whisper of the canyon blots out all other sound. For the first time in your life, you can actually hear distance. Welcome to the Grand Canyon.

The Artistry of Erosion

Grand Canyon National Park is the ultimate American travel destination. It's also the single most dazzling feature in the entire system of this country's national parks.

It's not the deepest or the largest canyon in the world but is certainly the most famous. Grand Canyon is an icon. It is a UNESCO World Heritage Site. An International Dark Sky Park. One of the Seven Natural Wonders of the World. The earth's most glorious wound.

For 277 miles it stretches across Northern Arizona, a crooked jack-o-lantern grin of a gorge. Up to 18 miles wide, the canyon is also a mile deep, a mile down to the basement where the Colorado River roars through, continuing its methodical work, chipping away at the walls little by little. The Grand Canyon isn't finished yet, but I love how the project is unfolding.

To enter the canyon is to descend through a stairway of life zones, quickly leaving forest behind. It's literally a journey back in time. The Kaibab limestone that forms the rim was laid down as ocean sediment 250 million years ago, while the black Vishnu schist found at the bottom alongside the Colorado River dates back about 1.8 billion years. So the rock layers were in place long before there was an inkling of a canyon.

Then about 70 million years ago, the grinding of tectonic plates uplifted the area resulting in the high and relatively flat Colorado Plateau. Around 6 million years ago, the Colorado River began to carve its way downward from the Rocky Mountains, cutting a channel across the plateau that would later become known as Grand. Sediment in the water, such as sand, rubs against rock as a river flows over it, causing it to slowly erode until a channel is formed. Tributary streams sliced the landscape and widened the canyon. Erosion remains nature's greatest artist.

Arizona's arid climate enhances the distinctiveness of the inner canyon. Sparse vegetation makes each layer clearly visible. Gazing into the canyon is like seeing an actual blueprint for the creation of the planet.

South Rim

Most canyon visitors come to the South Rim, which sits at an elevation of 7,000 feet above sea level and is open all year round. State Hwy 64 passes through the South Entrance near the town of Tusayan, and then proceeds to the canyon rim, reaching the commercial district. It then turns eastward, a segment known as Desert View Drive, as it winds through pine forest with multiple rim viewpoints before leaving the park through the East Entrance.

Grand Canyon Village serves as the heart of the commercial district containing most of the park's lodging, restaurants, shops, and museums, many of them housed in historic buildings. The village is spread along the edge of the canyon with soul-squeezing views at nearly every step. This is also where you'll access the famous Bright Angel Trail.

Despite the crowds, getting around on the South Rim proves remarkably easy, thanks to

A snowy canyon scene frames Desert View Watchtower at the eastern edge of the South Rim. Courtesy of Mike Koopsen, Sedona.

a free shuttle bus system. Buses run at frequent intervals from before sunrise to after sunset on an almost continuous loop. They follow three different routes, stopping at visitor centers, overlooks, lodges, markets, restaurants, and trailheads. Park your vehicle and take advantage of the big comfy shuttles to keep road traffic to a minimum.

Better yet, take a walk on the Rim Trail. This mostly paved 13-mile path passes through Grand Canyon Village and extends west to Hermits Rest and east to the South Kaibab Trailhead at Yaki Point. Hike as far as you like and then hop on a shuttle bus to return. For most of its length, you're only a few yards from the edge of the abyss, so you'll enjoy magnificent views. Once you're away from the hubbub of the village, you'll experience a quiet and personal connection to the canyon. And isn't that why you came?

At the edge of Grand Canyon Village, Hermit Road traces the canyon rim for 7 miles to the west and offers access to several scenic overlooks before ending at Hermits Rest. Built in 1914 by Mary Colter, this rambling stone structure was meant to resemble an old mountain man's hideaway. Inside is a soaring wood-beamed ceiling and arched fireplace, along with a snack bar and gift shop. Overlooks along Hermit Road include Maricopa Point, Hopi Point with its famous sunset views, the Abyss, and Pima Point. Hermit Road is closed to private vehicles except from December through February. And even though the road ends at Hermits Rest, Grand Canyon continues for another 180 miles, just in case you felt like you were finally starting to comprehend its size and scope.

Going in the opposite direction, Desert View Drive hugs the South Rim for 25 miles as it travels east and also ends at another Mary Colter masterpiece, the 70-foot-high lighthouse-shaped cylinder of stone known as the Watchtower. But you'll have several stops to enjoy along the way. Grandview Point also serves as a trailhead for steep and rugged Grandview Trail. Moran Point is a peaceful scenic overlook away from the crowds. Take a tour of the Tusayan Museum and Ruin, a small 12th-century pueblo. One of my favorite viewpoints in the park, Lipan Point makes another excellent sunset perch, providing dazzling views of the curving Colorado River and distinctive Unkar Delta.

Desert View is the easternmost developed area on the South Rim in the park. There's a

Hikers make their way down the South Kaibab Trail approaching the Black Bridge. Courtesy of Mike Koopsen, Sedona.

gas station, seasonal campground, general store/market, snack bar, trading post, and the iconic Watchtower perched right on the canyon rim. Constructed in 1932, Colter patterned the tower from architectural styles of the Ancestral Puebloan people. Several days a week, cultural demonstrations are conducted in or near the Watchtower by Native Americans.

Grand Canyon has been home to 11 different tribes. The Cultural Demonstration Program is designed to give members of the traditionally associated tribes a voice at Grand Canyon. The 11 tribes who have made Grand Canyon their home are Navajo, Havasupai, Hualapai, Hopi, Yavapai-Apache, Kaibab band of Southern Paiute, Las Vegas band of Southern Paiute, Moapa band of Southern Paiute, Paiute Indian Tribes of Utah, San Juan Southern Paiute Tribe, and Zuni.

North Rim

This is where you go when seeking solitude and a summer escape. Rising 1,000 feet higher than its southern counterpart, you'll see more elk and deer than tour groups here. There are no crowds or shuttle buses. Of the millions of people who visit Grand Canyon National Park each year, only about 10 percent venture to the North Rim. The two rims may be as little as 10 miles apart as the raven flies, but it's a 212-mile winding drive from one to the other.

Atop the lonely Kaibab Plateau, the North Rim feels like a free-floating sanctuary, cloistered and cocooned. This is an alpine outback of sun-dappled forests of ponderosa pine, blue spruce, Douglas fir, and quaking aspen, interrupted by lush meadows drenched in wildflowers. This is where you come to revel in tranquility and quietude.

The South Rim takes your breath away; the North Rim gives it back.

Due to heavy snowfall, North Rim maintains a short season, with services staying open only from May 15 through October 15. (Roads close by December 1, or earlier.) Don't expect much in the way of infrastructure. There's one lodge and one developed campground. There's also a general store selling groceries and snacks, a service station, a couple of restaurants, a saloon, hiking trails, mule rides, and scenic drives. What else do you need?

Unlike the South Rim, where the commercial district is more spread out, everything is compact on this side of the gully. Hwy 67 is the only entry point, and it ends on the doorstep of the visitor center surrounded by a small cluster of businesses that includes historic Grand Canyon Lodge, positioned at the edge of the abyss.

Walk through the front door of the lodge to discover giant picture windows across the lobby filled with stunning canyon views. If you want to have dinner in the elegant dining room, make reservations pronto. The restaurant fills up quickly. Then step out back to discover one of the world's all-time great porches, a sprawling stone patio atop the canyon rim. Enjoy a chair, a beverage, and a view you'll never forget.

The paved Bright Angel Point Trail tumbles off the lodge's back porch. It's only a half-mile round trip but with some ups and downs as it follows a narrow ridge with steep drop-offs and expansive panoramas.

The North Rim also offers a couple of spectacular scenic drives. The 23-mile Cape Royal Road traverses a wooded plateau and snakes past picnic areas and multiple canyon overlooks. It ends at the southernmost point on the North Rim. A paved level trail leads to an amazing diversity of views, including a vista of the natural bridge known as Angel's Window.

A short winding drive, a 3-mile side trip off Cape Royal Road, leads to Point Imperial with its regal vistas. At 8,803 feet, this is the highest point on either rim. Views stretch forever and take in such landmarks as Navajo Mountain, the Painted Desert, and Marble Canyon.

The Inner Canyon

From the rim, the inner canyon can only be reached on foot or by mule trip. There are no easy trails to the river. You're hiking at high elevation, on steep, rugged trails, often in extreme heat. And remember it gets hotter as you go down. Do not attempt to hike to the Colorado River and back in a single day.

Still, some people are unable to resist the pull of the gorge. But heed this word of warning: hiking into the Grand Canyon can change your life. Once you step below the rim, it's easy to fall under a spell you can't begin to understand. It can provoke an internal examination of priorities and perspectives. You may experience emotions ranging from serenity to excitement to unabashed joy. You may rediscover a part of yourself long forgotten.

It's a vastly different world when you drop below the rim. There are only two maintained

The rustic cabins of Phantom Ranch sit along Bright Angel Creek at the bottom of the Grand Canyon, offering welcome beds and food for hikers, mule riders, and river rafters. Courtesy of Mike Koopsen, Sedona.

trails into the canyon, the Bright Angel and the Kaibab (North and South) Trails. Unmaintained trails like Grandview, Hermit, Tanner, and Bass should only be attempted by well-prepared and experienced hikers.

Don't expect amenities along the journey. Other than an occasional restroom and the rare water spigot, there are none. Yet a surprising oasis known as Phantom Ranch does exist at the very bottom of the canyon. A collection of rustic cabins and dormitory-style bunkhouses are scattered beneath the cottonwood trees on the north side of the Colorado River. Designed by Mary Colter, Phantom Ranch is the only place in the national park where visitors can sleep in a bed below the rim. Nestled on the banks of Bright Angel Creek, the little outpost is paradise for weary hikers and mule riders.

It's 13.6 miles down the North Kaibab Trail to Phantom Ranch, 9.9 miles down the Bright Angel, or 7.4 miles on the shade-less South Kaibab. That's why Phantom should not be considered a day-hike destination. If you want a bed in a cabin or bunkhouse, it means entering an online lottery that accepts entries 15 months in advance. Beverages, snack items, and meals are offered at Phantom Ranch Canteen to everyone, but meals must also be reserved in advance. (888) 297-2757, www.grandcanyonlodges.com.

Magic of the Canyon

Yet anyone who is reasonably fit can venture at least a little bit into the depths. There are

Expansive views spread out below the North Rim vista of Point Sublime. Courtesy of Mike Koopsen, Sedona.

several day-hike options that allow visitors a chance to sample the wonders that exist below the rim.

From the South Rim, head down the switchbacks of Bright Angel Trail to Mile-and-a-Half Resthouse. Or descend on South Kaibab to Cedar Ridge. Both are 3-mile round trip hikes. From the North Rim, follow the North Kaibab Trail down to Coconino Overlook (2.6 miles round trip) or to Supai Tunnel (4 miles round trip). Rest, relax, and soak up the views before returning. Your knees might grumble, but your soul will thank you.

One of my favorite canyon day hikes is down South Kaibab to Skeleton Point, 6 miles round trip. Other trails that drop below the rim follow a fault line. They hug rocky walls as they zigzag into the depths. Views are spectacular but limited to only what's framed in front of you.

There's nothing coy about the South Kaibab. It's a torpedo of a trail, launching from the rim and chasing a ridgeline down and out across the canyon. It stays close to the cliffs only for the first mile, then pushes off and thrusts into the big empty.

At 0.9 miles the canyon cracks open wide at aptly named Ooh Aah Point. Breaking free of the canyon wall, this small promontory juts into the open and unveils resplendent views up and down the gorge. At 1.5 miles, I reach Cedar Ridge, a hefty mesa that includes restrooms and plenty of good sitting rocks. This is the logical stopping place for day hikers. But logic and I are barely on speaking terms. I continue my descent, a long traverse curving past O'Neill Butte named for Buckey O'Neill, a former Prescott lawman who was instrumental in bringing the railroad to the Grand Canyon. The views through here devastate me. Then there's a final stretch of moderately level trail—a sweet gift in the sharply angled terrain—before I reach my destination.

Skeleton Point is a high stone perch sitting atop the Redwall Limestone formation. We all need our safe harbors, those special places where we feel a special cosmic connection. This is one of mine. A narrow footpath traces the western edge of the cliff, and provides a first glimpse of the Colorado River, still some 2,700 feet below. I like to sit on this ledge for a lazy hour or three, listening to the distant croak of ravens, watching the cloud shadows sweep the Tonto Platform below me, and feeling the ancient bones of this canyon wrap around me.

I live in Arizona exactly for moments like this, for the sheer staggering potential this state holds. No matter what else is happening in my life, no matter what drama or stress, I can still manage to disappear for a while into the Grand Canyon. No one but an Arizonan has that option.

When You Go

(928) 638-7888, www.nps.gov/grca.

Admission

Admission fee is good for seven days and includes both the South Rim, and the North Rim during its season.

Facilities

The Grand Canyon Visitor Center Complex is located near the South Entrance, with plenty of parking, just a short walk to Mather Point. It includes interpretive exhibits, a gift shop, and a park orientation film.

Other visitor centers are at Yavapai Geology Museum, with detailed geology exhibits; Verkamp's Visitor Center, telling the story of early canyon pioneers; Tusayan Museum, highlighting American Indian culture; and Desert View Visitor Center, near the East Entrance.

The North Rim Visitor Center features interpretive exhibits, ranger programs, and a bookstore.

LODGING (SOUTH RIM)

Designed to resemble a European hunting lodge, the elegant and historic El Tovar Hotel is a crown jewel of the national park system. El Tovar Dining Room is a world-renowned fine dining restaurant with exquisite canyon views.

Bright Angel Lodge was designed by Mary Colter. Made of log and native stone, the lodge and rustic cabins incorporate the historic Buckey O'Neill Cabin, the oldest standing structure on the South Rim, just footsteps from the canyon edge. It also includes restaurants, a saloon, and gift shop. At the back of the building, Bright Angel Fountain serves up hot dogs, sandwiches, ice cream, and cold drinks, and always seems busy.

For contemporary accommodations, both Kachina Lodge and Thunderbird Lodge are conveniently located in the village. Request a canyon-side room for the views.

Maswik Lodge sits back from the rim about a quarter-mile in the pine forest. A large motel complex, the main building also includes a pizza pub and food court.

South Rim lodging is managed by Xanterra. Reservations can be made by calling (888) 297-2757 or online at www.grandcanyonlodges.com.

The exception is Yavapai Lodge, managed by Delaware North. Housed in several buildings at Market Plaza (about a half-mile from the rim), the lobby also includes a restaurant, coffee shop, and tavern. (877) 404-4614, www.visitgrandcanyon.com.

LODGING (NORTH RIM)

Grand Canyon Lodge offers motel rooms and cabins scattered among the rimside forest. The restaurant is renowned with a wall of windows facing the canyon. (866) 499-2574, www.grandcanyonnorth.com.

MULE RIDES (SOUTH RIM)

A Grand Canyon mule ride is a classic Southwestern experience and, for many folks, a lifelong dream. The most accessible option, and the easiest on your backside, is the Canyon Vistas Mule Ride, which meanders along through woodlands near the canyon edge for 4 miles. You'll spend about 2 hours in the saddle, enjoy some big views, and learn some lore from the knowledgeable wranglers. And all before lunch. This trip does not descend into the canyon.

The other trip offered is the Overnight Ride to Phantom Ranch. This strenuous ride clops down the Bright Angel Trail for 10.5 miles. You'll enjoy dinner (assuming you can still sit down) at Phantom Ranch, spend the night, and make the long ride out the next day.

South Rim mule rides may be booked 15 months in advance. Reservations for Phantom Ranch trips are made through an online lottery. For more information, call (888) 297-2757. To check on any last-minute cancellations, visit the Bright Angel Lodge transportation desk.

MULE RIDES (NORTH RIM)

Canyon Trail Rides offers mule rides (1 hour and 3 hours) through the lush forest along easy rim trails. They also offer a 3-hour excursion into the canyon down North Kaibab to the Supai Tunnel. (435) 679-8665, www.canyonrides.com.

MISCELLANEOUS (SOUTH RIM)

Grand Canyon Railway rolls out of Williams each morning crossing the high prairie and forested plateau. Vintage diesel engines pull beautifully restored train cars highlighting six classes of service. It takes a little over 2 hours to complete the historic journey that began in

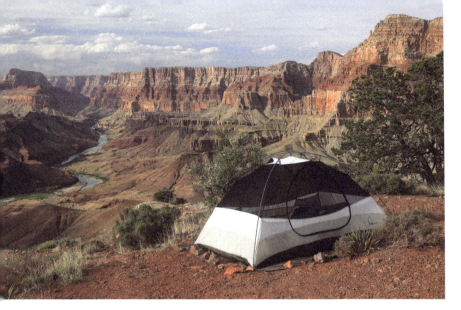

Backcountry camping permits allow visitors to experience some remarkable locations, like this room with a view along the Tanner Trail. Courtesy of Mike Koopsen, Sedona.

1901, before arriving at the log depot at the South Rim. Passengers who aren't spending the night have 3 hours to soak up the sights before returning to Williams, for a most memorable day. Don't be surprised if the train is "robbed" by the notorious Cataract Creek Gang on the way back. (800) 843-8724, www.thetrain.com.

Bright Angel Bicycles & Café rents bikes, strollers, and wheelchairs; offers guided tours; and dishes up healthy food and smoothies. (928) 679-0992, www.bikegrandcanyon.com.

Kolb Studio sits at the head of Bright Angel Trail, sells books and gift items, and tells the story of the pioneering photographers who built the studio.

Pets

SOUTH RIM

Leashed pets are allowed on trails above the rim, Mather Campground, Desert View Campground, Trailer Village, and throughout developed areas. Yavapai Lodge is the only in-park lodge with pet-friendly rooms.

Pets are not permitted below the rim, on shuttle buses, or in other park lodging. Pets may be boarded at Grand Canyon Kennel. (928) 638-0534.

NORTH RIM

Leashed pets are only allowed on the bridle path (greenway) that connects North Kaibab

Trail, and the portion of the Arizona Trail north to the park entrance station. There is no kennel on the North Rim.

Hiking

Know your abilities; choose an appropriate hike. Carry plenty of water and drink it. Replenish your electrolytes as well. Bring food to munch along the way. High-energy salty snacks are best.

Mules have the right of way. When encountering mule riders, step off the trail on the uphill side away from the edge. Follow the instructions of the wrangler. Remain quiet and stand perfectly still. Do not return to the trail until the last mule is 50 feet past your position.

Do not attempt to hike to the Colorado River and back in a single day.

There is no secret to hiking uphill in the Grand, except don't go too far down to begin with. When returning, set a comfortable pace, stop often to rest, hydrate, nibble snacks, and admire the views. It may be uphill, but you're still hiking in the Grand Canyon. Who's having a better day than you?

South Rim

RIM TRAIL

Panoramas are endless on this 13-mile long backbone path that is mostly paved and easy as it stretches along the edge of the South Rim from South Kaibab Trailhead to Hermits Rest.

BRIGHT ANGEL TRAIL

You won't find solitude on the Bright Angel but plenty of beauty. Located in the village, the route passes through two short tunnels along the upper reaches framed by massive cliffs. Look for a panel of pictographs—ancient images painted on the rocks—past the first tunnel. Many day hikers will make their way to 1 1/2-Mile Resthouse or 3-Mile Resthouse where toilets and seasonal water await. The shady oasis of Havasupai Gardens sits below the steep switchbacks of Jacobs Ladder at 4.8 miles. Dropping through the twisting Devils Corkscrew, the trail follows a splashy creek till joining the River Trail. The sandy path soon crosses the Colorado on the Silver Bridge and reaches Phantom Ranch in 9.9 miles.

SOUTH KAIBAB TRAIL

After a few tight switchbacks, this corridor trail bursts into the open as it chases a ridgeline down and out across the canyon, exposing wide-ranging panoramas. After just 0.9 miles you reach Ooh Aah Point, a rocky shelf with what feels like the entire canyon wrapped around it. Views go on forever. Another series of switchbacks deposits you on Cedar Ridge, a broad mesa with restrooms 1.5 miles from the rim. After passing Skeleton Point, the trail makes a steep plunge down the Redwall to the Tonto Platform and the Tipoff, with restrooms and an emergency telephone. A final descent ends at the Black Bridge spanning the Colorado River. This is also the bridge used by mule riders to cross the river. It's 7.4 miles to Phantom Ranch. But due to an unavailability of water, lack of shade, and steepness of the South Kaibab Trail, rangers recommend hiking down this trail only and using the Bright Angel for the hike out.

Be aware that parking is not allowed at the South Kaibab Trailhead (Yaki Point). Regular shuttle buses run throughout the day, and a Hikers' Express shuttle bus runs each morning from Bright Angel Lodge to South Kaibab Trail.

GRANDVIEW TRAIL

Upper sections of the very steep Grandview Trail are braced by logs and steel rods attached to sheer rock walls, originally built by an early prospector. Only experienced canyon hikers should attempt this trail, which begins from Grandview Point off Desert View Drive. The plunging grade descends 3 miles to Horseshoe Mesa atop the Redwall Limestone to find remnants of Last Chance Mine. Please leave artifacts in place. Spur trails fan out across the mesa and offer a variety of views.

TONTO TRAIL

The Tonto Trail provides east to west travel through the inner canyon for approximately 95 miles. It traverses the open benchland of the Tonto Platform about 1,200 feet above the Colorado River. It is often used to make multiday backpacking loops within the canyon, as it serves as a connector for several trails. It intersects the South Kaibab Trail at the Tipoff and rambles across open country to connect with Bright Angel Trail in 4.6 miles at Havasupai Gardens.

HERMIT TRAIL

Located at the end of Hermit Road, even the name of this historic route conjures up a sense of solitude. The Hermit Trail is rough, rocky, and relentlessly steep, for experienced hikers only. It is 2.5 miles to Santa Maria Spring, where a cool stone rest house guards the trail. Make this your turnaround point. Sit inside and pretend the entire Grand Canyon is your yard. It's 8.9 miles to Hermit Rapid on the Colorado River.

North Rim

NORTH KAIBAB TRAIL

The North Kaibab is the only maintained trail into the canyon from this side. It drops steeply through big timber with groves of Douglas firs, Engelmann spruce, and ponderosa pines following you downhill as you reach the Coconino Overlook. Supai Tunnel, 2 miles from the rim, is blasted from solid rock. With restrooms and drinking water, this makes a good turnaround point. Switchbacks zigzag down the Redwall Limestone, a dizzying combination of exposure and views. Roaring Springs gushes out of the cliffs to form Bright Angel Creek, which follows the trail all the way to the river. Passing Cottonwood Campground, watch for a short detour leading to the oasis of Ribbon Falls. The last segment travels through a narrow passage known as the Box, a dangerous stretch in summer as the heat radiates from the rock walls. It's 13.8 miles to Phantom Ranch.

TRANSEPT TRAIL

A short but beautiful ramble, following the canyon rim from Grand Canyon Lodge to the North Rim Campground; 1.5 miles one-way.

UNCLE JIM TRAIL

Leaving from the North Kaibab Trailhead, this 5-mile loop is named for a former game warden. It swings through a mixed conifer forest to an overlook of the canyon and North Kaibab Trail switchbacks.

WIDFORSS TRAIL

This is the essence of the North Rim experience, walking in a lush, wildflower-carpeted conifer forest that breaks apart just long enough to expose magnificent views. The trail ends at Widforss Point for a round trip hike of 10 miles.

CAPE FINAL TRAIL

This easy trail, 2 miles one-way, leaves from Cape Royal Road, cutting through woodlands of oak and juniper. It ends atop a sprawling promontory with eye-popping views of rocky formations falling away from the rim. Snippets of the Colorado River are visible far below, frothy with whitewater.

Rim-to-Rim

Most people start from higher North Rim, descending on the North Kaibab Trail and climbing out on the Bright Angel Trail, 24 miles of grueling, epic adventure. Since the North Rim is only open from May 15 through October 15, inner canyon temperatures can be scorching. It can be done in a single day by hikers who are extremely fit and fast, but the National Park Service strongly discourages that. Better to spend a night or two below the rim, which will require securing a bed at Phantom Ranch and/or the necessary camping permits. Research, train, and prepare for this adventure of a lifetime.

Camping

SOUTH RIM

Mather Campground is open year-round and features 327 sites. Each includes a campfire ring / cooking grate, picnic table, parking space, and room for up to six people, three tents, and two vehicles. There are flush toilets and drinking water throughout the campground. No hookups are available; however, there is a free dump station. Pine Loop is a tent-only area where generators are not permitted. From March 1 through November 30, most campsites are by reservation at www.recreation.gov or by calling (877) 444-6777.

Desert View Campground offers a peaceful setting at the east end of the park with only 49 sites. Open from April 15 through October 15, the campsites accommodate tents, small RVs, and vehicles with travel trailers. Reservations are required and should be made at www.recreation.gov or by calling (877) 444-6777.

Trailer Village RV Park is the only in-park campground with full hookups (sewage, water, and electric with 30-amp and 50-amp sites). Open year-round, Trailer Village offers paved pull-through sites that accommodate vehicles up to 50 feet long. Reservations can be made 13 months in advance by contacting the operator, Delaware North. (877) 404-4614, www.visitgrandcanyon.com.

NORTH RIM

The North Rim Campground is open only during their season, May 15 through October 15. It features 87 RV and tent sites. There are no hookups but a free dump station is available. Maximum RV length is 40 feet. Campgrounds include showers and laundry. Reservations are required and should be made at www.recreation.gov or by calling (877) 444-6777.

INNER CANYON

There are three campgrounds located along the corridor trails. To camp in one of these campgrounds you must obtain a backcountry permit by creating an online lottery application at www.recreation.gov.

Havasupai Gardens is located along Bright Angel Trail, 4.8 miles below the South Rim, in a beautiful riparian area shaded by cottonwood trees. There is a ranger station, emergency phone, year-round potable water, and toilets.

Bright Angel Campground is at the bottom of the canyon, 9.9 miles from the South Rim and 14 miles from the North Rim. The campground is 0.5 miles north of the Colorado River and sits along shady Bright Angel Creek, near Phantom Ranch. There is a ranger station, emergency phone, year-round potable water, and toilets. Seasonal ranger programs are offered. Beverages, snack items, and meals are offered at Phantom Ranch, but meals must be reserved in advance by calling (888) 297-2757.

Cottonwood Campground is a small campground 6.8 miles below the North Rim on the North Kaibab Trail. Bright Angel Creek flows nearby. There is an emergency phone and toilets. Potable drinking water is available from mid-May to mid-October. During other times you should be prepared to filter/treat water from the creek.

A limited number of last-minute permits are available exclusively for park visitors who wish to camp at Havasupai Gardens or Cottonwood Campground. These permits are issued in-person only, are for one night only, and cannot be purchased more than one day prior to the start of a hike. Last-minute permits are issued by the Backcountry Information Center on the South Rim and North Rim.

Programs/Events

Rangers offer an extensive selection of programs, often several times a day at different locations. They include guided walks, discussions on geology, wildlife, history, night skies, and more. Programs take place throughout the village and at Desert View on the South Rim and at various locations on the North Rim. Check the calendar on the park website or at visitor centers for a current schedule.

Cultural demonstrations are offered at Desert View Watchtower. These demonstrations of traditional Native practices and crafts are conducted by members of the 11 tribes associated with Grand Canyon allowing for interaction with the public.

There are also several highly anticipated annual events in the park. Grand Canyon Star Party takes place every June on both rims with astronomers sharing their telescopes and expertise with park visitors.

Grand Canyon Music Festival dates back to 1984 and attracts an incredible lineup of musicians performing near Shrine of the Ages on the South Rim in August and September.

Celebration of Art in September features artists on the South Rim creating plein air art while visitors watch their process. All pieces will be sold at Kolb Studio.

Native American Heritage Days take place in late summer on the North Rim and celebrate the canyon's associated tribes with demonstrations of music, dance, and artwork.

Special Notes

Stay on trails and keep a safe distance from the edge of the rim. In areas where there is a railing or fence, do not climb over the barrier. Keep an eye on children. Never throw rocks, coins, trash, or any other objects over the edge. Feeding deer, squirrels, and other wildlife is illegal.

Summer temperatures on the South Rim at 7,000 feet are warm but pleasant, generally in the 80s, and cooler on the North Rim at 8,000 feet. Within the canyon, summer temperatures will be hotter, often exceeding 100 degrees at Phantom Ranch.

Winter weather varies greatly and can change suddenly. Be prepared for cold, rain, ice, and, snow. Roads can be treacherous. Trails and walkways may be icy.

All vehicles, including mountain bikes, are restricted to maintained roads.

Located far from paved roads, Grand Canyon–Parashant National Monument is one of the most remote locations in the continental United States. Courtesy of Mike Koopsen, Sedona.

Grand Canyon–Parashant National Monument

Overview

The most remote corner of the contiguous United States encompasses a land of extremes, from harsh desert to rugged mountains, lonely cliffs to ancient volcanoes, while offering exquisite views of the neighboring Grand Canyon. But it is also extremely difficult to reach and explore, so come prepared.

Nearest Cities

St. George, UT; Mesquite, NV; Fredonia, AZ.

Established

January 11, 2000.

Size

1,048,321 acres.

When you're ready to step off the edge of the known world, head for Parashant.

Arizona keeps more than a million acres of rugged frontier—a chunk of land bigger than Rhode Island—tucked away in the far northwestern corner, snugged up against the Grand Canyon and the Nevada state line and just south of Utah. Established by President Bill Clinton in 2000, Grand Canyon–Parashant National Monument is the lonely hind end of the Arizona Strip, the piece of state cut off from the rest by the Colorado River. That's very much how it feels. You're cut off from everything here.

Remote doesn't even begin to describe the place. The monument is so far off the grid, the grid takes it personally. Cell phone navigation apps will try to strand you here amid the desolation. They often route visitors in Las Vegas or St. George searching for Grand Canyon viewpoints through Parashant. Don't listen to them! Out here your tires will be eaten and your axles snapped like twigs and the tow job will cost more than your vehicle is worth.

Doom Awaits

You're probably better off not going to Parashant. There are no services. Forget about your cell phone working. I'm not even sure it's the 21st century out here. You'll run out of pavement long before you even reach the border of the monument. There really is nothing here. It's the Big Empty.

All you'll find at Parashant are tall cliffs painted in sunlight, sagebrush steppes that break apart against the flanks of towering mountains capped with ponderosa pines, desert scrub, deep canyons, natural springs, weathered cowboy shacks, ancient petroglyphs etched into boulders, a silence so rich it cradles and comforts you, and a big night sky glittering with stars and planets. Hardly worth a trip.

Even the park website reads like a big jangly warning alarm. They're really not trying to talk you out of visiting, but they want your attention. Spend some time reading the information provided and follow their advice.

Grand Canyon–Parashant National Monument is likely the most isolated, remote area in the lower 48 states. It is crisscrossed by hundreds of miles of dirt roads that range from "rough" to "you can't seriously call that a road." High clearance is a must for even the gentlest routes in ideal weather, and four-wheel drive with all-terrain tires is required for anything beyond the fringes. Inclement weather makes everything terrible. Come fully prepared with all-terrain spare tires (preferably more than one), plenty of water, food, first-aid kit, and extra gas. You are far from any kind of safety net and must be prepared to self-rescue. Whatever dangerous jackpot you find yourself in, you've got to pull yourself out. If that doesn't scare you off, then maybe Parashant is for you after all.

Into the Wild

Fortunately for me since I don't have four-wheel drive, my friend Mike Koopsen needs little coaxing to venture into the backcountry. We set out in late September, stopping first at the Bureau of Land Management Arizona Strip Field Office in St. George, Utah, for the latest road conditions. Good thing, too. A late monsoon storm had washed out a section of narrow road high on the shoulder of Mount Trumbull, one of the routes we had hoped to explore.

From St. George, it's 50 miles of washboardy but gentle dirt road just to reach Mount Trumbull schoolhouse, which sits in a long meadow outside the monument border. The historic one-room schoolhouse is a replica (the original burned down in 2000) and is open to the public, filled with signs, photos, and maps. Mormon settlers began farming here around 1916, and a small community developed, reaching a high population of 250 during the 1930s. The Hurricane Cliffs and Mount Trumbull define the eastern skyline. We continued driving south into Parashant and left all hope behind.

Just kidding about the hope thing. Weather was ideal and it was a beautiful day. The road turns much rougher in the monument, dropping through broken hills and sharp little valleys—but Mike is an experienced jeep driver and we had no issues. We paused long enough to check in at the Bar 10 Ranch, the only speck of civilization in Parashant and our lodging for the night, before pushing on.

The "Grand Canyon" portion of the monument's name refers to the crucial watershed

The Bar 10 Ranch offers visitors to Parashant hot meals, hot showers, and a bed in a covered wagon. Courtesy of Mike Koopsen, Sedona.

that feeds the Colorado River and also the proximity of the two parks. Parashant—a Southern Paiute Indian family name—is how the monument is commonly referenced to avoid confusion between the locations. We were on our way to a rare and stunning viewpoint of the sister property.

The road to Whitmore Canyon Overlook crosses an ancient lava flow, dropping 1,500 feet in 7 miles in a series of tight turns and rocky ledges. Four-wheel drive and all-terrain tires are essential here, as the sharp basalt through this section is noted for its tire-slashing prowess.

After passing through groves of barrel cactus, mingled with prickly pear and hedgehog, the road ends at a wide turnaround atop a volcanic shoulder peering into the Grand Canyon. This lava flow once dammed the Colorado River for thousands of years, forming a massive lake behind it. And that was not an isolated event. Lava from the Uinkaret volcanic vents altered the course of the river numerous times during the past 700,000 years.

I've never experienced a rimside Grand Canyon overlook like Whitmore. There's an intimacy to it that is jarring. Just 900 feet above the Colorado, I can hear the flow of water, and it seems close enough to feel the spray of the rapids. Taller cliffs rise overhead and views extend up and down the river.

While on the rim we're still in Parashant. But there's a hiking trail that switchbacks down the canyon wall to the river. We start down and almost immediately enter Grand Canyon National Park. Yet as tempting as it would be to spend a little time beside the river, we can only go partway. We didn't want to be late for dinner.

Bar 10 Ranch

Started as a working cattle ranch in the 1970s, the Bar 10 ((435) 628-4010, www.bar10.com) expanded to become a stopover for Grand Canyon river rafters and lodging for adventurers

Lonely Whitmore Point shows off a quiet side of the Grand Canyon. Courtesy of Mike Koopsen, Sedona.

navigating the monument. Most rafters arrive via the ranch's landing strip and helipad. It's a welcome oasis to find a bed, hot meal, and showers in the middle of nowhere.

Mike and I enjoyed a heaping country dinner in the warm wood-paneled lodge with its wagon-wheel chandeliers and big picture windows. Also dining and spending a couple of nights was a group of ATVers exploring some of the sketchy roads in the monument by day. They had been coming to Parashant and the Bar 10 Ranch for years. After dinner, groups spilled outdoors on patios and porches for storytelling, music, and possibly a little drinking. Some, like me, wandered away from the buildings to savor the star-laden sky. Not surprisingly, Parashant is an International Dark Sky Park.

Although there are a few dorm-style rooms upstairs at the lodge, most guests prefer sleeping in the vintage covered wagons set on the hillside overlooking the ranch. Don't expect luxury—each of the 14 wagons is equipped only with a bench seat, a battery-powered lantern, and a bed. But it all feels just right in this lonely place. And how many opportunities do you have to sleep in a covered wagon?

After an equally hearty breakfast, we were once again bouncing along dirt roads with no sign of civilization in sight.

Floor to Roof

Jointly managed by the Bureau of Land Management and the National Park Service, Parashant is a land of startling extremes. The monument climbs from 1,400 feet above sea level amid the twisted Joshua trees of the Mojave Desert to 8,000 feet atop snowcapped Mount Trumbull. Two geologic provinces meet here—the Basin and Range, and the Colorado Plateau. The Grand Canyon falls away to the south. Such abrupt transitions and overlapping ecosystems lead to a remarkable diversity of plant and animal life.

Four wilderness areas are scattered across Parashant. The massive upland of the Shivwits Plateau pushes through the middle of the monument, forcing the Colorado River into a long sweeping bend. The Grand Wash Cliffs rise in stair steps from the Mojave Desert in the west, forming a scenic spine of highlands, and the Hurricane Cliffs snake their way along the eastern edge. This is a broken land with a rowdy geological past. Here the earth was bent and twisted and flooded and scorched, and Parashant still carries the barely healed scars.

Human residents have left significant but less noticeable marks on the land. Small bands of hunter-gatherers roamed the region during the Archaic Period. The Southern Paiute replaced the Pueblo groups sometime after AD 1300. Ancient artifacts, agave roasting pits, faint trails, and shelters mark their time here. A short hiking trail on the flank of Mount Trumbull leads to Nampaweap, one of the largest petroglyph sites on the Arizona Strip, with hundreds of images chipped into basalt boulders.

Historic structures and ruins scattered across the monument tell the stories of the early settlers who tried to scrape out a living here. The most noted of these is the Tassi Ranch, where a few buildings still stand beside a flowing stream in the western corner of the park. Ruins of the Grand Gulch Mine can be found down a treacherous road in the Grand Wash Cliffs.

Pakoon Springs, one of the monument's largest natural springs, is being restored to its natural state. But when it was impounded as a ranch site many years ago it was home to a famous Parashant resident, Clem the alligator.

A rancher named Charles Simmons received Clem as a gift in the 1980s from friends with strange senses of humor. Simmons turned the small toothy reptile, barely a foot long, loose in one of his ponds and left him to fend for himself. For an animal more suited to southern swamps, the dry summers and cold winters couldn't have been easy, but Clem survived for nearly 20 years at Pakoon Springs as Arizona's only wild alligator.

The rancher sold the property to the BLM in 2002 with the stipulation that no harm befall Clem. In 2005, after a couple of tries, a very malnourished Clem, 8 feet long and weighing only 130 pounds, was captured and relocated to the Phoenix Herpetological Society, where he quickly began putting on weight and growling and hissing at everyone he saw. He soon tipped the scale at over 600 pounds. Today he is known for his immense size and cranky attitude. And of all the dangers you might encounter in Parashant, at least being eaten by a gator is no longer one of them.

Hard to Reach, Harder to Leave

Grand Canyon–Parashant National Monument isn't for everyone. It's too lonely, too swarming with peril. And that's the way it's going to stay. There are no plans to change anything. Roads will stay feral. No cell towers are going up. The information center will remain conveniently located in another state. That's part of the bargain if we want to keep wild country intact.

It's good to know that the frontier still exists. Solitude and silence and starry skies still have value. Clean air and unobstructed views matter. Protected places far from the din of civilization, even rough and dangerous ones, enhance us all.

On a final note, I'll provide no directions at all. You have to do your own research to determine if your vehicle and your comfort level are right for the adventure you plan. And then once you've prepared, be certain to check in with monument rangers by phone or in person for current conditions. A list of scenic drives—road quality and best seasons for each—are listed on the website. Just remember, the only good adventures are ones you come back from.

When You Go

BLM: www.blm.gov/national-conservation-lands/arizona/grandcanyon-parashant.
NPS: www.nps.gov/para.

Admission

Free.

Facilities

None. The BLM Arizona Strip Field Office is in St. George, UT. Passport stamps are available here.

Pets

Pets must be restrained or kept on a leash. Please respect wildlife. Saddle or pack animals are allowed in recreation sites only where authorized by posted instructions.

Hiking

There are only a handful of official semi-maintained hiking trails in the monument. But there are plenty of peaceful roads that serve the same purpose.

The most popular—popular by Parashant standards, which means you'll probably be the only person hiking—include trails to the summit of Mount Trumbull (5.1 miles round trip, strenuous), to the summit of Mount Dellenbaugh (5.9 miles round trip, strenuous), and Pakoon Springs Trail (1 mile round trip, easy), which is being restored to its natural habitat.

Camping

There are no developed campsites. Camping on the monument requires planning, preparation, and care to protect the fragile desert and mountain ecosystems. Use existing sites if possible. Choose a durable surface such as gravel. Locate your camp away from any wash or drainage. Avoid camping or stepping on cryptobiotic soil crusts. Pack out all trash. Return your campsite to a natural appearance.

Programs/Events

None.

Special Notes

Before setting out take some time to really plan your visit and make certain you are prepared with the proper equipment, maps, and knowledge of the region. You will need to plan for potential hazards such as unmarked rugged roads, extreme heat, flash floods, and venomous reptiles.

Road conditions vary based on weather conditions. Many roads become impassable in winter or following monsoon storms. Call ahead before coming to the monument. Always carry extra water, food, matches or lighter, a signal mirror, and foul-weather gear. No vehicles are allowed in wilderness areas. Always tell someone your itinerary. A satellite phone could be helpful but be prepared to self-rescue. Help is not on the way.

Ganado Red is a style of Navajo rug characterized by red interior, black borders, and intricate design. Photo by the author.

Hubbell Trading Post National Historic Site

Overview
History still lives and breathes at the oldest continuously operating trading post in the Southwest, even while it still serves its original purpose, and also offers visitors a glimpse into Navajo culture.

Nearest City
Ganado.

Established
August 28, 1965.

Size
160 acres.

On the high plateau of the Navajo Nation sits a sandstone building, just footsteps from the Pueblo Colorado Wash. Long and low with a flat roof, the structure is unadorned except for a few wood-framed double-hung windows. Pull open the screen door, push through the entryway, and step inside. Let your eyes adjust to the dim lighting. If you just came in out of the summer sun, it will feel cool and welcoming. If it's winter, the heat from the stove will wrap around you.

You're inside the store, also known as the bullpen. The space is cozy, crowded with goods, and spicy with old aromas. Long U-shaped counters are stacked with bolts of cloth, skeins of wool, and baskets full of sundries. Groceries and supplies line the shelves. Frying pans, horse collars, and kerosene lanterns hang from the ceiling in a joyful cacophony of clutter. Scuffed wooden floors creak at every step. It feels like you've wandered back in time.

Adjacent to the store, a trader sits in the jewelry room, which also contains carvings, paintings, kachinas, and pottery, all for sale. On any given day, visitors might see a trade negotiated as Navajo artisans bring in their work. In a third room, gorgeous handwoven rugs are stacked in casual piles and draped over wooden rails. The color and detail in the designs are breathtaking.

Walking into Hubbell Trading Post is very much a step back in time. Photo by the author.

Living, Breathing History

While many national parks include stores, there's only one that actually IS a store. And it's a magnificent store, a slice of American retail that is almost impossible to find these days and brimming with stories of tragedy and triumph. Hubbell Trading Post is the oldest continuously operating trading post in the Southwest.

Nestled in the cottonwood trees alongside a wide arroyo, the national historic site is part museum and part art gallery. Most importantly, it's still a fully functioning trading post, virtually unchanged since it first opened in the 1870s.

For generations, Hubbell Trading Post has served as a bridge between Navajo and Anglo cultures. While the trading post was a place of business it also served as the center of social life for Navajo, or Diné, which means "the people." They came to trade their goods like wool, corn, and pinion nuts, and later their handcrafted jewelry and woven rugs for the supplies they needed. But it was also a gathering spot to meet old friends and relatives.

John Lorenzo Hubbell was born in 1853 in a small village south of Albuquerque. His father was Anglo, his mother was Spanish. He first came to the Ganado area in 1876 at the urging of a Navajo friend. In 1878 he bought a small trading post from William "Old Man" Leonard and immediately began to expand. The site would be his permanent home for the next 50 years.

Hubbell's understanding of Navajo life and culture and his ability to speak Navajo earned him the trust of the local people. He had a reputation for fairness and honesty in his business dealings, and was admired for his unfailing hospitality.

The Long Walk

Hubbell opened his trading post at a critical time for the Navajo. They were still trying to adjust to reservation life following their brutal exile.

Believing that gold existed in Navajo country, General James H. Carleton established Fort Defiance in the heart of the Diné homeland. After years of conflict, Carleton made a push to forcibly remove the Navajo. He unleashed Colonel Christopher "Kit" Carson, who

The store, or bullpen, at Hubbell Trading Post has changed very little in the past century. Photo by the author.

launched a brutal scorched-earth campaign—burning crops, killing livestock, and massacring men, women, and children.

Facing starvation, most of the remaining Navajos surrendered. In 1864 they were led on a forced march more than 300 miles to the Bosque Redondo Reservation, a desolate tract of land near Fort Sumner in the New Mexico Territory. Hundreds died on what came to be known as the Long Walk. Many more perished from disease and starvation at the barren and overcrowded Bosque Redondo along the Pecos River. Water from the Pecos proved alkaline. Crops failed and food was scarce. Finally, in 1868 the Navajo were allowed to return home. Their homesteads, livestock, and crops were all gone. The Navajo now relied on a small allotment of food, supplies, and sheep. Faced with this world, trade with men like Hubbell became increasingly important.

Hubbell was respected by the Navajos, often writing and translating letters for his customers and helping explain and navigate government policies. He donated land for a school to be built. During an outbreak of smallpox in the 1880s, he turned his home into a makeshift hospital and cared for the sick and the dying.

As a trader, Hubbell was there to supply merchandise and food to the Navajos, but he also helped create an industry by encouraging and then promoting Diné arts and crafts. Hubbell's influence can be seen in Navajo silversmithing and especially weaving.

The Art of Weaving

By the early 1800s, Navajo weavers were known for finely woven nearly weatherproof blankets that became popular trade items. As machine-made blankets became available, the market began to dry up. Traders like Hubbell encouraged the weaving of rugs. He insisted on the highest quality and encouraged weavers to re-create designs of the past. His preference for the color red and passion for certain motifs led to the distinctive style of rug known as Ganado Red.

Visitors to Hubbell Trading Post get to see this historic art form come to life. On most days, Diné weavers work at an upright floor loom in the visitor center, demonstrating the skill, technique, and patience that go into each rug. Travelers from around the world pause to watch. They ask questions and learn about weaving and cultural traditions. It has been one more way that Hubbell Trading Post stays connected to its rich past.

After watching the weaver at work, guests can try their hands on the visitor's loom set up in the next room. Or better still, wander over to the trading post and examine the colorful rugs with a fresh perspective. They are even more beautiful when you understand all that goes into making them.

Many of the rugs created at the visitor center, and others that have been purchased or bartered from local artisans are for sale in the rug room, just off the bullpen. Prices range from $50 all the way up to $10,000. The prices vary based on size, difficulty of the pattern, and the artist who created it.

All in the Family

Hubbell married a Spanish woman named Lina Rubi in 1879. The couple had two daughters and two sons. Over the years, Hubbell established the most successful trading empire in the Southwest. He opened other posts across Navajo lands, operated freight and mail lines, and ranches and farms, as well as other businesses. Yet the trading post at Ganado remained his home base.

Navajo workers began construction on the current trading post building in 1883. The Hubbell home was built directly behind it. Over the years the family hosted a steady stream of notable guests such as former president Theodore Roosevelt, novelist Lew Wallace, and painter Maynard Dixon.

John Lorenzo Hubbell—known as Naakaii Sani (Old Mexican) or Nak'ee sinili (Eyeglasses) to the Navajo, and Don Lorenzo to local Hispanics—died in 1930. He is buried on the cone-shaped hill behind the home. Several family members and a longtime Navajo friend are also buried on what is now known as Hubbell Hill.

The youngest son Roman Hubbell continued to operate the trading post until his death in 1957. His wife Dorothy managed the post for another decade until the National Park Service acquired it. While the history is carefully preserved, the commercial enterprise—the original intent of the trading post—continues unabated. The National Park Service manages the property while their partner, the nonprofit Western National Parks Association, operates the trading post.

The site consists of the original 160-acre homestead, including the trading post, family home, and visitor center with exhibits. Short guided tours, or peeks, of the Hubbell home are offered daily as staffing permits.

Tour the grounds that include corrals, gardens, farm animals, and other historic buildings. When completed about 1900, the two-story barn was the largest in Northern Arizona. A full-time baker manned the big bread oven behind the house. He often made up to 400 loaves a week for the family and the store. The guest hogan still welcomes visiting artists, researchers, and volunteers. Enjoy a quiet stroll along the Veterans Healing Trail as it winds through the cottonwoods above the Pueblo Colorado Wash.

A few picnic tables are found in a shady grove beside the visitor center. Buy a snack or a drink or an ice cream from the store and relax for a bit. Imagine the sound of wagon wheels rolling up the lane, the murmur of voices in several different languages, the aroma of fresh-baked bread wafting past on the breeze. Suddenly the past doesn't seem so distant after all.

When You Go

(928) 755-3475, www.nps.gov/hutr.

Admission

Free.

Facilities

The visitor center has museum exhibits and features Navajo rug-weaving demonstrations.

The trading post offers a variety of Native American arts and crafts including jewelry, baskets, kachinas, rugs, and more. Among the goods sold in the store are drinks, snacks, and groceries.

Pets

Pets are not permitted in any of the buildings. Leashed pets are allowed on the grounds.

Hiking

The short Veteran's Trail follows Pueblo Colorado Wash for a brief out-and-back hike.

Camping

Park is day use only.

Programs/Events

Short guided tours, or peeks, of the Hubbell home are offered daily as staffing permits. Ranger talks and other presentations take place throughout the year.

Native American Art Auctions are held in May and September in Gallup, New Mexico, by the nonprofit Friends of Hubbell Trading Post as fund-raising events to support the park and provide economic assistance to the artists and community. www.friendsofhubbell.org.

Sheep, Wool, and Weaving Workshops give visitors a chance to learn the importance of Churro sheep to the Navajo people. Hands-on learning includes dyeing, spinning, and weaving.

Lantern Tours are conducted in October.

Luminaria Night every December creates a little holiday magic as hundreds of flickering candles are lit across the grounds as part of a time-honored Southwest tradition.

Special Notes

The Navajo Nation observes daylight saving time from March through November. The rest of Arizona does not.

Do not climb on fences or machinery. Do not approach or feed animals, tame or wild. All plants, animals, and natural and historic features are protected by federal law.

Kayakers navigate the clear waters of Lake Mohave. Photo by the author.

Lake Mead National Recreation Area

Overview

A startling contrast of water and desert, mingled with mountains and canyons, creates an epic playground spread across two states.

Nearest Cities

Bullhead City, AZ; Kingman, AZ; Boulder City, NV; Laughlin, NV; Las Vegas, NV.

Established

On October 13, 1936, the National Park Service and the Bureau of Reclamation formalized a memorandum of agreement creating Boulder Dam National Recreation Area. The name was changed to Lake Mead National Recreation Area in 1947. On October 8, 1964, the new Lake Mead National Recreation Area was established under the sole jurisdiction of the National Park Service.

Size

1,495,855 acres.

There is a fine bit of madness to Lake Mead National Recreation Area (NRA). Giant sparkling lakes are wrapped in mountains and spread across a gaunt and boney landscape that just happens to be one of America's most beloved playgrounds. And it was all made possible by a bunch of unemployed gas station attendants and shoe salesmen.

Millions visit Lake Mead each year, designated as the country's first national recreation area. They come seeking fun, adventure, natural beauty, or possibly just the wild exhilaration of discovering water in one of Earth's hottest, driest regions. Lake Mead was formed following the construction of Hoover Dam.

Man-Made Wonder

When Hoover Dam was built to control the mighty Colorado River, it was the highest dam in the world, over 726 feet from foundation rock to the roadway on top. Its base is thicker than the length of two football fields. The amount of concrete in the dam would be enough to build a two-lane highway stretching from San Francisco to New York City. Or to build a sidewalk that would go completely around the earth at the equator.

The engineering marvel of Hoover Dam created the impoundment of Lake Mead. Courtesy of Rick Mortensen, Phoenix.

Construction took place from 1931 to 1935. As hard as it is to imagine today, the engineering marvel of Hoover Dam was designed not by high-powered computers, artificial intelligence, and intricate software but with slide rules and pencil and paper. The labor was not led by an elite squad of seasoned dam builders but by an army of unemployed fry cooks, factory workers, and plumbers—men just desperate for work during the Great Depression. They began showing up in 1931 before construction even began, often bringing their families and camping in the blistering heat.

Such a large concrete structure had never been built before, and some of the techniques were unproven. The project cost the lives of 96 men. Despite the insurmountable obstacles, the dam was finished almost two years ahead of schedule and well under budget. It forever changed the face of the Southwest, providing power and a reliable source of water.

Blue, Blue Water

The dam's original name was Hoover Dam. Then during the Roosevelt administration, it was called Boulder Dam. In 1947, it became Hoover Dam once again. The reservoir was named after the Bureau of Reclamation commissioner, Elwood Mead.

Once the dam was built, the impounded river began filling parched desert canyons along the Arizona-Nevada border. Water backed up from the dam all the way to the Grand Wash Cliffs at the mouth of the Grand Canyon. It stretches for 110 miles, the largest man-made lake in the country. In 1951, Davis Dam was built downstream, creating Lake Mohave and adding even more miles of shoreline and some spectacular canyons. Then in 1964, both lakes became part of the first national recreation area in the National Park Service.

Millions of visitors flock to the shimmering seductive lakes, etched with coves and beaches. Boaters, swimmers, anglers, sunbathers, hikers visit the vast park. At 1.5 million acres, it's twice the size of Rhode Island and allows plenty of room for peaceful solitude, even when it's crowded.

That's one thing that always amazes me when visiting Lake Mead. The park is one of the most popular in the country, yet I always seem to find a big chunk to claim all for myself. The trails are seldom crowded, there are plenty of quiet overlooks, and I spend lots of time sitting on an isolated stretch of beach watching kayakers paddle by in the shadow of slanted rock mountains. I always scan the cliffs for movement because these hills are lousy with bighorn sheep and watching them scramble among clefts and ledges is a rare treat. As a desert dweller I am soothed by the soft kiss of water lapping against rocks. Surely there can be no sweeter sound.

Perhaps I feel so at home here because I am a desert lover, and this place is a collision of deserts. Lake Mead sits at the sun-blasted intersection of three of North America's four deserts. The Mojave, Sonoran, and Great Basin Deserts all converge here in a hardscrabble landscape that felt far-flung and barren. At least until they started pouring concrete for a big old dam.

All those deserts bring something different to the table. Despite the sparseness of the landscape, the park is home to 900 species of plants and 500 species of animals, including 24 that are rare and threatened, such as the desert tortoise. Be sure to keep an eye out for the big lumbering reptile.

Lakes Mead and Mohave also offer some of the country's best sport fishing. Species found in both lakes include largemouth bass, striped bass, crappie, rainbow trout, channel catfish, and bluegill. Since waters in the lakes share borders with Arizona and Nevada, please be aware of all fishing laws in both states. In Arizona, a valid fishing license or combination license is required for resident and nonresident anglers 10 years of age and older. Two species of protected fish, the razorback sucker and the bonytail chub, may be found in the lakes. If these fish are caught, they should be returned to the water.

Boats, Barrels, and Bodies

Of course, recent years have not been kind to Lake Mead. Increased water demand combined with the ongoing drought that's throttling the Southwest has caused lake levels to drop dangerously low.

As waters receded, all sorts of strange artifacts surfaced. Handguns, baby strollers, tackle boxes, dozens of sunken boats including a WWII-era landing craft, and even human remains. Some of the bodies were undoubtedly drowning victims. Others—especially the

Bighorn sheep enjoy the luxurious lawn of Hemenway Park in Boulder City, Nevada. Photo by the author.

ones stuffed in barrels—seemed to come with a more sinister backstory. While drowning can't be ruled out because it would certainly be difficult to swim while inside a barrel, a mob hit seems to be more likely. Police estimated one victim had been shot in the mid-1970s or early 1980s, based on the person's Kmart shoes. Viva Las Vegas!

Yet unlike Lake Powell, no one is suggesting draining Lake Mead. This is the key reservoir for the region. The hydropower it produces is important; the water it supplies is irreplaceable. More than 25 million people rely on water from Lake Mead.

How Lake Mead will change going forward is impossible to say. Some areas and launch ramps have already been closed for years. Always stop by the visitor center for the latest information on conditions of roads, ramps, and lake levels.

Getting Around

Lake Mead National Recreation Area is surprisingly accessible for adventures on the water or dry land. The lakes make up only 13 percent of the park, so there's a whole lot of backcountry to explore.

FROM THE ARIZONA SIDE

You can visit Temple Bar Resort Marina perched along the southern shore of Lake Mead, if you don't mind a little extra driving. Once you turn off US 93 it is 27 miles through a sea of creosote flats just to reach this quiet little outpost, which is sadly watching the water slip farther away. There's a motel with cabins, an RV park, campground, store, restaurant, and saloon. You can also rent boats and watercraft. (855) 918-5253, www.templebarlakemead.com.

Another lonely drive (starting from Kingman or off US 93) crosses one of the largest and densest Joshua tree forests in the world atop Grapevine Mesa. This is near the small town of Meadview, which offers food, gas, and lodging. The road continues on to South Cove, the farthest east you can launch a boat in the recreation area. Always check on road conditions before setting out. Four-wheel drive is recommended for South Cove.

I have to admit my favorite section of the park is Lake Mohave, which flows directly south from Hoover Dam for approximately 67 miles. Both narrow and shallow compared to Lake Mead, much of it retains the feel of the old Colorado River. Especially the first section leaving the dam, which is enveloped by the steep dark walls of Black Canyon. In 2014, this 30-mile portion was designated as the Black Canyon National Water Trail, the first in the Southwest, and the first to flow through a desert. It's a kayaker's dream as the river winds past beaches, caves, coves, waterfalls, and hot springs beneath towering cliffs of volcanic rock. You can access the water trail through a guided tour at the base of Hoover Dam, or from Willow Beach, on the Arizona side. Launching at the dam requires a permit. Tours are offered by a limited number of vendors. A list of authorized tour guides can be found on the park website.

Surrounded by steep canyon walls 15 miles south of Hoover Dam, Willow Beach captivates visitors with an intimate connection to the river. Many visitors take a guided raft or kayak tour from the base of the dam to Willow Beach. Others drive straight here to rent boats or paddlecraft, or fish from the accessible pier along this sliver of a river. Another popular adventure from Willow Beach is a kayak tour to Emerald Cave, 2 miles upstream. The right slant of sunlight turns the water a glowing green, illuminating the small cave. Willow Beach Harbor also offers a full-service marina, with a restaurant, store, RV park and campground, and watercraft rentals. (855) 918-5253, www.willowbeachharbor.com.

At the bottom tip of Lake Mohave, Katherine Landing sits just north of Bullhead City and Davis Dam. It's the best of all worlds here where the lake has widened out but still feels intimate. You'll find plenty of creature comforts, because Katherine Landing offers motel rooms, full hookup RV sites, tent camping, a restaurant, store, a public swim beach, and watercraft rentals ((928) 754-3245, www.katherinelanding.com). Yet if you want a little seclusion, just north of the marina you'll find a series of inlets—Princess Cove, Cabinsite Cove, North Telephone Cove, and South Telephone Cove. These are quiet places with nothing but a few picnic tables and long stretches of beachfront.

FROM THE NEVADA SIDE

While I'm an Arizona guy right down the line, I do love our neighbors. And Nevada has plenty of can't-miss spots in this big park. Start at the Alan Bible Visitor Center, a first-class facility with lots of maps, brochures, exhibits, and, most importantly, knowledgeable rangers. Conditions can change so rapidly at Lake Mead; it's good to get the latest info.

Near the visitor center, take a hike on the Historic Railroad Trail. This is the original railroad bed that trains used to haul equipment during construction of Hoover Dam. It passes through five tunnels, each about 300 feet long and 25 feet wide, with nice lake panoramas along the way.

Take a drive on scenic Lakeshore Road. This leads to Boulder Beach, Hemenway Harbor, and several other pullouts for picnic areas, viewpoints, and hiking trails.

Lake Mead Cruises lets you explore the lake in style. They offer brunch tours, midday tours, and dinner cruises aboard an authentic three-level Mississippi-style paddlewheeler known as the *Desert Princess*. (866) 292-9191, www.lakemeadcruises.com.

Here's a bonus tip for those hoping to spot desert bighorn sheep. It's outside the recreation area, but check out Hemenway Valley Park in Boulder City with a nice view of the lake. An entire herd of bighorn has claimed the 10-acre park as their own backyard and show up frequently to water and feed. Sometimes dozens of sheep can be seen grazing on the manicured lawns or relaxing in the shade. But as calm as they seem, please treat them like the wild animals they are. Do not try to feed, pet, or approach.

Hoover Dam straddles the Nevada-Arizona border and can be approached from both states. There is free parking on the Arizona side if you want to walk across the top of the dam and admire the architecture and the stunning Art Deco sculptures. Several tour options are available from the Bureau of Reclamation, including a self-guided tour of the visitor center, and a tour of the power plant. Tickets can be purchased online for those. For the full-blown guided dam tour, a truly impressive experience, tickets must be purchased on-site. (702) 494-2517, www.usbr.gov/lc/hooverdam/service.

When You Go

(702) 293-8990, www.nps.gov/lake.

Admission

Admission fee is good for seven days.

Facilities

The Alan Bible Visitor Center includes museum exhibits, a theater, and a gift shop. Don't miss the large walk-around relief map of the area and its history.

Pets

Pets are welcome in developed areas, on hiking trails, along many beaches, and in campgrounds and some lodging facilities. Historic Railroad Trail and Owl Canyon are favorite trails among pet owners. Keep pets on a leash no longer than 6 feet. Pets are prohibited on designated beaches and in public buildings.

Hiking

Lake Mohave Hikes (Arizona)

FISHERMAN'S TRAIL

The trail begins southeast of the Katherine Landing launch ramp and follows the southern outline of the harbor, offering stunning looks of the water fringed by rugged mountains. There's an impressive sand dune often covered with wildlife tracks. Trail ends at the sandy beach at Ski Cove; 1.9 miles round trip.

LAKE VIEW TRAIL

Parking for this trail is next to the Katherine Landing day-use picnic area. The hike provides a sampling of Mojave Desert vegetation mingled with mountain and water vistas as it winds its way to South Telephone Cove, a 4.7-mile round trip outing.

Three trails share a trailhead located just off US Hwy 93, south of Hoover Dam before milepost 4. These hikes are considered strenuous or very strenuous, and can be deadly in hot temperatures. For your safety, these trails are closed May 15–September 30. The three trails are:

LIBERTY BELL ARCH TRAIL

The trail follows a wash and old roads over hills and down through canyons. Hikers will pass the remains of an old mine before reaching an impressive natural arch and Colorado River overlook. This strenuous hike is 5.5 miles round trip.

WHITE ROCK CANYON TRAIL

This very strenuous route leads hikers to Arizona Hot Spring, dropping through a deep, narrow gorge to the river. It turns downstream for 0.5 miles to Hot Spring Canyon. A short ascent leads to a 20-foot waterfall and a ladder. Climbing the ladder brings hikers to the Arizona Hot Spring; 6.5-miles round trip.

ARIZONA HOT SPRING TRAIL

Another very strenuous hike to be taken very seriously. With a 750-foot elevation change and some steep scrambling, this leads to the hot spring near the Colorado River. It can be combined with the White Rock Canyon Trail to form a loop. Always grab maps and get current information at the visitor center. It's 5.2 miles round trip using this trail as an out-and-back, 5.8 creating a loop with White Rock Canyon.

Warning! Naegleria fowleri, an amoeba common to thermal pools around the world, may be present in the hot spring and could enter through the nose, causing rare infection and death. Do not dive into pools, splash water, or submerge your head.

Lake Mead Hikes (Nevada)

HISTORIC RAILROAD TRAIL

This 3.7-mile easy trail traces the route of the original railroad used during the construction of Hoover Dam. The wide smooth path passes through five cavernous tunnels and past historical remnants of the dam construction era while offering panoramic views of Lake Mead. The trail can be accessed near the Lake Mead Visitor Center. The first tunnel is about 1 mile from the trailhead, and it's 2.2 miles to the fifth tunnel. From there, the trail climbs another 1.5 miles to Hoover Dam parking garage.

RIVER MOUNTAINS LOOP

This 35-mile paved trail connects Boulder City, Henderson, Lake Mead NRA, and the rest of the valley. Popular with bicyclists, segments can be enjoyed by anyone and can be accessed from two main trailheads in the park: the Historic Railroad Trailhead and off Lake Mead Parkway just west of the entrance station.

OWL CANYON

Dramatic winding canyons below the Lake Mead high-water line have been revealed as the water level has dropped. The hike is 2.2 miles round trip through this intimate little slot canyon where owls are often seen. Trailhead is located at the first parking lot on the left from 33 Hole turnoff.

BLUFFS TRAIL

This well-defined route, 3.9 miles round trip, scrambles among the bluffs overlooking Las Vegas Bay with views of distant mountains. The trailhead starts next to site #72 in the Las Vegas Bay Campground. Watch for birds and wildlife.

WETLANDS TRAIL

Birders love this short path that leads down to the flowing Las Vegas Wash. It's 1.5 miles round trip and don't forget the binoculars. Trail starts on Northshore Road just past milepost 1, across the bridge.

REDSTONE TRAIL

Wander among a cluster of petrified sand dunes on this easily accessible 1.1-mile loop. Geologic forces have turned the ancient dunes into wildly eroded sandstone hills clumped near the roadside. Start from the Redstone Picnic Area near milepost 27 on Northshore Road.

Camping

ARIZONA

Katherine Landing anchors the southern tip of Lake Mohave, so the 173-site landscaped campground is popular. Campsites feature picnic tables, fire rings with cooking grills, restrooms, and showers. The 24-site RV park comes with water, sewer, and electrical hookups. All spaces are back-in, with the largest accommodating 40-foot vehicles. Laundry and shower facilities are on-site. (928) 754-3245, www.katherinelanding.com.

Willow Beach, another beautiful Lake Mohave spot, offers an RV park and campground with 28 full-service (water, sewer, electric) RV sites and 9 tent sites. All sites have picnic tables, fire rings, and showers and restrooms available. (855) 918-5253, www.willowbeachharbor.com.

At Temple Bar, on the south shore of Lake Mead, the NPS maintains a 71-site campground with fire pits / grills, picnic tables, restrooms, a dump station, and running water. RVs, trailers, and tents are welcome. It can be booked through www.recreation.gov. A park concessioner operates an RV park with 10 full hookup sites, showers, and laundry. (928) 767-3211, www.templebarlakemead.com.

NEVADA

Boulder Beach Campground stretches nearly a mile along the shoreline of Boulder Basin on Lake Mead. This is sort of the center of the action, with swimming, kayak, and Jet Ski beaches nearby, as well as the fishing pier and boat launch in Hemenway Harbor, Lake Mead Marina, and the Lake Mead Cruises paddlewheeler all close by. The campground features 135 large paved sites. RVs are welcome but there are no hookups. Reservations can be made through www.recreation.gov.

Lake Mead RV Village is within walking distance of Boulder Beach, and includes 115 sites (many pull-through sites), all with water, sewer, and electricity. There's also a recreation area with picnic tables, horseshoe pits, and a bocce ball court. (844) 311-5678, www.lakemeadmohaveadventures.com.

Programs/Events

Park rangers offer a variety of programs including talks, night-sky tours, and guided hikes.

Special Notes

Nevada is in the Pacific time zone. Arizona is in the mountain time zone and does not observe daylight saving time, except on the Navajo Nation.

Always wear a life jacket for any recreation activity in the water. Never use pool toys in the lake; winds can blow you far from shore. There are no lifeguards. Swim at your own risk.

Boaters should be aware that water levels change throughout the year. Approach the shore cautiously; watch for shallows and submerged debris. Never let a passenger ride on the bow. Wear a life jacket. Operating a boat while drinking alcohol is illegal.

Off-road driving is prohibited. Get the free Approved Backcountry Roads maps at the visitor center or on the park website.

The Aspen Trail offers views of deep-cut Tsegi Canyon. Courtesy of Mike Koopsen, Sedona.

Navajo National Monument

Overview

Three extremely well preserved 800-year-old cliff dwellings are protected among the sandstone mesas and canyons of the Navajo Nation.

Nearest Cities

Kayenta, Tuba City.

Established

March 20, 1909.

Size

360 acres.

The name is not misleading, but neither does it tell the whole story. The name gives you the location, not the history. Three ancient pueblos are tucked away in the rugged canyons of the Navajo National Monument. They are found on the Navajo Nation—but the Navajo people did not build them, nor live in them.

It was the ancestors of the Hopi, the Hisatsinom, who hunted game and farmed the canyon floors. They were the builders of large stone villages in the Tsegi Canyon system of the Shonto Plateau, occupied between AD 1250 and AD 1300. Archaeologists call them the Ancestral Puebloan people. The communities they built are Betatakin, set in the alcove of a magnificent sandstone arch, Keet Seel, the largest cliff dwelling in Arizona, and Inscription House, a smaller cliff dwelling named for wall markings etched there in historic times.

Canyon Cultures

The Zuni, also pueblo builders, know that several of their clans began in this area. While their home is now in New Mexico, they consider the Tsegi Canyon region in the monument an essential part of their traditions. Later, the San Juan Southern Paiute moved into this area and lived near Inscription House, hunting, gathering, and raising crops. They are famous for their basket-making skills. Today, the Navajo Nation land surrounds the monument. The Navajo, or Diné as they call themselves, moved into this area in the fifteenth century.

The Ancestral Puebloan culture probably emerged about 2,000 years ago, descended from nomadic hunters and gatherers who migrated with the seasons. Through trade they eventually acquired seeds of corn and other food crops. Agriculture allowed them to become more stationary. They lived first in underground pit houses. But then they left their most distinctive mark on the land by constructing multistoried stone masonry houses clustered in villages.

Betatakin, Keet Seel, and Inscription House were all built in large natural alcoves cut from the towering sandstone cliffs. This likely served several purposes. It preserved more farmland in the narrow canyon bottoms. Natural overhangs offered protection from the elements. Each of the alcoves faced south or southeast, offering shade in the summer while allowing the low slant of winter sun to provide some welcome warmth.

It also assured their remarkable condition more than 700 years later. Other structures nearby that were built in the open did not fare nearly so well, with little evidence of their existence remaining. But beneath the alcove, even perishable items such as roof beams and foodstuffs were protected.

Betatakin

Tucked inside a cavernous arch, Betatakin was completely sheltered by the overhanging canyon wall. Betatakin is a Navajo word that translates to "ledge house." With a nearby flowing stream, this really was an excellent spot for a village. Approximately 135 rooms were built in the alcove, filling virtually every bit of space, with some even spilling outside. Rooms were constructed of sandstone, mud mortar, and wood beams.

Yet while the village seemed to flourish, it was not for long. Inhabitants only lived here between 1250 and 1300. Today only about 80 rooms remain due to rock falls inside the alcove.

The only way to visit Betatakin is with ranger-led hikes that are generally offered Memorial Day through Labor Day. Hikes are scheduled on weekends, and occasional weekdays as staffing permits. A signup sheet is posted in the visitor center and all tours are first-come, first-served. Reservations are not required. Tours are limited to 20 people but seldom fill up. The tours are free.

These strenuous hikes (either a 3-mile round trip or 5-mile round trip, depending on which route is taken) climb into and out of a steep canyon on unpaved trails. They are not recommended for anyone with health issues. Tours generally last for 3 to 5 hours. Wear proper footwear, a hat, and sunscreen—and carry plenty of water and snacks. No water is available along the trail. Due to potential rockfalls, hikers will not enter the site but can view Betatakin from a safe distance.

Keet Seel

It looks like the village was only recently abandoned. That's the immediate impression of most visitors. Evidence of the people who lived here remains. Keet Seel is a rough translation of a Navajo name meaning "broken pottery scattered around." According to some archaeologists, Keet Seel is the best-preserved Ancestral Puebloan ruin ever discovered.

Two large pots, almost entirely intact, sit on top of a roof. Pieces of pottery, fragments of yucca-fiber rope, corncobs, and squash rinds are strewn about. Pictographs adorn the walls. Many rooms still retain their original roofs.

The big alcove had offered shelter to earlier groups of people as well. Tree-ring dating indicates that people settled here as early as AD 950. Construction on the large Keet Seel village began in 1250. It eventually grew into a town with as many as 150 people. Formal streets are rarely found in Ancestral Puebloan villages, but Keet Seel has three.

Yet by 1300, the village lay unoccupied. Some families sealed granaries full of corn before leaving, as if they expected to return.

To visit Keet Seel requires a strenuous 17-mile round trip hike over the course of two days. Led by park rangers, the hike takes place during the summer and is a group experience. Each hike is limited to 15 participants and slots are available on a first-come, first served basis. Sign up on the park website. Registration usually opens in March.

Expect a 1,000-foot climb down a cliff face and multiple stream crossings along the canyon floor, including the possibility of quicksand. Hikers must bring all needed food and water for the backcountry experience, and all trash and solid human waste must be packed out. The primitive campground has no facilities. Check the website for a complete list of everything you'll need to carry. For resource protection, no one will enter the Keet Seel village, remaining approximately 30 feet from the site.

Inscription House

The third village protected by the monument sits in a high, shallow alcove. Like Betatakin and Keet Seel, it was permanently occupied from about 1250 to 1300. Many of the rooms are constructed partly using a form of adobe bricks rather than the stone blocks that comprise the other two sites. It was named for wall markings left behind by Mormon settlers from the mid-1800s. Modern Indian tribes still hold ceremonies here.

Due to its fragile nature and unstable conditions, Inscription House is closed to the public, and has been since 1968.

A Spiritual Journey

In 1276, a 23-year drought settled over the Southwest, devastating the agricultural economies of the large Ancestral Puebloan villages. After years of faltering crops, they would have been compelled to abandon their towns and disperse across the land.

At least that's how archaeologists see it. The Hopi have a different version.

According to their oral tradition, the villages of Tsegi Canyon were abandoned as part of

Ranger-led tours to Betatakin cliff dwelling are available on summer weekends. Courtesy of Mike Koopsen, Sedona.

a spiritual quest. The Hopi believe their ancestors emerged into this, the Fourth World, and that they spent many years wandering. They would often stop and build communities but would always abandon them and continue with their migrations until all the clans came together to settle on the three fingers of Black Mesa in northeastern Arizona.

The Hisatsinom, ancestors of the Hopi, built the cliff dwellings contained within the monument. Many of the pictographs on the canyon walls have been identified as Hopi clan symbols. In the Hopi language, Talastima (Betatakin), Kawestima (Keet Seel), and Tsu'ovi (Inscription House) remain spiritual and physical links between past, present, and future. Hopi elders still make regular pilgrimages to visit the old villages.

When You Go

(928) 672-2700, www.nps.gov/nava.

Admission

Free.

Facilities

The visitor center has interpretive exhibits and a gift shop.

Pets

Pets are not allowed in buildings or on trails. Leashed pets are permitted in parking lots and campgrounds.

Hiking

While the ancient pueblos of Navajo National Monument are hidden away in the lower portion of the canyons, the landscape atop the rim is beautiful as well. There are three mesa-top trails that can be enjoyed by visitors.

SANDAL TRAIL

This 1.3 miles round trip hike crosses a rock ledge leading to an overlook with a cross-canyon view of Betatakin. This is the only point in the park where visitors can view the cliff dwelling other than on guided tours.

ASPEN TRAIL

A short (0.8 miles round trip) path branches off the Sandal Trail and drops steeply through the forest to view an ancient stand of aspen. Some stair climbing is required.

CANYON VIEW TRAIL

Another scenic walk, Canyon View (0.8 miles round trip) skirts the high rim of Betatakin Canyon, offering big vistas, and finally leads to a historic ranger station.

Camping

Two campgrounds are available in the monument. Both are free and offer sites on a first-come, first-served basis. Dry camping only. Neither campground offers RV dumpsites or hookups. Vehicle length is limited to 28 feet total.

Sunset View, near the visitor center, is open year-round, contains 31 sites, and offers potable water. Canyon View, on a narrow unpaved road, has 14 sites and is only open during summer months. Please enjoy this campground for its silence and spectacular night skies.

Programs/Events

Lectures, presentations, educational programs, and star parties are offered as staffing permits.

Special Notes

The Navajo Nation observes daylight saving time, while the rest of Arizona and the Hopi Reservation do not. Be alert and safety conscious. This is an area with cliffs and canyons and steep drop-offs. Falling rocks, lightning, and flash floods are just some of the hazards. Navajo Nation law prohibits alcohol on the reservation.

If you do take a guided tour to the cliff dwellings, do not remove any artifacts. Never enter a dwelling, or leave the tour group.

The first version of the Old Spanish Trail followed an earlier route forged by Franciscan missionaries Dominguez and Escalante, skirting the Vermilion Cliffs on the way to Pipe Spring. Photo by the author.

Old Spanish National Historic Trail

Overview

This trade route linked Santa Fe, New Mexico, with Los Angeles, California, from 1829 through 1848. It was known as "the longest, crookedest, most arduous pack mule route in the history of America."

Nearest Cities

Kayenta, Page, Fredonia, Colorado City.

Established

December 4, 2002.

Size

2,680 miles (approximately 200 miles in Arizona).

The name Old Spanish Trail is a bit misleading, because it's not really a trail and Spain never could make it work. The idea was to connect two frontiers of the extensive Spanish empire, the growing trade center of Santa Fe with the southern California coast. But attempts at establishing an overland trade route were thwarted by unforgiving terrain and harsh weather.

It wasn't until eight years after Mexico gained independence from Spain, that the first successful journey was completed. In November 1829, Antonio Armijo, a merchant from Santa Fe, set out with 60 men and a large caravan of pack mules loaded with blankets, rugs, serapes, and other goods. They left from Abiquiú, New Mexico.

The 1,200-mile journey traversed the Colorado Plateau and crossed the Mojave Desert. They forded rivers, climbed mountain passes, and navigated a trackless expanse. They did without water and had to eat a few of their mules. After 86 days they arrived at the San Gabriel Mission and traded their textiles for California-bred horses and mules. The return trip to Santa Fe took only about half the time, and they sold the animals for a healthy profit. Armijo was 25 years old. The way west was now open.

The Armijo Route

The Armijo Expedition crossed Arizona. The young trader pieced together segments of trails developed by American Indians, trappers, explorers, and missionaries as he blazed his own way. He took the shortest and most direct route, cutting a slice through the hardscrabble land that today is known as the Arizona Strip.

The Armijo Route cuts a pretty straight line westward from Abiquiú, crossing the San Juan River and entering Arizona near Four Corners. The traders passed north of the Carrizo Mountains to Church Rock, east of present-day Kayenta and on through Marsh Pass. It's believed they traversed Tsegi Canyon, now part of Navajo National Monument. From there they angled northwest and forded the Colorado River at the Crossing of the Fathers, above present-day Glen Canyon Dam. The expedition continued, pushing west to Pipe Spring and on to the Virgin River, slicing through the northwest corner of Arizona before continuing on to the artesian springs of Las Vegas. Then they crossed the Mojave Desert to Cajon Pass and dropped into the Los Angeles Basin.

But once was enough. The brutality of that journey prompted future expeditions to travel hundreds of miles out of their way by arching through Colorado and central Utah where rivers and streams and green pastures were more common.

Over the next two decades, traders led caravans along variations of the route pioneered by Armijo, creating a network of parallel and intertwined trails. This collection of routes spanning six states—New Mexico, Colorado, Utah, Arizona, Nevada, and California—is known today as the Old Spanish Trail.

The Fathers

The only way the Armijo Route could work was if a way across the Colorado River could be found in the rugged canyon country of Arizona. That key piece of information had been uncovered 50 years before by two Franciscan priests in an early Spanish effort to find a route from Santa Fe to the newly established missions in Monterey.

Fathers Atanasio Dominguez and Silvestre Vélez de Escalante set out with a small group of men in July 1776, heading north through Colorado and into Utah. They were the first Europeans to travel through much of the region. Aided by Utes acting as guides, the padres made it to western Utah before encountering an October blizzard. Fearing the onset of an early winter and with supplies running low, the party decided to return to Santa Fe.

Turning south into Arizona and now without a guide, they struggled to navigate the deep gorges of the Colorado River. They finally located a spot, east of the intimidating Grand Canyon. They carved steps into the stone to help the livestock make the treacherous descent to the river. This would become known as the "Crossing of the Fathers." Today, this ford is submerged beneath the waters of Lake Powell.

Although the Dominguez-Escalante Expedition did not fulfill their quest, their maps and journals would prove invaluable. Their journey became an early template for the Old Spanish Trail, and their return to Santa Fe, though fraught with hardship and peril, formed the backbone of the Armijo Route.

End of the Trail

For 20 years after Armijo's successful venture, caravans left Santa Fe in late summer or fall and returned in the spring with fresh grass providing forage for the animals. The Mexican-American War forever changed the geopolitical landscape. With the victory, the United States took control of the Southwest in 1848. Use of the Old Spanish Trail sharply declined as easier and safer routes opened to carry troops, gold-rush miners, emigrants, and others into the West.

The Old Spanish Trail faded not just from use but also from history. Interest in the trail's significance began to revive in the 1920s with the publication of a few scholarly works. In 1954, historians LeRoy and Ann Hafen published some eye-opening articles and a comprehensive book on the topic. They called the Old Spanish Trail "the longest, crookedest, most arduous pack mule route in the history of America," inspiring even more research.

Today, you'll find no old wagon tracks marking the Old Spanish Trail. It was always a pack route. In fact, it's difficult to find any trace of the trail in the modern landscape, especially in Arizona. Various states and associations have marked portions of the trail, but Arizona seems to be lagging in this effort. Even though Antonio Armijo laid the foundation of the Old Spanish Trail with the first trek across Arizona, all later expeditions created, and then traveled, the northern branches.

There are a couple of historic markers commemorating the Dominguez-Escalante Expedition that paved the way for the Old Spanish Trail. One of my favorites can be found at the edge of the Vermilion Cliffs, near milepost 557 off US 89A. Sitting on the broad sagebrush plains, there's a pullout with parking, a simple stone marker, and signage with information and maps showing the routes of the Dominguez-Escalante Expedition, the Old Spanish Trail, and the Honeymoon Trail used by Mormons in the late 1800s traveling to the new temple in St. George, Utah, to be married. In a harsh and arid land, trails often overlapped because they relied on the same waterholes.

In 2002, Congress passed the Old Spanish Trail Recognition Act, and today it is known as the Old Spanish National Historic Trail. It became America's 15th National Historic Trail.

When You Go

BLM: (435) 688-3200, www.blm.gov/office/arizona-strip-district-office.
NPS: www.nps.gov/olsp.

Admission

Free.

Facilities

None. Passport stamp locations for the Old Spanish Trail are Navajo National Monument, Glen Canyon National Recreation Area, Powell Museum in Page, the Red Pueblo Museum and Heritage Park in Fredonia, and Pipe Spring National Monument.

Pets

It will vary from location to location.

Hiking

Since only the original Armijo Route of the Old Spanish Trail cuts through Arizona, and much of that crosses the Navajo Nation, hiking options are limited.

Hiking trails are available at Navajo National Monument and Pipe Spring National Monument.

Camping

Camping is available at Navajo National Monument and at Paiute RV Park and Campground adjacent to Pipe Spring National Monument.

Programs/Events

None.

Special Notes

Vehicles must remain on existing roads and hikers should stay on designated trails. Please respect all private boundaries.

The Navajo Nation observes daylight saving time, while the rest of Arizona does not.

A short loop trail curls through the colorful moonscape of Blue Mesa. Courtesy of Mike Koopsen, Sedona.

Petrified Forest National Park

Overview

The world's largest collection of petrified wood lies scattered across rolling plains and tucked in the folds of brilliantly colored badlands where giant reptiles and early dinosaurs once roamed.

Nearest City

Holbrook.

Established

Petrified Forest was designated a national monument on December 8, 1906. It was one of the first four national monuments in America. Petrified Forest became a national park on December 9, 1962.

Size

221,390 acres.

Petrified Forest always reminds me of the suburbs of the moon.

This vast beautiful thin-grass prairie stretches for mile upon uninterrupted mile until it suddenly breaks apart against a cluster of inhospitable badlands, a virtual lunar landscape, except one drenched in vibrant hues. Layers of siltstone, mudstone, and shale are stacked in weird configurations and banded with color—a shocking palette of pastels. The rumpled, crumpled hills appear more gnawed than eroded.

It throws you for a loop coming out of the empty grasslands like it does. When you enter the park from the north, you swoop through a corner of the Painted Desert. From overlooks, gazing across the naked layer cake of clay, it feels like you've landed someplace strange and distant.

The magnificent desolation intrigues me. I like to wander out into the Painted Desert, find a comfortable spot, and eat a sandwich. I'm not sure why. I did it once and it became a weird tradition. In preparation, I left home with a sandwich, but it didn't survive the journey. To be honest, I was barely out of sight of my house when my sandwich mysteriously vanished. I need a cooler with a time lock.

Fortunately, I was able to sandwich up at the visitor center—a premade salami, pepperoni, and provolone number that really hit the spot. I hiked cross-country into the soft labyrinth of hills colored like hearts, bruises, and bones. I sat here on the bright side of the moon and savored my sandwich. When it comes to otherworldly picnic spots, Arizona is tough to beat.

It doesn't matter whether you come for the scenery, the epic sky, the haunting quiet, the surprising colors of the fossil fields, or the mind-boggling span of history, you'll find it all at Petrified Forest.

Welcome to Triassic World

A single 28-mile scenic road winds through Petrified Forest National Park north-to-south, carving out a visitor-friendly experience filled with photogenic pullouts, exhibits, archaeological sites, and short hiking trails.

The Puerco River divides the park into two distinct sections. North of the river, broad tilted plains crash against the edge of a steep cliff overlooking the colorful badlands. South of the Puerco is where visitors will find the largest concentration of petrified wood, which happens to be Arizona's official state fossil. Jasper Forest, Crystal Forest, and Rainbow Forest mark significant collections.

Hard to imagine while traveling this wind-scoured terrain, but 200 million years ago this was a tropical jungle filled with rivers and streams. Freshwater sharks swam here. Crocodile-like reptiles, giant carnivorous amphibians, and small dinosaurs prowled the lush landscape in the late Triassic Period. In 1985, paleontologists discovered the fossil of a previously unknown small carnivore, Chindesaurus bryansmalli. It was nicknamed "Gertie" and later determined to be one of the very first dinosaurs.

The massive trees of the jungle eventually died and toppled into swamps where they were buried beneath volcanic ash. Slowly the woody tissue was replaced by dissolved silica and other minerals. The minerals added a kaleidoscope pattern of colors and preserved minute details of the wood. Now these ancient trees—trees that once offered shade to dinosaurs—lie tumbled amid the hills and desert grasslands of the park.

Believed to shelter the largest concentration of petrified wood on the planet, Petrified Forest delivers scenic and scientific wonders in equal measures. The fossils of the plants and animals unearthed tell the story of a time when the world was young.

In the North

Visitor centers anchor both ends of the park road. The Painted Desert Visitor Center in the north is the largest. Here you'll find information, books, gifts, and food. A short film provides the lowdown on the petrification process and opens your eyes as to just what a remarkable assortment of fossils are still being dug up in the park.

Guests also have a chance to chat with a paleontologist on certain days. Behind the visitor center, the Museum Demonstration Lab is the scientific equivalent of an open-kitchen restaurant. You get to peer through big windows overlooking the workstation where fossils are cleaned and studied and ask questions of the resident brainiac. Ask where they're cloning the velociraptors, I'm sure they'll get a kick out of that.

Multiple overlooks of the badlands dot the rim of the plateau and are connected by short trails. The Painted Desert Inn also perches here. What started out as a trading post built in the 1920s was taken over by the Fred Harvey Company in the 1940s. Built in the Pueblo Revival style, the stylish inn, now a National Historic Landmark, was restored and turned into a museum with exhibits, gifts, and views from its high roost overlooking the Painted Desert. Downstairs they serve up big scoops of ice cream, a nice bonus after I come hiking out of the badlands below with my sandwich nothing but a faint memory.

Petrified Forest is the only national park that includes and protects a section of historic Route 66. They've got a poignant memorial established, just a few hundred yards north of I-40, which replaced the old highway. There's some commemorative signage and a rusted 1932 Studebaker marking the spot where Route 66 once carried travelers across such a haunting expanse. A string of weathered telephone poles traces the old alignment, a silent reminder of what once existed as cars and semis hurtle past on the interstate.

In the South

After passing over I-40 (no access to the interstate), you'll cross the bridge spanning the Puerco River. Of course, a water source in the high desert attracted human habitation. A paved 0.3 mile loop trail circles past the remnants of Puerco Pueblo, an Ancestral Puebloan village occupied between AD 1250 and AD 1380. Nearby boulders are adorned with petroglyphs.

For the largest collection of rock art found in the park, stop at Newspaper Rock. Spotting scopes are set up at an overlook above a grouping of boulders. Hundreds of petroglyphs are etched into the stone faces, some dating back 2,000 years.

Blue Mesa should not be missed. The roadside formations known as the Teepees give hints of what's to come. Named for their conical shape, the Teepees are banded with grays, blues, and purples. Soon afterward is the turnoff to Blue Mesa. A 3.5-mile loop road leads through an astonishing collection of bluish badlands, log falls, and pedestal logs. A 1-mile loop trail curls through the heart of the hills formed of bentonite clay, laced with minerals.

The overlook at Agate Bridge highlights a 110-foot-long petrified log bridge. Jasper Forest offers a panoramic peek at an area with a high concentration of petrified wood. At Crystal Forest you can hike a 0.75-mile paved loop through some softly carved hills and many intact petrified logs.

Near the southern end of the park sits a complex of buildings and trails. The Rainbow Forest Museum and Visitor Center is a stone building housing books, exhibits, and monster skeletons. Here's where visitors get a glimpse of some of the giant reptiles and early

Petrified wood is Arizona's official state fossil. Courtesy of Mike Koopsen, Sedona.

dinosaurs that once prowled this humid swamp. It's an impressive display. Kids will love it—if they can elbow their way around me to actually see anything.

Walk out the back door and onto the short Giant Logs Trail. Although there are some steps, this short (0.4 miles) paved loop is easy to manage as it weaves through an assortment of the largest logs in the park, including "Old Faithful," 35 feet long and weighing 44 tons.

Across the parking lot, a large gift shop offers cold drinks and snacks. The Long Logs and Agate House trails lead to another impressive collection of petrified wood and a small pueblo dating back 700 years, which feels like the blink of an eye here in dinosaur country.

Set in Stone

The park is a dream scenario for those with limited time or mobility issues. All the highlights I've listed above can be seen from roadside overlooks and short paths, meaning the park can be enjoyed as just a scenic drive if that's all you have time for. I've done that plenty, pulling off I-40 for a quick detour just to immerse myself in this quiet backcountry.

Yet a small taste only whets my appetite for more. I don't want to say that Petrified Forest is the most soothing, relaxing place in Arizona but then again, maybe I do. The vastness of the landscape always startles me—an endless prairie broken by clusters of clay hills seamed with color. There's something hypnotic about it. An immense sky, this wild canopy of blue, drapes over it all. Without a nearby horizon to hold on to, it feels like I am unmoored and free-floating.

Stress just seems to melt away in the face of such expanse and eerie quiet. You experience that sensation in small doses from roadside stops. But it really takes hold when you walk away from the highway.

Designated trails in Petrified Forest are short but spectacular. Additionally, the park offers several Off the Beaten Path routes posted on the website, steering visitors to backcountry adventures. Some are quick and relatively easy. Others are more complicated treks requiring navigational skills. These are not trails—you're just making your way across open terrain.

There's also 50,000 acres of wilderness spread among the rolling badlands of the Painted Desert at the far northern end of the park. Day hikers can explore at their leisure. What's less well known is that permits for overnight backpacking are also offered. Permits are free and available from both visitor centers on the day you want to backpack. No other camping is available in the park.

When You Go

(928) 524-6228, www.nps.gov/pefo.

Admission

Admission fee is good for seven days.

Facilities

The Painted Desert Visitor Center is at the northern entrance to the park and includes interpretive exhibits, a video presentation, and a gift shop. Also in the complex you'll find a restaurant, gas station, travel store, and post office.

Rainbow Forest Museum and Visitor Center anchors the southern end of the park. It includes a gift shop, snack bar, and museum.

Pets

Pets must be kept on a leash and are permitted on any paved road or trail, as well as all designated wilderness areas in the park. Pets are not allowed in buildings.

Hiking

TAWA TRAIL

From the Painted Desert Visitor Center, the easy path (1.2 miles one-way) winds through the grasslands to Tawa Point, overlooking the Painted Desert.

PAINTED DESERT RIM TRAIL

A short half-mile trail that traces the edge of the plateau above a sea of badlands connects Tawa Point and Kachina Point, where you'll find the historic Painted Desert Inn.

PUERCO PUEBLO

A paved 0.3-mile loop visits a partially stabilized village of Ancestral Puebloan people dating back almost 700 years. Wayside exhibits and petroglyphs can be viewed from the trail.

BLUE MESA TRAIL

This 1-mile loop makes a sharp descent to the valley floor to wander up close among a striking arrangement of bluish bentonite clay badlands sprinkled with a colorful collection of petrified wood.

CRYSTAL FOREST TRAIL

Paved, easy, and lovely, this short (0.75 miles) loop crosses hills adorned with an impressive display of petrified logs.

GIANT LOGS TRAIL

Walk through the back door of the Rainbow Forest Museum into a toppled stone jungle. The trail is a 0.4-mile loop but there are some stairs. Look for "Old Faithful" at the top of the hill, almost 10 feet wide at the base.

LONG LOGS TRAIL

Starting in the Rainbow Forest Museum parking area, Long Logs makes a 1.6-mile loop through a large concentration of petrified wood, even an ancient logjam at the base of gray badlands. The first half-mile is paved.

AGATE HOUSE TRAIL

Also beginning at Rainbow Forest, this 2-mile loop leads to a small pueblo occupied about 700 years ago. The first half-mile is paved. Long Logs and Agate House Trails can be combined for a total 2.6-mile loop.

Stay on designated trails while in developed hiking areas. Bicycles are not permitted on trails, only on paved roads.

Off the Beaten Path routes are posted on the website, and maps are available in the visitor centers. These are off-trail backcountry adventures across the open landscape. They range from short and easy to more difficult.

Camping

There are no established campgrounds in the park. Overnight hiking/camping in the wilderness area requires a free permit, obtained at Painted Desert Visitor Center or Rainbow Forest Museum and Visitor Center.

Programs/Events

Ranger talks, guided walks, cultural demonstrations, and other programs are offered throughout the year.

Special Notes

Please leave all petrified wood for others to enjoy. Theft is always a serious issue for the park. Report any removal of petrified wood or other materials. Petrified wood collected from private lands is for sale at shops in and outside the park.

Do not climb on petrified logs. Do not climb on the walls of any archaeological site. Federal law prohibits collecting petrified wood, fossils, plants, animals, and archaeological objects.

The old Mormon fort known as Winsor Castle anchors the historic buildings of Pipe Spring National Monument. Courtesy of Mike Koopsen, Sedona.

Pipe Spring National Monument

Overview

A source of life-giving water amid the vastness of the Arizona Strip once sustained Ancestral Puebloans, the Kaibab Paiutes, and the Mormon pioneers who constructed the fort that still occupies the site.

Nearest City

Fredonia.

Established

May 31, 1923.

Size

40 acres.

Anyone who roots for the little guy has to love Pipe Spring. This lightly visited national monument, located 15 miles west of Fredonia on State Route 389, is about the most remote location in Arizona that can be reached via paved road. I discovered that early on, as I mentioned in the introduction, and have loved making the long scenic journey ever since.

Pipe Spring is a 40-acre speck amid the vastness of the Arizona Strip, the nearly 8,000 square miles of the state cut off by the Grand Canyon. The Strip is near the bottom of the geologic formation known as the Grand Staircase. In this neighborhood, nearby parks are epic/massive/legendary. Besides one of the Seven Natural Wonders of the World, there's Vermilion Cliffs and Grand Canyon–Parashant. Just across the border in Utah is Zion National Park, and Bryce Canyon National Park is close by.

Pipe Spring offers a chance to reset from all the grandeur, to pause and savor the details. Tucked away in a sprawling wilderness, there is a spring, an orchard, and a garden.

Stephen Mather, the first director of the National Park Service, originally envisioned Pipe Spring as a stopover for early travelers exploring western parks, a place to picnic, stretch their legs, and fill their radiators. Yet the more Mather learned about the multilayered history of the Pipe Spring, the more enamored he grew. When the time came, he even used his own money to acquire the land and dilapidated buildings. He understood that this place needed to be saved, that this story needed to be told.

Long Way from Anywhere

Across the rolling plains of the Arizona Strip, life revolves around water. The water of Pipe Spring has long been a cherished and sacred commodity. As early as 300 BC, the Ancestral Puebloans lived and farmed here. They were followed by the Kaibab Paiutes, who adapted to the harsh environment by living in small nomadic groups, moving seasonally to hunt game while also gathering grass seeds, pinion nuts, roots, and cactus fruit. Not surprising as they lived among a virtual sea of grasslands, the Paiutes were known for their exquisite basketry.

In 1776, a weary band of Spanish explorers stumbled through the region. If not for the kindness of the Paiute tribes, the Dominguez-Escalante Expedition would have been lost to history. The Paiutes fed the starving missionaries and told them of a route that skirted a little obstacle that would come to be known as Grand Canyon. Dominguez, Escalante, and their men survived and made it back to Santa Fe. They had failed in their quest to blaze an overland route to California, but their notes and maps would pave the way for others.

Trader Antonio Armijo forged a route in 1829–1830 from New Mexico to Los Angeles with a stop at Pipe Spring. His would be the first commercial caravan to complete the journey. This expedition, and other ones that followed, would form a network of routes that evolved into the Old Spanish Trail.

Utah Gets Grabby

Mormon missionary Jacob Hamblin stopped at the spring in 1858. Other Mormon ranchers began settling and running livestock on this vast tract of land. It was James Whitmore who first claimed Pipe Spring. He traveled to St. George, Utah, and filed for a land certificate giving him title to 160 acres surrounding the source of the water. Officials granted the request in April 1863, which was quite generous considering that Pipe Spring lay in Arizona, 8 miles south of the Utah line.

Amid such isolated frontier, boundaries were mostly theoretical. It wasn't until John Wesley Powell and his intrepid team of federal surveyors came through during 1872–1873, climbing the high hogbacks of the Vermilion Cliffs to triangulate positions, was it learned that Pipe Spring was actually part of the Arizona Territory.

As Mormons pushed herds of cattle onto the grasslands, it devastated a way of life for the Paiutes. Adding to the conflict, small bands of Navajos were raiding livestock across the Arizona Strip in 1864. These were among the few Navajos that evaded forced relocation to Bosque Redondo in New Mexico. They had lost everything in the scorched-earth campaign waged by the US Army, and began stealing livestock for food and trade. In 1866, Whitmore and his herdsman were killed while trying to recover stolen cattle. The Mormon militia retaliated, slaughtering a band of Paiutes that likely had no involvement in the incident.

A Castle Rises

In 1870, construction began on a fort atop the main spring. Plans called for two sandstone buildings facing a courtyard that would be enclosed by sturdy wooden gates. Gun ports provided additional security. The fort soon became known as "Winsor Castle" after Anson Winsor, the ranch manager. It was never attacked, even though the building cut off the Kaibab Paiutes from a sacred water source used by them and their ancestors.

Even before the fort was completed, a telegraph was installed, serving as one of the stations of the Deseret Telegraph Company. This subsidiary line consisted of hundreds of miles of spindly juniper poles capped with glass insulators. It connected remote Utah outposts to the transcontinental line that passed through Salt Lake City. Suddenly, the region was a bit less isolated. This was the first telegraph in Arizona, once the actual location of Pipe Spring was determined. Most operators at Winsor Castle tapping out messages were young women.

From 1871 to 1876 the ranch served as a beef and dairy operation. Every day dozens of cows were milked, producing cheese and butter, a distinctive luxury for such a rural location. The lower floor of the castle's south wing was set up as a creamery with butter churns, cheese presses, and vats. Water from the spring flowed through a cement trough, cooling the rooms. Every two weeks a wagonload of dairy products was driven to St. George to help feed workers building the temple there.

Once the temple was completed, Pipe Spring proved instrumental in supplying other raw material—brides and grooms. In the 1870s, Mormon settlers moved to the Little Colorado River in eastern Arizona, establishing new communities. To get married, couples traveled back to St. George by wagon over a long rugged road that became known as the Honeymoon Trail.

The trail began from the Little Colorado near present-day Cameron and headed north following water. It passed Echo Cliffs and Bitter Springs, crossing the mighty Colorado River at Lees Ferry. After skirting the Vermilion Cliffs and traversing the Kaibab Plateau, couples stopped for water, food, and rest at Pipe Spring before continuing on their journey.

In later years, some of those same brides returned. Pipe Spring became a refuge for wives hiding from federal marshals enforcing stricter anti-polygamy laws. Faced with confiscation of church property under the new laws, the Mormon church sold Pipe Spring ranch in 1895.

The Kaibab Paiutes continued to struggle. New settlements displaced them from their traditional lands. Overgrazing livestock decimated their food supply. Finally, in 1907 the Kaibab Indian Reservation was created, returning a small portion of lands to the people who called it home for centuries. Pipe Spring remained a private ranch, surrounded by the reservation.

The small size of Pipe Spring National Monument belies the significant role it played in the history of the Arizona Strip. Courtesy of Mike Koopsen, Sedona.

Water Still Flows

Pipe Spring National Monument offers a vivid and unblinking look at American Indian and pioneer life on this lonely prairie. Start with the excellent museum housed in the joint Tribal–National Park Service visitor center. A short film plays in the theater that presents a comprehensive overview of the area's rich history, told from the perspective of Mormon ancestors, historians, and Paiute tribal members.

As soon as you exit the visitor center, you walk into the high-desert frontier. Native grasses are being restored on a section out back. Nearby is a re-created Paiute seasonal camp. Follow the paved path that crosses the grounds. A thin orchard provides a smattering of shade. A screen of trees line spring-fed ponds that were first dug in the 1870s. Just beyond stands Winsor Castle and a handful of stone buildings at the base of a rocky hill.

It is a surprising little oasis that always puts a smile on my face, this far-flung huddle of trees and buildings. Cross a small wooden bridge for a closer look at the big shaggy garden that includes several indigenous crops. Horses and longhorn cattle graze in the corrals, and wildflowers spill across the grounds. A couple of wagons are parked on the hardpack, as if visitors only just arrived at the castle.

Step inside the walled compound where a ranger waits to answer questions and point out some intriguing details. Rooms in both buildings look very much like they would have more than a century ago. Step into the cellar chilled by the spring's flow. Here in the cool darkness, in the middle of nowhere, cheese was made a long time ago.

Take time to explore the other cabins with their exhibits on cowboying, the early telegraph, and historic preservation. Then hike the short Ridge Trail up the hillside for the kind of broad vistas that put the whole story of the Arizona Strip into focus.

Just as Stephen Mather originally intended, Pipe Spring still makes a pleasant stop along a lonely highway. Just don't be surprised if you plan a quick rest break and end up spending most of the day at this fascinating little oasis. It may even inspire you to seek out other little underdog parks just like it did me. To Pipe Spring, I owe a big debt of gratitude.

When You Go

(928) 643-7105, www.nps.gov/pisp.

Admission

There is an admission fee.

Facilities

The visitor center has museum exhibits, video presentation, and a gift shop.

Pets

Dogs on a leash are permitted in the park but not allowed in the historic buildings or on the Ridge Trail.

Hiking

RIDGE TRAIL

A half-mile loop, climbs a rocky slope behind Winsor Castle. Interpretive signage presents more of the Pipe Spring story as you hike. From the mesa top you'll have an excellent overview of the ranch below, as well as dramatic panoramas of the Arizona Strip, Mount Trumbull, and the Kaibab Plateau.

Camping

The park is day-use only.

The Paiute RV Park and Campground ((928) 643-6601)—with full hookups, tent camping, showers, and laundry—sits adjacent to the monument and is connected by a short walking path.

Programs/Events

Open-house-style tours of Winsor Castle are offered most days. Guided tours are conducted occasionally. Ranger talks, cultural demonstrations, and guided hikes are offered seasonally.

Special Notes

The park's livestock are not tame; keep a safe distance.

The colorful rim of the volcanic cone prompted the name Sunset Crater. Courtesy of Mike Koopsen, Sedona.

Sunset Crater Volcano National Monument

Overview

Protecting Arizona's youngest volcano, this pine forest conceals the haunting desolation of old lava flows that have transformed into twisted rock, porous black cliffs, spatter cones, and other intriguing formations that defy description.

Nearest City

Flagstaff.

Established

May 26, 1930.

Size

3,137 acres.

So much of Arizona is shaped by geological forces that are ponderous and complicated. But a volcano is easy to grasp. It's fast and dirty. The earth goes boom and then rains fire. That's apocalyptic kind of stuff. The big adios. End times. Yet all this bleak drama can be found in a pine forest filled with birdsong, where stunted aspen trees fight for footholds, and flowers poke through gnarled slabs of basalt.

Sunset Crater has always been a frequent stop on my travels. It's a quiet peaceful getaway that just happened to be born of unimaginable violence. There are hiking trails, picnic areas, viewpoints, and ranger programs to enjoy. And it's all set amid a ragged, jagged forlorn landscape.

Starkly Serene

I love the dynamic terrain of Sunset Crater, so dark and mysterious. I'm drawn to places that bend our perception of reality—places that teach us new ways to interpret beauty. So I took it especially hard when I heard that flames consumed the national monument in the spring of 2022.

That's when the Tunnel Fire exploded. On April 19, the wind-driven blaze roared toward the park, requiring immediate evacuation. Rangers fanned out, searching for visitors. They ran down trails, and checked every side road and parking area with precious few minutes to worry about any of their own on-site residences and personal possessions. They led everyone north, a caravan of frightened people through the high desert dotted with junipers into Wupatki National Monument.

It was a historical déjà vu moment. Folks fleeing fire and ending up at Wupatki is very much the story of Sunset Crater, which erupted around 1085. Although that exodus was less frantic since a few weeks of earthquakes likely preceded the eruption, giving the Sinagua people time to realize that the neighborhood was about to undergo some drastic changes.

Curtain of Fire

Part of the broad San Francisco volcanic field, Sunset Crater is the youngest lava-geyser of the bunch. The field contains more than 600 volcanoes, including the San Francisco Peaks, a hulking stratovolcano that once rose to a towering height of 16,000 feet before blasting itself apart. The first eruptions began 6 million years ago, with Sunset Crater being the most recent.

When Sunset Crater erupted, it sprayed lava 850 feet into the air through a long fissure, an event called a "curtain of fire." The curtain cooled and rained down in a barrage of lava bombs and smaller rocks known as cinders. The cinders piled up around the volcano's vent, forming the 1,000-feet-high cone-shaped mound. A final blast deposited red and yellow oxidized cinders onto the rim that seems to forever glow with the rays of a setting sun. The fiery hues led to the volcano's name. The entire event may have lasted a few months or a few years.

Such cataclysmic activity forced the Sinagua people living nearby to abandon their settlements. Before their pit houses were submerged beneath a flaming river of lava, many migrated north relocating to what today is known as Wupatki. A period of increased rainfall followed the eruptions, and the layer of volcanic ash added nutrients to the soil. It helped the ground absorb moisture and prevented evaporation. Crops could be grown where they couldn't before, and the adaptable Sinagua took full advantage.

Starting Over

The eruption turned the immediate vicinity of Sunset Crater into an ash-covered wasteland. Decades passed before vegetation sprang up. The rebirth was led by tiny lichens that latch onto rocks. The lichen secretes a weak acid that slowly converts rocks to soil, giving other plants a chance to take root. It is a slow process and a challenging one in a land of scant precipitation. Many of the trees remain stunted by lack of water, twisted by strong winds. The vibrant red flowers of the Sunset Crater penstemon, a rare splash of color amid the somber lava flows, evolved new traits allowing it to live in cinder soils while also trapping it in this rarefied habitat. It has become an endemic species and cannot survive elsewhere.

Growing plants brought animals back to the landscape. Birds of the monument include Steller's jays, pinion jays, black-chinned hummingbirds, white-breasted nuthatches, ravens, hawks, and occasionally golden eagles. Mammals such as mule deer, elk, pronghorn, bobcats, coyotes, Abert's squirrels, cottontails, and porcupines find habitat in the surrounding pine forests.

A few species of lizards scurry about on the lava flows, but you might not notice them. They are dark in color to blend in with the terrain. Lighter-colored lizards, easier to spot, have mostly been weeded out of the gene pool long ago by hungry predators.

A Resilient Landscape

In 1928, a movie company proposed dynamiting the slopes of Sunset Crater Volcano so they could film the ensuing landslide. Citizens of Flagstaff rallied to prevent such wanton destruction and then continued their lobbying efforts to gain more permanent protection. In 1930 President Hoover established Sunset Crater National Monument. (The name was changed to Sunset Crater Volcano National Monument in 1990.) The Civilian Conservation Corps left their distinctive mark on the new monument by building roads and some visitor facilities during the Great Depression.

Devastation-wise, it remained pretty quiet at Sunset Crater for almost 1,000 years. Right up until April 2022. The Tunnel Fire entered the park in late afternoon and in a matter of hours had burned through the entire national monument. About 60 percent of the monument was scorched. Maintenance equipment was destroyed and guardrails were melted.

Yet there was good news as well. Much of the fire consisted of low burn severity and was beneficial in removing ground debris. The fire went through Bonito Meadow near the entrance to the monument. Yet later that summer the bowl-shaped meadow was blanketed with wildflowers. Most importantly, the visitor center was spared, as were staff residences. All the culturally significant items were safely removed before the fire. As soon as they were able, staff began the cleanup and repair work required to get the park back on its feet.

Sunset Crater Volcano National Monument reopened a few months later. I visited as soon as they did, braced for the worst but was pleasantly surprised. The damage was not nearly as pronounced as I had expected. The Tunnel Fire moved so fast it burned in a mosaic pattern, scorching swaths of ponderosa pines while barely singeing others, and leaving behind big patches of green. The scars of the Tunnel Fire are visible. Yet they seem to blend in easily with the eruption scars the terrain has worn for centuries. This is a land that was swimming in lava less than a millennium ago. Fire is nothing new.

What to Expect

Sunset Crater Volcano and Wupatki National Monument are connected by a 35-mile loop road that intersects US 89 at mile marker 430 at the southern entrance (Sunset Crater) and 444 on the northern end (Wupatki). These parks, along with Walnut Canyon National Monument, are managed collectively as Flagstaff Area National Monuments. Together, these three sites protect more than 40,000 acres and 3,000 archaeological sites, in a landscape of high deserts, canyons, mountains, mesas, and volcanoes.

The stories of the Flagstaff Area National Monuments are inextricably linked—the journey of the Sinagua people set in motion by a cataclysmic event less than 1,000 years ago.

The volcano rimmed with sunset hues rises above midnight lands, black, black, and blacker still. Rocks are twisted and curled in unexpected ways. Among the cinder hills are a scorched crust of dunes and tortured lava flows. The park contains a few short hiking options, although climbing to the summit of Sunset Crater isn't one of them. Park officials closed the route to the top in 1973 because of deep ruts that that hikers carved in the loose surface.

But if you're itching to scale a volcano, scramble up the crunchy cinder slope of the Lenox Crater Trail. As for me, I like hiking the Lava Flow Trail. It's only a mile-long loop but it cuts through the dark heart of the Bonito Lava Flow. Jagged, twisted lava slabs are mingled with strange volcanic accessories like spatter cones, squeeze-ups, and ice caves.

Sunset Crater Volcano National Monument remains resilient, eerie, and starkly beautiful. This is a land that swallowed the sun and then spat it back out. It wears its scars with a jaunty pride and will continue to be one of my favorite stops when I yearn to have my sense of reality upended.

When You Go

(928) 526-0502, www.nps.gov/sucr.

Admission

Admission fee grants entry to both Sunset Crater and Wupatki.

Facilities

The visitor center has museum exhibits and a gift shop.

Pets

Pets are not allowed in buildings or on trails with the exception of the paved portion of Lava Flow Trail. Leashed pets are permitted on the US Forest Service lands surrounding the monument.

Hiking

LAVA'S EDGE TRAIL

Sample the hard and the soft of the monument as this trail meanders through a ponderosa pine forest along the jagged fringe of the Bonito Lava Flow. When lava broke out from the base of the volcano it formed the Bonito Flow, now a frozen river of black shrapnel. You'll encounter loose cinders, rough basalt, and lovely vistas along this 3.4-mile round trip hike.

A'A TRAIL

The monument's shortest trail (0.2-mile loop) delivers big drama including rough basaltic lava known as a'a that formed as the Bonito Lava Flow cooled more than 900 years ago.

Old lava fields are still evident on the flanks of Sunset Crater. Courtesy of Mike Koopsen, Sedona.

LENOX CRATER TRAIL

Climb almost 300 feet up the soft crumbly slope of Lenox Crater for sweeping views of the national monument and the largest of all volcanoes in the field, the San Francisco Peaks; 1.6 miles round trip.

BONITO VISTA TRAIL

This paved stroller-friendly path offers intriguing views of the Bonito Lava Flow and surrounding volcanoes; 0.3 miles round trip.

LAVA FLOW TRAIL

Stretching along the base of Sunset Crater Volcano, a 1-mile loop provides a close-up look at a wide variety of exotic volcanic formations. An upper 0.3-mile loop has a concrete surface. Leashed pets are allowed on the paved portion only.

Stay on designated trails for your safety and to protect fragile rocks, soils, and plants.

Camping

Hidden in a stand of ponderosa pines, the US Forest Service operates Bonito Campground near Sunset Crater. Facilities include running water and restrooms, but there are no showers or trailer hookups. The campground is open from late spring through early fall. There are 22 reservable sites and 21 sites that are first-come, first-served. Reservations are available at www.recreation.gov or by calling (877) 444-6777.

Programs/Events

Rangers offer interpretive talks, hikes, and other programs as staffing permits.

Special Notes

All plants, animals, and archaeological objects in the park are protected by federal laws. Sunset Crater is closed to climbing to protect its fragile resources. You may climb other cinder cones in the area, such as Lenox Crater and Doney Mountain at Wupatki.

The high wall of distinctly colored cliffs are just one geological feature in a landscape renowned for them. Courtesy of Mike Koopsen, Sedona.

Vermilion Cliffs National Monument

Overview

Hidden away behind a fortress of cliffs are some of the most seductive and dangerous destinations of the Southwest, including Paria Canyon, Buckskin Gulch, and the legendary Wave.

Nearest Cities

Page, AZ; Kanab, UT.

Established

November 9, 2000.

Size

293,689 acres.

I rolled out of my tent in the predawn gloom, then tromped through sand to reach the stony floor of White Pocket. Shadows peeled away and colors began to emerge in the muted light as I scrambled up a curving spine of rock to an exposed perch overlooking the basin. Last night's sunset proved to be a delicious show, and I wanted a front-row seat for the sunrise sequel.

Just as that fiery ball kissed the eastern horizon and a creamy, dreamy light washed across the waves of multihued sandstone, a coyote began yipping off to my left. Soon, the animal was joined by a second coyote off somewhere in the sand and sagebrush to my right. It was a lovely chorus. And while I didn't know the words, it was obviously a song of welcome aimed at the dawn. Naturally, I couldn't resist. I sang along.

If anyone else was up yet, I didn't see him or her. The world was empty and pure. It was just two coyotes and me greeting a new day in Arizona. Together we hoisted the sun and allowed the earth to keep spinning onward.

Opening a Geologic Toy Box

The Vermilion Cliffs are Arizona's Atlantis. They're a lost land, full of legends and mysteries. The fortunate few who visit come stumbling out of wild country raving about slot

A hiker explores the narrows of Paria Canyon. Courtesy of Mike Koopsen, Sedona.

canyons that never end, freakish hoodoos, formations stretched like taffy, and jagged rocks protruding from the sand like the spiny fin of some ancient beast lying in wait.

Hidden away among megastar national parks Grand Canyon, Zion, and Bryce Canyon, Vermilion Cliffs National Monument was once overlooked by travelers. That's not the case anymore for those with an adventurous spirit. Despite the lack of amenities such as a visitor center, or even paved roads, people now vie for the chance to snag coveted permits to wander into this hallowed expanse.

The towering escarpment of the namesake Vermilion Cliffs runs for more than 30 miles, stretching between Lees Ferry and House Rock Valley and reaching heights of 3,000 feet. Fierce, stark, and drenched in sunshine, this massive wall of eroded stone is a defining feature of the lonely Arizona Strip. Explorer John Wesley Powell named the cliffs that now form the southern and eastern boundary of the national monument. The park extends to the Utah border and is supplemented by the Paria Canyon–Vermilion Cliffs Wilderness Area.

Much of the land corralled by these lofty ramparts consists of high desert scrub stretching northward from the top of the cliffs and is defined by solitude, far-ranging views, and a conglomeration of startling features. The monument, managed by the Bureau of Land Management (BLM), contains some of the most outlandish geologic formations in the country including Coyote Buttes and the Wave, White Pocket, Buckskin Gulch, and Paria Canyon.

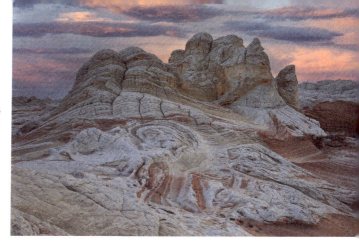

The soft hues of sunset blend exquisitely with the sandstone formations of White Pocket. Courtesy of Mike Koopsen, Sedona.

Young Pterodactyls

First, you have to find a way in. Don't expect a welcome mat. Out here, you're not really a guest. You're just part of the food chain, as one ranger put it. But don't worry. If you die in the monument, at least there's the possibility your carcass might be eaten by some of the most rare birds on the planet. Sort of an honor when you think about it that way.

Passersby can enjoy an easy-breezy view of the Vermilion Cliffs as they cruise along US 89A between Lees Ferry and the Kaibab Plateau. The paved road cuts straight across the Arizona Strip along the base of the long rock wall and is traveled by those venturing to the North Rim of the Grand Canyon or heading for Page and Lake Powell. Views of Vermilion Cliffs are gorgeous but access is scarce.

Turn north on House Rock Valley Road near the edge of the Kaibab Plateau. The dirt road is simply marked BLM 1065 but is hard to miss since it sits near a small stone house, the only building within miles. The gravel and graded dirt is generally manageable during dry weather in any high-clearance vehicle. Yet even a little bit of rain can make the road utterly impassable.

House Rock Valley Road traces the western edge of the monument. About 3 miles in, amid a landscape renowned for scenic wonders, you'll find an unassuming but very significant little pullout marked by a few panel signs. This is the Condor Viewing Site. It was here among the high cliffs that the California condor, North America's largest flying land bird, battled back from the brink of extinction.

In 1982, only 22 condors were left in the wild. A captive breeding program was initiated, and, starting in 1996, condors have been released here yearly. A number of condors now roost on the ledges and in the caves high off the valley floor and can often be seen circling above the grasslands. With a nearly 10-foot wingspan, these giant birds look like something that filled the sky when dinosaurs still stomped around. They feed on carrion.

Cliffs and Canyons

Scenic House Rock Valley Road continues for almost 30 miles, crossing into Utah and connecting with US 89. And through those lonely miles are a handful of trailheads and turn-offs offering access to the monument's roster of attractions.

Soon after you cross the Utah state line, you'll find Wire Pass Trailhead. This provides the easiest entry to the mother of all slot canyons, Buckskin Gulch. Buckskin is the longest and deepest slot canyon in the United States, probably the world. Wavy sandstone walls stretch for 16 miles across the wilderness until it connects to Paria Canyon. There are no limits on day hikers. You can purchase permits online or at the trailhead by scanning a QR code with your smartphone.

Starting out, you'll hike a dry streambed for a mile with not much hint of what's to come. Finally, the hills begin to crowd around, and you enter the tight confines of Wire Pass. Consider this your introductory slot canyon, an appetizer before the main course. Slither through the stony clasp of the narrow passageway as water-smoothed walls spiral upward. There's a tight squeeze or two and a downclimb of about 8 feet before it suddenly bursts open into a big cathedral of light and stone. This amphitheater with its towering cliffs marks the junction with Buckskin Gulch. Look for the petroglyphs at the base of the alcove on the right.

When entering Buckskin Gulch, turning left leads upstream through a long twisting corridor where the gorge will eventually widen out as it approaches Buckskin Gulch Trailhead (also on House Rock Valley Road) in about 3 miles. Turning right, or downstream, leads through 13 miles of this subterranean realm, a dark cool world wrapped in stone. Sky that seemed so broad out on the plateau is pared down to a pale ribbon when visible at all. Sunlight corkscrews in, kindling rich hues of reds and golds in the upper walls that tower hundreds of feet overhead. Yet the passage may only be a dozen feet wide.

You quickly realize why *Backpacker Magazine* named Buckskin Gulch as one of its 10 most dangerous hikes in America. Once you're in, you're in. There are only a couple of escape points throughout its length so the flash-flood danger is extreme, especially during the summer monsoon season. Never enter a slot canyon if rain is a possibility anywhere in the region. While the canyon floor is generally flat and dry, you may encounter deep pools, mud, quicksand, logjams, and chockstones. Go as far as you're comfortable before turning around.

If you've got an overnight permit for Paria Canyon, continue downstream through the miles of twisting corridor until reaching the confluence with the Paria River, corralled by another high-walled canyon. No camping is permitted in Buckskin. You must wait until you reach Paria Canyon. You can camp in Paria and return back through Buckskin Gulch. Or turn upstream (left) through Paria Canyon and it's about 7.5 miles to the White House Trailhead (21 miles total) where you've wisely stashed a second vehicle. If you turn downstream, it's about 30 more miles to Lees Ferry, the only other exit point.

The Paria River is an important tributary to the Colorado River, flowing for 38 miles from a wide valley at White House Trailhead through a dramatic canyon streaked with desert varnish to join the Colorado at Lees Ferry. While Paria Canyon includes miles of narrows, primarily surrounding the junction with Buckskin Gulch, it also offers sandstone arches, huge amphitheaters, wooded terraces, and hanging gardens. Not surprisingly, the BLM limits the number of overnight campers to protect it from overuse. Permits must be secured in advance. As with Buckskin Gulch, there is no limit on day hikers, and permits are available online or at trailheads.

For those that want to avoid Buckskin and just slosh through Paria Canyon, White House Trailhead (off US 89) in southern Utah serves as the main entry point. The muddy, shallow Paria River flows through a wide valley for more than 4 miles before the canyon walls close in. The Narrows last for a few miles, extending beyond the junction with Buckskin Gulch before opening up again. Most backpackers take 3–5 days to complete the epic wet-footed journey to Lees Ferry, a total of 38 miles.

The Wave

In recent years Coyote Buttes has emerged as a bucket list destination for adventurers worldwide. That's largely because of the Wave, an exotic sandstone bowl laced with ribbons of swirling strata. The undulating curves, the radiant pastels create a hypnotic scene beloved by photographers as the rocks seem to flow past the camera lens in long, graceful swoops.

Visiting the Wave is complicated because permits are required and very hard to come by. Demand far outstrips availability. Once you've acquired a permit, expect a moderately difficult shade-less hike of 3.2 miles across the sand and sandstone to reach the Wave.

To protect the delicate structure, the BLM limits access to only 16 groups (no more than 64 people per day). Of those, 48 people or 12 groups (whichever comes first) are chosen in an online lottery 4 months in advance. Sign up at www.recreation.gov. The other option is to sign up for a Daily Lottery. Permits are issued 2 days in advance, but you can only apply on a mobile device within a geofence area in Northern Arizona / southern Utah. While within the geofence area, this lottery is only available by going to www.recreation.gov in your browser or by installing the www.recreation.gov app.

As an alternative to the Wave, White Pocket requires no permit—although that may change in the future. However, you do absolutely need a high-clearance four-wheel-drive vehicle to navigate many miles of deep tire-sucking sand. Having the right vehicle and knowing how to drive in sand is imperative. If you don't have four-wheel drive, there are companies in Page and Kanab that offer day tours to White Pocket.

What you'll find is an alien island of multihued stone amid the high desert landscape. That same mystical feel permeates White Pocket. It is larger and more untamed than the Wave, a chaotic jumble of windswept curves, bent and buckled and veined with color. This is Medusa's playground, where puffy clouds, scoops of sherbet, and ancient beehives have all turned to stone. The anarchy overwhelms the senses. These are earth bones with muscle and tendon still attached. In Arizona, sandstone is the canvas for geological masterpieces.

And if you hear howling, it's either a coyote or me. In either case, feel free to chime in.

When You Go

www.blm.gov/national-conservation-lands/arizona/vermilion-cliffs.

Admission

Free.

Facilities

There are no facilities within the national monument.

Paria Contact Station is a seasonally staffed information center primarily focused on assisting guests visiting Vermilion Cliffs National Monument, Paria Canyon–Vermilion Cliffs Wilderness, and nearby sites within the Grand Staircase–Escalante National Monument. The station also serves as a pickup location for Paria Canyon overnight permits. Drinking water is available year-round in the parking area. The station is located between mile markers 20 and 21 on Hwy 89 between Kanab and Page.

The BLM Arizona Strip Field Office is in St. George, Utah. Passport stamps are available here.

Pets

Dogs are permitted to hike with you in Coyote Buttes North (the Wave), Coyote Buttes South, and for overnight trips in Buckskin Gulch and Paria Canyon, but both you and your pup must obtain a permit in advance.

Hiking

Vermilion Cliffs doesn't have marked trails, just routes and adventures.

Permits are required to explore Coyote Buttes North (the Wave), and Coyote Buttes South. These are backcountry wilderness areas and contain no facilities or developed trails. Practice Leave No Trace principles to preserve the pristine quality of this fragile landscape. Much of the time you'll be hiking in deep sand using landmarks to plot a course. You should be in good physical condition and have navigation skills. Find more details on the park website, or book permits at www.recreation.gov.

Revered for its scenic beauty and seclusion, Paria Canyon is a beloved backpacking hike. Permits are required to enter. Day-use permits for Paria Canyon are available by using your smartphone to scan a QR code at each trailhead. (Since Buckskin Gulch is considered part of Paria Canyon, the same guidelines apply for all permits.) Display your day-use permit receipt on your vehicle windshield.

Overnight permits must be reserved in advance at www.recreation.gov. There is a limit on overnight use in the canyon to 20 people per day.

Four trailheads provide access to Paria Canyon. Lees Ferry, part of Glen Canyon National Recreation Area, is the only one in Arizona. This is most often an ending point for an outing just because it's easier to hike downstream. There is no trail; you'll simply follow the canyon and quite often you'll be hiking in the river.

The other trailheads are White House, Wire Pass, and Buckskin Gulch, which is the least popular because it adds extra mileage. Buckskin Gulch Trailhead is located 4 miles north of Wire Pass on House Rock Valley Road. To access White House Trailhead from Page, Arizona, travel west on US 89 for 30 miles to the turnoff for the Paria Contact Station. Continue on the dirt road past the station for 2 miles to the campground and trailhead.

All slot canyons are inherently dangerous for flash-flood potential. Hiking in Buckskin Gulch and Paria Canyon is best from April to June or September to October. Never enter a slot canyon if rain is a possibility anywhere in the region.

Both Buckskin Gulch and Paria Canyon are rife with potential dangers beyond the threat of flash flood. Deep stagnant pools of cold water may require swimming, and canyon obstructions such as rock and logjams may involve the use of ropes to ensure a safe descent. All trash and solid human waste must be carried out. Do your research beforehand.

Camping

Dispersed camping is allowed outside the wilderness area in previously disturbed areas. When camping at White Pocket, or elsewhere in the monument, use existing campsites, and keep them small. Bury human waste 6 inches deep, and well away from the campsite. Pack out all your trash, including food scraps and toilet paper. Do not damage trees or collect firewood.

There are two developed campgrounds outside the monument.

Stateline Campground is located on the border of Arizona and Utah on House Rock Valley Road. The campground contains seven sites with a pit toilet and shade structures but no water. This also marks the northern terminus for the Arizona National Scenic Trail. There is no camping fee.

White House Campground is located approximately 43 miles east of Kanab, Utah, 2 miles to the south of US 89 and the Paria Canyon Contact Station at the end of Monument Road 751. White House is open year-round and contains seven car camping sites (including parking), and five walk-in, tent-camping sites. Amenities include vault toilets, fire rings, picnic tables, and tent pads. Drinking water is available at the nearby Paria Contact Station.

Campsites at White House are highly sought after and are available on a first-come, first-served basis. They cannot be reserved. Campers will claim and pay for their spot upon arrival using Scan and Pay through the www.recreation.gov mobile app.

Programs/Events

None.

Special Notes

Visiting Vermilion Cliffs National Monument requires special planning and awareness of potential hazards. Risk is inherent in backcountry areas, and rescue is not guaranteed. Expect rugged and often unmarked roads, extreme heat and cold, deep sand, flash floods, rattlesnakes, and quicksand. Bring a full-sized spare tire and plenty of water, food, and gasoline.

Visitors experience the Sinagua cliff dwellings of Walnut Canyon at a personal level. Photo by the author.

Walnut Canyon National Monument

Overview

Experience a rare intimacy in this small, forested canyon with ancient cliff dwellings lining the path and soot-darkened rooms inviting you inside.

Nearest City

Flagstaff.

Established

November 30, 1915.

Size

3,588 acres.

Like everyone else, I come to Walnut Canyon for the rich history. Dozens of prehistoric cliff dwellings are tucked away in the contours of the canyon walls, an actual cliff city. Yet while I am walking through the past, I never lose sight of the beauty and ever-changing scenery. This small gorge highlights a smorgasbord of diversity rarely found with surprises tucked in every fold and bend of the sloping walls.

Walnut Creek is a sporadic, seasonal little stream flowing east to join the Little Colorado River en route to the Grand Canyon. And never bet against the relentless patience of water. Over millions of years, the little creek carved a picturesque gorge, a long thin slash cut from the rolling plateau country east of Flagstaff. Walnut Canyon is 20 miles long, 400 feet deep, and one-quarter mile wide.

Plant life in the canyon is varied, abundant, and rapidly changing as it goes from fir trees to cactus in just a few steps. That biodiverse bounty no doubt helped seal the deal for the Sinagua, who were always shopping for real estate. A period of increased rainfall following the eruption of Sunset Crater benefited many communities.

Canyon Life

The Sinagua were a resilient and adaptable people who inhabited the varying terrain of central and Northern Arizona from AD 600 through AD 1450. By 1100 the Southwest's

The steeply forested gorge of Walnut Canyon was once home to hundreds of Sinagua families. Courtesy of Mike Koopsen, Sedona.

population had swelled. People were looking for new places to live and farm. Walnut Canyon proved irresistible. When the Sinagua discovered the forested gorge, they realized that half their work was complete before moving in. The eroded canyon walls with overhanging cliffs and deep-cut alcoves provided excellent building sites with floors, back walls, and leak-proof ceilings already installed. All that was left for builders was to enclose the front and sides with rock and mortar, and they quickly had a snug, protected shelter.

From about 1125 to 1250, Walnut Canyon provided a home to hundreds of Sinagua people. While most of their dwellings were built in the canyon walls, they planted crops in the deep soil of the terraces atop the rim. The Sinagua relied heavily on growing a drought-resistant corn, and also planted squash and beans. They hunted deer and small game, gathered plants in the canyon for food and medicine, and were at the center of a large trade network.

The Sinagua built more than 80 dwellings within the canyon and occupied both rims. Many of the structures are secreted away around a U-shaped promontory of rock that juts into the canyon, forming a kind of "island."

The Kaibab limestone that forms the upper strata of Walnut Canyon was scoured by water, leaving behind shallow alcoves. Builders constructed extra walls as needed out of blocks of limestone and mud mortar. The walls were plastered both inside and out, and layers of clay were used to smooth out the bedrock ledges serving as floors. Wooden beams reinforced the openings for doorways. Many of the homes were built in cliffs facing south or east to maximize winter sun and summer shade.

While the Southern Sinagua of Montezuma Castle and Tuzigoot enjoyed a relative abundance of water near their villages, the Northern Sinagua were not as fortunate. The land near present-day Flagstaff atop the Colorado Plateau lacked flowing rivers and streams. (Sinagua comes from the Spanish words sin agua, or "without water.") At Walnut Canyon, they built check dams to catch runoff. They hauled water from pools in the creek bed, harvested rainwater draining off cliffs, and packed snow into large pots. Farming at 7,000 feet with a short growing season is challenging in the best of times.

A Trip to the Island

For more than 100 years, the Sinagua navigated the steep walls of Walnut Canyon as part of their daily lives, tending crops, gathering firewood, hunting, and trading. They utilized game trails and natural breaks in the cliffs. Visitors today have it easier, but exploring the heart of the monument still requires some effort.

The moderately steep Island Trail is a highlight of any visit to Walnut Canyon. It circles around the distinctive promontory following the cliff edge while leading you past 25 dwellings. The signed trail starts from the back door of the visitor center and after a couple of switchbacks descends quickly. It's only a mile-long loop, but you'll encounter 736 stair steps along the way. So carry plenty of water and take it slow.

The trail drops 185 feet down a series of steps, crossing a small saddle. At the junction, bear to the right to begin the loop. This portion of the path stays mostly level with a few stairs. It also takes on an intimate feel, hugging the canyon wall as it dips beneath tree branches and under limestone overhangs. Here in these quiet woods, amid a patchwork of sun and shadow, you suddenly find yourself on the doorstep of Sinagua culture.

The remains of the old dwellings line the ledges, one after another. Up close the rooms seem small. They averaged 80 square feet—enough space to sleep and store a few things but that's about all. Much of the Sinagua daily life spilled outside. Several walls are still blackened with soot from ancient fires. Some rooms can be entered. Please be respectful.

Take time to enjoy the remarkable setting. The twists and turns of the canyon create different exposures allowing for a variety of life zones to coexist almost side-by-side. Walk through a shady grove of Douglas fir and ponderosa pines, and then just around a bend in the trail you're likely to find prickly pear cactus and desert yuccas thriving. The walnut trees, from which the creek and canyon were named, grow along the streambed.

Gaze across the canyon and you may spot additional cliff dwellings. Walnut Canyon was very much an interconnected community with families and neighbors working together.

A Walk on the Rim

Walnut Canyon created the two necessary worlds for the Sinagua to survive. The inner gorge provided them with shelter, protection, and resources. The world of the rim gave them the arable land for their crops. They farmed these open spaces with digging sticks and stone-bladed hoes.

The Rim Trail traces the edge of the canyon and loops back through a once-cultivated area. The easy path wanders through pinion-juniper woodlands to scenic overlooks complete with handy benches. On the loop portion of the trail, you'll find an excavated pit house and the remains of a freestanding pueblo. They may have served as homes or storage, or both.

With no stair steps to negotiate, the Rim Trail makes for a peaceful outing. Enjoy the wide canyon views and the music of songbirds filling the forest. Don't be surprised if you also hear the faint echo of Sinagua voices, the laughter of children.

The Sinagua occupied the cliff dwellings of Walnut Canyon for a little more than a century. They began to drift away and by 1250 the canyon was abandoned. No one knows what prompted the exodus. There may have been tensions with neighboring tribes. Or their growing population may have put too much of a strain on the local resources. Or it may have simply been time to move on.

Many settled in new villages like the ones at nearby Anderson Mesa. It is generally believed the Sinagua were eventually assimilated into Hopi culture. According to Hopi beliefs, the early migrations of their ancestors were part of a religious quest to bring all the clans together.

These carefully constructed dwellings remained undisturbed for hundreds of years. But the arrival of the railroad in the 1880s brought curiosity seekers and souvenir hunters. Digging up archaeological sites was not universally frowned upon. Dwellings were destroyed, and sacred relics and valuable knowledge were lost forever.

Then, as often was the case, such wanton destruction inspired others to step forward. Local citizens lobbied for federal protection, which finally came in 1915 when President Woodrow Wilson designated Walnut Canyon a national monument.

When You Go

(928) 526-3367, www.nps.gov/waca.

Admission

There is an admission fee.

Facilities

The visitor center contains museum exhibits, a gift shop, and a panoramic view of the canyon.

Pets

Leashed pets are allowed on the Rim Trail and in the parking lot. Pets are not permitted in buildings or on the Island Trail.

Hiking

ISLAND TRAIL

This is the centerpiece of the park, dropping steeply 185 vertical feet. It's the best way to experience the habitat and the dwellings up close. Interpretive signs line the trail. The staircase into the canyon consists of 273 stair steps that will be waiting for you on the way out. The loop portion of the trail includes another 190 stair steps. That means 736 stair steps if you're keeping score. As the National Park Service emphasizes: Going down the Island Trail is optional. Returning is mandatory.

RIM TRAIL

This gentle path takes visitors on a stroll through a mixed juniper and pinion-pine forest, staying level all the way. The trail is 0.7 miles round trip and offers benches, signage, and overlooks into the canyon. Along the way, you'll pass an excavated pit house and pueblo.

Camping

Park is day use only.

Programs/Events

Rangers offer a variety of interpretive programs throughout the year including talks and guided hikes.

Special Notes

Do not sit or stand on walls. Stay on trails to protect unexcavated areas. Leave artifacts in place.

Built atop a rock shelf overlooking a narrow canyon, Lomaki once contained nine rooms. Courtesy of Mike Koopsen, Sedona.

Wupatki National Monument

Overview

A collection of intricately constructed stone pueblos bearing the signatures of multiple cultures rises from the high grasslands of Northern Arizona.

Nearest City

Flagstaff.

Established

December 9, 1924.

Size

35,401 acres.

It's the blowhole that gets me every time.

I love the history of Wupatki National Monument and the sweeping vistas that stretch across miles of desert grasslands to the towering San Francisco Peaks. I love the aching quiet and the ancient stone houses that blend so exquisitely with this stark environment. Hard to imagine thousands of people once lived and farmed here. But it's still a single weird geological feature that always intrigues me.

Down the slope from the large Wupatki Pueblo, near a ceremonial ball court, is the blowhole, a small crevice in the earth's crust where air blows out or gets sucked in depending on temperature and atmospheric conditions. The park straddles an extensive underground system of fractures. When it's colder outside and air pressure is higher, the heavier, denser air is pulled into the hole. When it is warm and outside pressure is lower—just when you need it most—air comes blasting out of the hole up to 30 miles per hour. It's like feeling the earth breathe.

I sat there listening to the soft freight train whoosh roaring through underground chambers and sampling that fountain of wind. More than the dwellings, the signage, or the artifacts, somehow the blowhole connects me with the ancient residents of Wupatki. I can envision them after a spirited bout on the ball court hurrying over to this little fracture in the ground. There was probably some playful shoving as they jockeyed for position. And then would come the smiles and laughter as they leaned over the opening, taking a refreshing blast of chilled air right in the face.

The tower of Wukoki still contains original wood beams from the roof and ceiling structure. Courtesy of Mike Koopsen, Sedona.

How miraculous it must have seemed on a warm summer day. It still does to me, all these centuries later.

The Falling Sky

Wupatki National Monument sits about 20 miles north of Sunset Crater along the same loop road that drops from the pine forests to the rolling grasslands of this high desert country. Wupatki borders the Navajo Nation. The Little Colorado River and Painted Desert lie to the east. The rising bulk of the San Francisco Peaks dominate the skyline to the west.

Wupatki and Sunset Crater are connected by more than just geography. They are interwoven into the same transformational story. When Sunset Crater erupted in 1085, it filled the air with lava, rock, and cinders. What may have seemed like the end of the world spurred a building boom and a sudden migration to the region. The stone villages of Wupatki sprang up more than 900 years ago in the shadow of devastation.

The calamitous event changed the agricultural fortunes of this dry landscape. A period of increased rainfall followed the eruptions, and a layer of volcanic ash added nutrients to the soil. It helped the ground absorb moisture and prevented evaporation. The dry terrain suddenly turned arable, and communities sprang up across the plains.

A population influx began during the 1100s, with construction at numerous settlement sites. Pueblos were constructed from thin blocks of Moenkopi sandstone, giving them their distinctive red color. A clay-based mortar provided strength and stability to the buildings that kept them partially intact through the centuries. Archaeologists have cataloged hundreds of sites in the national monument but only a few are open to the public, accessible by short easy trails.

The Pueblos

There's no place in Arizona like Wupatki National Monument. It is rare to find so many structures of the time in one area, influenced by different cultures. While larger ancient structures can be found in the state, none feel as animate. At Wupatki, the multistory masonry pueblos are rooted in the landscape, worn and weathered like natural formations, and pinned beneath an ever-changing sky. They rise like red-boned ghosts above the swaying grasses. Instead of being tucked away in canyons or cliff alcoves, these dwellings occupy prominent points in the park, atop an isolated butte or perched on the edge of a steep-walled canyon. Although uninhabited since the 13th century, they command attention.

These are the pueblos you'll encounter, traveling from south to north.

WUKOKI PUEBLO

A side road branches off to the east leading to one of the best-preserved and most distinctive pueblos in the park. Perched atop a sandstone outcrop, Wukoki dominates the surrounding landscape. It is anchored by a square tower three stories tall. A complex of rooms are built to the side of the tower in an unusual design. A short trail (0.2 miles) loops around the pueblo and offers excellent views of the San Francisco Peaks.

WUPATKI PUEBLO

Behind the visitor center, a self-guided paved trail leads to Wupatki Pueblo, the largest in the park. In fact, it's the largest freestanding pueblo in Northern Arizona. The sprawling three-story structure contains 100 rooms and straddles an outcropping of sandstone. Once a regional center of trade, Wupatki features a circular community room; a ball court, which happens to be the northernmost ball court ever discovered; and a refreshing blowhole. By 1182, approximately 85 to 100 people lived at Wupatki Pueblo. It's estimated that a population of thousands were within a day's walk.

CITADEL AND NALAKIHU PUEBLOS

Even from a distance you'll have no problem spotting the Citadel spread across a hilltop like a fortress. Nalakihu, a smaller pueblo, sits near the beginning of the trail. Many settlements in the park were designed this way, with small family structures surrounding larger community pueblos. The stone walls of the Citadel lie tumbled about the hilltop. Yet it's still a powerful feeling walking through this quiet place with commanding views that include assorted satellite pueblos and distant horizons.

LOMAKI AND BOX CANYON PUEBLOS

Just a half-mile round trip hike leads visitors to the weathered remnants of three small but picturesque pueblos perched on the rocky edge of a narrow gorge. First up are the twin Box Canyon structures guarding both sides of the defile. You can walk into Lomaki Pueblo located at the end of the trail through narrow doors. *Lomaki* means "beautiful house" in the Hopi language. Gaze through the windows across the sun-kissed prairie and you'll understand.

Crossroads of Culture

Post-volcanic life in Wupatki Basin lasted for more than a century. Despite the beneficial layer of volcanic ash that fell from the sky, farming in the arid landscape proved difficult. Agriculture was based mainly on maize and squash without the use of irrigation. There are few springs or seeps in the area, and the Little Colorado River is miles away. Harvesting water from infrequent rains became a way of life at Wupatki.

What makes Wupatki special is the overlap of cultures. Those that lived and farmed here included at least three archaeologically separate Ancestral Puebloan cultures—the Sinagua, Cohonina, and Kayenta. Most sites in the area reflect this population pattern, showing traits such as building styles, pottery, and tools from multiple cultures. Wupatki may have been a rare melting pot of intermingled cultures, although not all archaeologists are convinced that these different peoples had such close relationships here in the shadow of the volcano. Some argue that each village should be classified as Sinagua in origin.

By the mid-1200s, the Ancestral Puebloans left the Wupatki Basin for still undetermined reasons. An ongoing drought, decreased food supplies as the soil became increasingly unproductive, and disruption to their trade networks are all possible causes for departure. Life in the high desert is precarious at best, and even slight changes can make it untenable. The former inhabitants of Wupatki are thought to have traveled east, merging with other pueblo tribes on the Colorado Plateau. Hopi people refer to the Ancestral Puebloans as Hisatsinom, or "people of long ago."

Although they are no longer physically occupied, Hopi believe the people who lived and died at Wupatki remain as spiritual guardians. The pueblos are remembered and cared for, not abandoned.

To protect the abundance of archaeological resources, President Calvin Coolidge established Wupatki National Monument in 1924. More than 2,500 archaeological sites including multiroom pueblos, pit houses, hearths, stone quarries, burial grounds, shrines, and reservoirs have been cataloged within the monument. The recovery of at least 125 different types of pottery, as well as shells, copper bells, and macaw feathers and bones, suggest a thriving trade network that extended into Mexico, possibly Central America.

During the monument's early days, park officials attempted to reconstruct several collapsed pueblos. National Park Service policies evolved, and for decades they have focused on stabilizing the ancient dwellings but in a manner consistent with the original buildings.

When You Go

(928) 679-2365, www.nps.gov/wupa.

Admission

Admission fee grants entry to both Wupatki and Sunset Crater.

Facilities

The visitor center has museum exhibits and a gift shop.

Pets

Pets are not permitted in buildings or on any park trails. Leashed dogs are allowed at the Doney Mountain Picnic Area and trails in the adjacent Coconino National Forest.

Hiking

Each pueblo open to the public can be reached by short easy trails, ranging from 0.2 miles to 0.5 miles round trip. The trail to Nalakihu is ADA accessible. Parts of the trails to Wupatki and Wukoki are also accessible.

Apart from the short trails to the pueblos, one other path is available, climbing to an old cinder cone on the side of Doney Mountain. The moderate trail begins at the Doney Mountain Picnic Area, just off the main road, and makes a steady climb up the barren hillside. Interpretive signs line the way and hikers are rewarded with expansive views from the top. The Doney Mountain Trail is 1 mile round trip.

There is no off-trail unguided hiking within the monument.

Camping

Park is day use only.

Programs/Events

Ranger talks and guided walks offer a variety of interpretive programs throughout the year.

Discovery Hikes are offered from November through March as staffing permits. These moderate hikes provide the only public access to some of Wupatki's backcountry.

Crack-in-the-Rock Hikes are offered in April and October. These strenuous overnight ranger hikes take visitors on a backpacking trip to the Crack-in-the-Rock Pueblo. The hike includes visits to rock-art sites. Reservations are required for all guided hikes.

Special Notes

Do not climb on walls. Stay on designated trails. All plants, animals, and archaeological objects in the park are protected by federal laws.

STATEWIDE ARIZONA

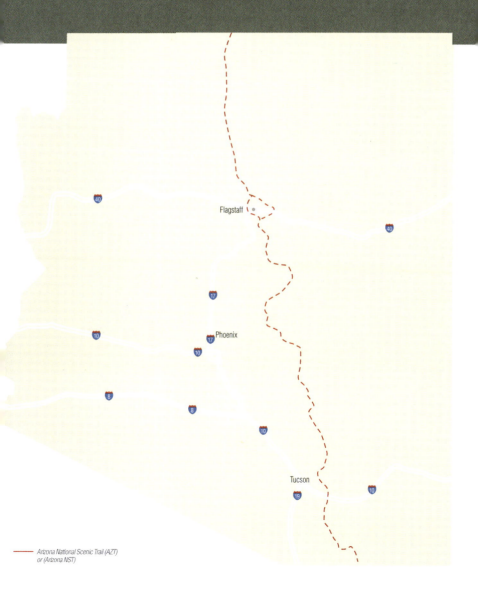

Arizona National Scenic Trail (AZT) or (Arizona NST)

The southernmost segment of the Arizona National Scenic Trail rambles through the desert scrub in the shadow of Coronado Peak. Photo by the author.

Arizona National Scenic Trail

Overview

Traversing the entire length of the state, this monumental route threads together Arizona's immense diversity while connecting communities and backcountry. It can be sampled whole or in parts.

Established

March 30, 2009.

Size

800 miles.

Arizona is a big old state—the sixth largest in the nation—and one way to get a sense of that expanse is to walk the length of it.

The Arizona National Scenic Trail is a long, lanky route cleaving the state as it stretches from Mexico to Utah. The trail begins at the Coronado National Memorial on the US-Mexico border and rambles north for 800+ miles crossing isolated mountain ranges, rolling grasslands, sun-spanked desert, forested plateaus, and the grandest of all canyons.

First Steps

A Flagstaff teacher, Dale Shewalter, began hatching the idea for the ambitious trail in the 1970s. He made his first complete statewide—or state-long—hike in 1985. It was that journey and his subsequent research into creating a route across public lands that became the basis of the Arizona Trail (AZT).

Shewalter's enthusiasm proved contagious as more agencies and people became involved with the project. The AZT began to materialize, pieced together from existing trails with new segments being built as needed. In 1994, the Arizona Trail Association was formed as a nonprofit organization, overseeing trail work and planning, coordinating with various agencies, and unleashing an army of passionate volunteers to create maps, provide GPS coordinates, locate potential water sources, and raise money for and awareness of the trail.

The AZT was designated a State Scenic Trail in 2006. Then in 2009, it became a National Scenic Trail. Others that have received such prestigious designation include Appalachian,

It couldn't really be considered the Arizona Trail unless it crossed the Grand Canyon. Courtesy of Mike Koopsen, Sedona.

Pacific Crest, and Continental Divide Trails. These are the premier long-distance routes in the country. While the Arizona Trail is relatively short compared to these other epic journeys, it presents its own unique set of challenges.

Hikers may encounter extreme weather swings from intense heat to deep snow, brutal elevation gains and losses, ever-changing habitats, venomous animals, and a scarcity of water—just for starters. Tackling the AZT is not to be taken lightly. No trail crosses such a startling diversity of terrain, passing through the same number of life zones as if traveling from Mexico to Canada, all within Arizona's borders.

Hike Your Own Hike

The Arizona Trail is closed to motorized vehicles, which means you'll have lots of time to savor the backcountry solitude. If you're planning on thru-hiking all 800 miles, start getting in shape and do a deep research dive into logistics. If setting out in spring, begin at the border with Mexico (generally in March) for your northbound (NOBO) hike. Southern terminus is located at Coronado National Memorial. In fall, start in September/October heading southbound (SOBO) from Stateline Campground in Utah, at the edge of the Vermilion Cliffs National Monument.

Expect to spend six to eight weeks to trek from one end of the state to the other. That will average out to approximately 14–19 miles of hiking each day. Of course, that's only a broad estimate. Some hikers are speed freaks and others like to move at a distinctly slower pace. You'll also be dealing with uncontrollable factors such as weather, illness, and injury. The most important thing is to hike your own hike.

It's the mantra of long-distance hikers. Hike your own hike (HYOH) means that there is no single right way to hike a trail. What works for you may be all wrong for someone else. Make the trail experience your own. Yet also be respectful and don't try to tell others what they should be doing. Just HYOH.

Arizona Trail Association

The Arizona Trail Association provides a wealth of information, from detailed maps and descriptions, necessary trail gear, water sources, information on gateway communities, and trail angel contacts. Trail angels offer invaluable support including shuttle service, water caching, laundry/shower facilities, food, and lodging. www.aztrail.org.

The association also does a terrific job of updating their site. They'll steer you toward the best apps for navigation and to provide current trail information, good camping spots, water sources, and more. There are also Facebook groups established each year for those attempting to thru-hike the AZT that season.

Section hiking is another option to cover the entire 800 miles. Hike the AZT in sections over a long period of time rather than completing a continuous thru hike. Once again, you'll have lots of planning ahead.

Mountain biking is allowed but some segments are off-limits due to wilderness restrictions. Preferred biking routes have been developed to provide alternatives. Likewise, dogs are allowed on the AZT, except in a few specific areas. Always consider the temperature, terrain, lack of shade, and availability of water before bringing your canine companion on any long-distance hike.

Certain sections of the trail require permits for overnight camping: Colossal Cave (Passage #8), Saguaro National Park (Passage #9), and Grand Canyon (Passage #38).

While the AZT crosses rugged lonely country, it also threads its way through several towns and cities. This was part of Dale Shewalter's original vision, forging a connection between the trail and the people and businesses along the way. There are 33 Gateway Communities offering supplies and a few creature comforts when needed. They range in size and include small towns like Patagonia, Superior, Pine, and Jacob Lake, and also cities like Tucson and Flagstaff.

Day Hikes

The association is also a great resource for those seeking shorter jaunts, with plenty of day-hiking options. The Arizona Trail is divided into 43 passages, ranging from 8.6 to 35.3 miles long, and even those can be tackled in more bite-sized chunks.

While many segments ramble through rugged backcountry, other portions are close to towns or are easily accessed, making for good day-hiking possibilities all up and down the state. Here are a few choice spots where you can break off pieces of the Arizona Trail.

SANTA CATALINA MOUNTAINS: PASSAGE #11

The northern trailhead for this passage sits amid the timber at the very end of the Catalina Highway below the summit of Mount Lemmon. The high elevation makes this a good late spring through early fall hike. Start out on Marshall Gulch Trail as it plunges into the deep forest following the thread of a slender creek. Thin though the stream may be, the music of falling water is a welcome song in any woods.

The trail scrambles out of the gulch as it reaches Marshall Saddle and a five-way trail junction. While the Arizona Trail continues down the mountain slope, hang a left on the Aspen Trail. Soon you'll pass a cluster of big boulders, a perfect viewing platform known as Lunch Ledge. Most of this section ambles downhill and, of course, passes through some lovely aspen groves before returning you to the trailhead for a 4-mile loop.

Where

From Tucson, drive 30 miles up the slope of Mount Lemmon on the Catalina Highway. Pass through the town of Summerhaven to the Marshall Gulch Picnic Area.

Additional Details

(520) 749-8700, www.fs.usda.gov/coronado.

ORACLE: PASSAGE #13

For its entire length, the Arizona Trail passes through only one state park. Oracle State Park sits in the rolling hills north of Tucson. The centerpiece of the park is the historic Kannally Ranch House, a sprawling Mediterranean Revival Style building completed in 1932. From the ranch house parking lot, start out on the Wildlife Corridor Trail as it crosses scrubby grasslands with views of distant mountains. After 1.6 miles, it connects with the Arizona Trail.

Turn right on the AZT as if heading toward Mexico. (You can also make a short detour to Kannally Wash and a rustic windmill by first turning left on the AZT, then backtracking.) The trail rambles southeast for a couple of miles before connecting with the Manzanita Trail. Turn right on Manzanita and head back toward the parking area for a 6-mile loop. Along the way, it dips in and out of small ravines as the vegetation grows heavier. Keep a sharp eye because Oracle is a wildlife refuge teeming with a roster of animals that includes white-tailed deer, javelina, coyote, fox, skunk, bobcat, and mountain lion.

Where

Oracle State Park is located in the town of Oracle, 35 miles north of Tucson off Arizona 77.

A sign guides hikers on Passage #40 of the Arizona Trail across the Kaibab Plateau. Photo by the author.

Additional Details

(520) 896-2425, www.azstateparks.com.

GILA RIVER CANYONS: PASSAGE #16

The key to this hike is simply forcing yourself to stop. It pulls you into isolated country along the Gila River. Starting from the Kelvin Bridge south of Superior, the trail traces the route of the river, sometimes overlooking it from above, occasionally venturing closer. You'll pass beneath a ridge of mine tailings early but then enjoy big vistas of the river valley framed by mountains and mesas. This was the last segment of the Arizona Trail to be completed, and a small survey post commemorates that fact 2 miles from the trailhead. Enjoy the riparian corridor and surrounding desert, have a riverside snack, and then return the way you came.

Where

From Superior, drive south on AZ 177 for 15 miles, and then turn right onto Florence-Kelvin Highway for 1.2 miles to Kelvin Bridge.

Additional Details

BLM Tucson Field Office, (520) 258-7200.

FLAGSTAFF: PASSAGE #33

While there's wild country on both ends of this section, it also rambles up and down streets right through town. This is the only passage through an urban area. The Arizona Trail meets another icon when it crosses Route 66, and gets incorporated into the Flagstaff Urban Trails System. For great scenery that's easily accessed, hike the section through Buffalo Park. The wide smooth path crosses grassy meadows atop McMillian Mesa. Along the way you'll pass a Dale Shewalter Memorial, a nice tribute to the "Father of the Arizona Trail," who passed away in 2010. A broad panorama of Mount Elden, Dry Lake Hills, and the San Francisco Peaks dominates the skyline.

The Arizona Trail cuts across the heart of Buffalo Park to junction with Oldham Trail, which will climb the southern slope of Mount Elden. You can stay on level ground by connecting to the Nate Avery Trail, a 2-mile loop around the perimeter of the park.

Where

Buffalo Park is located off Cedar Ave. northeast of downtown.

Additional Details

www.Flagstaff.az.gov.

KAIBAB PLATEAU SOUTH: PASSAGE #40

Save this for a summer treat when the weather is ideal and all the facilities are open at Grand Canyon's North Rim. From the trailhead a paved path leads to East Rim Viewpoint, where you'll be gazing across the Saddle Mountain Wilderness to Marble Canyon and the line of the Vermilion Cliffs. The Arizona Trail follows the rim in both directions for a bit. If you turn south, it's several miles to the national park boundary. Go north and the trail ambles through lush forest, conifers mingled with aspens. It would make a colorful early autumn treat as well. Hike as long as you want and then return by the same route.

Where

From Jacob Lake, drive south on Arizona 67 for 27.5 miles, then left on FR 611 for 4.5 miles.

Additional Details

(928) 643-7395, www.fs.usda.gov/kaibab.

When You Go

Arizona Trail Association, www.aztrail.org.

Acknowledgments

The author wishes to acknowledge the invaluable assistance of several people, most notably the dedicated men and women of the National Park Service. They make these places so incredibly special through their hard work, passion, and knowledge. A big shout-out to the countless volunteers who expend time and energy improving the parks in so many ways. Thanks to the folks at the Bureau of Land Management, US Forest Service, and US Border Patrol for preserving and protecting some of our most remote and scenic parks.

I gratefully acknowledge the Native peoples who were the original stewards of these lands. Many national parks are ancestral homelands and important places for maintaining cultural identity. It is imperative that Native voices become a larger part of the national park story, and I'm encouraged to see such efforts being made in recent years.

Thanks to Jill Cassidy, the kind of editor an unschooled freelance writer only finds once in a career, if he or she is fortunate. I was fortunate. Thanks to Stephen Hull for his guidance and supreme patience. Rick Mortensen's enthusiasm is always appreciated, as are his wonderful photographs. I'm grateful to Ken Lapides for his sharp-eyed diligent work. Of course, none of this would be possible without the support, strength, and soul-sustaining love of my wife, Michele.

About the Author

Roger Naylor is an award-winning Arizona travel writer and author. He has been swoony in love with Arizona since arriving as a wide-eyed college student. For decades he has explored his adopted state while writing about his discoveries. He specializes in national and state parks, lonely hiking trails, twisting back roads, diners with burgers sizzling on the grill, small towns, ghost towns, and pie. Naylor's work has appeared in the *Arizona Republic*, *USA Today*, *The Guardian*, *Country Magazine*, *Arizona Highways*, and dozens more. He was inducted into the Arizona Tourism Hall of Fame in 2018. He is also the narrator of the Verde Canyon Railroad.

Naylor has authored several books including *Awesome Arizona: 200 Amazing Facts about the Grand Canyon State*, *Arizona's Scenic Roads and Hikes*, *Arizona State Parks*, *The Amazing Kolb Brothers of Grand Canyon*, *Arizona Kicks on Route 66*, and *Crazy for the Heat: Arizona Tales of Ghosts, Gumshoes, and Bigfoot*. For more information, visit www.rogernaylor.com.

The Southwest Adventure Series
Ashley M. Biggers, SERIES EDITOR

The Southwest Adventure Series provides practical how-to guidebooks for readers seeking authentic outdoor and cultural excursions that highlight the unique landscapes of the American Southwest. Books in the series feature the best ecotourism adventures, world-class outdoor recreation sites, back-road points of interest, and culturally significant archaeological sites, as well as lead readers to the best sustainable accommodations and farm-to-table restaurants in Arizona, Colorado, Nevada, New Mexico, Utah, and Southern California.

Also available in the Southwest Adventure Series:

Slow Travel New Mexico: Unforgettable Personal Experiences in the Land of Enchantment by Judith Fein
Arizona Family Outdoor Adventure: An All-Ages Guide to Hiking, Camping, and Getting Outside by Chels Knorr
Colorado Family Outdoor Adventure: An All-Ages Guide to Hiking, Camping, and Getting Outside by Heather Mundt
New Mexico Family Outdoor Adventure: An All-Ages Guide to Hiking, Camping, and Getting Outside by Christina M. Selby
South Mountain Park and Preserve: A Guide to the Trails, Plants, and Animals in Phoenix's Most Popular City Park by Andrew Lenartz
New Mexico Food Trails: A Road Tripper's Guide to Hot Chile, Cold Brews, and Classic Dishes from the Land of Enchantment by Carolyn Graham
Arizona's Scenic Roads and Hikes: Unforgettable Journeys in the Grand Canyon State by Roger Naylor
Arizona State Parks: A Guide to Amazing Places in the Grand Canyon State by Roger Naylor
Eco-Travel New Mexico: 86 Natural Destinations, Green Hotels, and Sustainable Adventures by Ashley M. Biggers
Skiing New Mexico: A Guide to Snow Sports in the Land of Enchantment by Daniel Gibson